RITA'S
STORY

God bless you

Rita Klaus

Medjugorje – A Shining Inspiration
Other titles available from Paraclete Press

RITA'S STORY

Rita Klaus

PARACLETE PRESS
Brewster, Massachusetts

To protect the privacy of the individuals involved, in certain instances names have been changed and some locations have been altered.

3rd Printing, February 1997

ISBN: 1-55725-056-1
Printed in the United States of America

To
the honor and glory
of God,
the Father of us all,
and Mary,
the mother of us all,
and my loving families:
Ron, Kristen, Ellen, and Heidi Klaus,
all the McLaughlin clan,
and my dear Servite Sisters,
this book is
gratefully dedicated.

Contents

Editor's Note ix

Foreword xi

1   "Totally Yours" 1

2   Gateway to Heaven 10

3   The McLaughlin Kids 17

4   Lost—and Found 25

5   Upside-down Pieces 32

6   To be a Saint 43

7   Home, Sweet Home 49

8   A Proper Environment 64

9   Home 76

10 The Way of the Cross............................84

11 A Day in the Life 93

12 The White Veil 106

13 The Black Veil....................................116

14 Sister Mary Raphael 132

15 Balance 143

16 Massena 150

17 Vaya con Dios 165

18 MS 176

19 Pieces 189

20 The Hardest Part 202

21 Goodbye, Mary Raphael.......................213

22 Maryville..219

23 Mars 230

24 Ron 240

25 Timmy...251

26 The Plunge 258

27 With a Little Help 264

28 Downhill...271

29 The Bottom.......................................281

30 Hugged by God...................................287

31 Uphill..293

32 The Feast Day of St. Julianna 303

33 After the Healing................................313

    Postlude 321

Editor's Note

Passage—the word refers to a journeying, a leaving behind of the known and cherished, to venture forth into the unknown. In earlier times such a transition was often marked by an ocean voyage: one was said to have "booked passage"—to India, or America, or wherever destiny awaited.

Rita's Story is a diary of such passages—from Iowa schoolgirl to Servite Sister, from nun to wife and mother, from embittered cripple to joy-filled sign that God is still among His people.

As a child, her one goal in life was to one day be numbered among the heroes of the faith whose lives she so admired. But sainthood is a dangerous ambition (even for a child); it says to God that you agree to be tested in a special way—an agreement which, as you grow older and wiser, you may have reason to regret.

While this is not meant to imply that Rita is a candidate for future canonization, there is no denying that she has been through some pretty extraordinary testing, and her response to it is an encouragement. For in a sense, all who love God are called to become saints—to ultimately embrace the cross that each is given to bear. *If any man would come after me, Jesus challenged His disciples, let him deny himself, pick up his cross daily, and follow me.*

What Rita's story shows us is that while we may have no control over the trials and tribulations placed in our path, we have total control over how we choose to respond to them. And even in those dark times when we are tempted to hate God, His love for us never wavers.

Rita's healing is a sign to the unbeliever that God *is* God. To the believer, her story is an inspiration, for each of our lives is a passage, an ongoing journey into the unknown. We are all voyagers, embarked on the Way of the Cross—but we are not on that way alone, and it is a journey home.

— *David Manuel*

Foreword

I want to say something about this book, and then I want to say something about its author. The book reads like a novel, holding the reader in suspense as he wonders what will happen next. It is also a beautifully told, refreshingly positive look at the life of a sister (reminding me of the sacrificial love of those who taught me when I was a child). Altogether, it is a remarkable account of a very powerful life experience.

The author in person is as remarkable—and genuine—as her book. I first heard of Rita Klaus in 1987 from Mel McDermott, one of my parishioners in Dubuque who happened to be her godfather. From all he told me, I looked forward one day to meeting this woman who had been miraculously healed of Multiple Sclerosis after suffering from it for 26 years.

Two years later I did meet her—at a conference in Texarkana, at which we had both been invited to speak. I listened to her story, enthralled. But three more years would pass before I got a glimpse of the real Rita Klaus, the one far from the speakers platform.

It happened at the 1992 Marian Conference in Des Moines, where once again she was a speaker. For that conference I was a guest in the home of Dr. Charles and

Lucy Gutenkauf, and as I arrived Friday evening, Lucy asked if I knew Rita personally. When I said yes, she told me of her close friend Janie, a recent convert who was in the hospital, near death with M.S. Was there any possibility of my prevailing upon Rita to visit Janie?

I did not hold out much hope; there would be more than 9,000 people at the auditorium. And even if I could find her, many people would be wanting to speak to her privately, to ask about her healing, seek her advice, or simply request prayer. But I would try.

By the time we got there, the meeting had already begun. Starting up the steps, there were only two other people in sight—Rita and her sister Ruthanne.

I told Rita about Janie, and asked if she could possibly go see her.

"Yes," she said without a moment's hesitation. "Just let me see when I can get away."

We arranged to meet the following afternoon at 4:30. From the conference I called Janie's husband Gary to tell him of our plans; he was delighted. But late that night when I returned to the Gutenkauf home, there was discouraging news: Janie's father had called to say she was far too ill to receive any visitors. Cancel the plan.

The next morning I found Rita and informed her. "No problem, Father," she smiled. "I understand."

That evening, however, when I returned to Charles and Lucy's for dinner, there had been two frantic calls from Gary: Janie had overruled her father's concern. She wanted very badly to see Rita; please try to get her to come.

But—could I find her in that vast crowd? And would she be free? It would have to be tonight; she was the lead speaker in the morning, and would be flying home immediately afterward. But that also meant this evening would be the last chance for people to talk to her; she would be mobbed. Still, I would try.

The auditorium was packed. I looked everywhere for my tall friend with the white hair, but there was no sight of her. Time was slipping away. I asked conference coordinator, Jerry Morin, the security staff, members of Rita's large Iowa family, other mutual friends—had they seen her? No one could help.

More time passed—till I began to think we would need a small miracle of our own. And then, in that sea of people in the crowded auditorium, I saw a hand waving to me. It was Rita's brother Russ; she was in the bookstore.

As I had expected, she was surrounded by people— including some Servite Sisters whom she had not seen since leaving the convent, 25 years before.

Haltingly I explained that Janie desperately wanted her to come, but given the lateness of the hour I would certainly understand if that were not possible.

"Let's go," she said.

"You mean, right now?"

She nodded. "If Janie needs me, then that is what Mary wants me to do tonight."

We went to the hospital. For nearly an hour, Rita sat by Janie's bed, sharing, chatting, praying.

When it came time to leave, Rita said to her, "I've got something I want you to have," and she gave her the stunning plaque of Mary and Child which had been blessed by the Holy Father, and which she had been given as one of the conference's speakers.

Janie died six weeks later. Her husband related that one of the happiest occasions in all that time was the visit from Rita, and how much she had treasured Rita's gift.

That weekend Rita Klaus had been a Very Important Person—the key attraction of the largest Marian conference in the United States. But that was not why she was a V.I.P. in God's eyes—what most pleased Him was what occurred offstage, where no one would know, as she reached out to a sister in pain.

Now I understand *Rita's Story.*

— *Rev. Msgr. Francis P. Friedl*
Dubuque, Iowa

1

"Totally Yours"

A breeze stirred the surface of the swimming pool, breaking the sun's reflection into a million dazzling diamonds. Though the sun was warm that Saturday morning in July, I was shivering. Our swim class had already been in the pool to get wet and were now assembled at the edge, listening to the instructor. Hugging myself with goose-bumped arms, I wished she would hurry up.

"You little ones will learn the flutter kick, holding onto the gutter here in the shallow end. And bobbers," she surveyed the eight and nine-year-olds which included my sister Ruthanne, "you'll also be in the shallow end, with me. Remember to stay close to your buddy."

Finally she said, "Rita, you can entertain yourself, until I can work with you on your stroke. But you stay in the shallow end, too." She paused and looked at each of us. "You know the rule: we never go in the deep end, unless someone is with us."

As the oldest in the class (by one year) and the only one who had passed their length-of-the-pool test, I did not have a buddy. And while I was a confident (albeit brand-new) swimmer, I had no intention of going into the deep end: rules were rules.

The instructor slipped into the pool and called for

1

the rest of us to join her, showing us that the water was only up to her waist. With much splashing and shouting, we all jumped in. Soon the little ones were furiously churning the water at the end of the pool, while the bobbers were practicing letting out their breath underwater. Just beyond them I dog-paddled around, waiting for it to be my turn with the instructor.

There was only one problem with the community pool: it was heavily chlorinated. I had a severe allergic reaction to chlorine: if even a little water got in my eyes, it would turn them so red that people would be alarmed. And if I ever opened them underwater, they would literally swell shut. So whenever I swam, it was with my eyes tightly closed.

Never having gone near the deep end, I had paid scant attention to it. When I had done my length, I had been close enough to the side that I could have reached out and grabbed the gutter, had I needed to. So I never really noticed that the deep end was L-shaped, or that the arm of the L, accommodating the one-meter and three-meter boards, was extremely deep.

What was taking her so long? Tired of dog-paddling in circles, I decided to swim across the pool in my best impression of the Australian crawl. Standing up in the shoulder-deep water and opening my eyes, I waded over to the side. Then taking a bearing on the opposite side, I shut my eyes and pushed off.

Somewhere around the middle, I must have gotten slightly off course—just enough to miss the opposite side and swim into the arm of the L.

With my eyes closed, I had no idea where I was; it just seemed to be getting awfully long. . . .

Too long! Never mind reaching the other side, I was

getting tired; it was time to stand up. I reached my legs down for the bottom and found—nothing.

No bottom! Panic swept over me—and all my newly-acquired swimming skills abandoned me. Suddenly I was floundering—and sinking. Somewhere I had read or heard that a drowning person got three chances to cry for help. Well, I'd better start: "Haa—" I managed, before water gurgled into my mouth, choking off the rest. Down I went, then fought my way back up to the surface. "Haa—" same result.

One more chance: *"Haal—"* It was louder, but still no one heard, or saw me frantically waving. I was terribly afraid as I went down for the third time, because you only got three tries, and then you died. I waited for my life to flash before my eyes, like it was supposed to. Only it never did; I just kept sinking deeper and deeper. . . .

Not that I'd lived all that much of a life in my ten years. I was born in Dubuque, Iowa, on January 25, 1940—the Conversion of St. Paul, at the end of the Church Unity octave.

Two weeks later, I was baptized in St. Patrick's Church, after which my parents took me to Cedar Rapids two hours away, to see my grandparents and my great aunt who were unable to attend the baptism. My great aunt was Sister Mary Helen of the Sisters of Mercy, and we drove up the long hill to the motherhouse, for her blessing.

Years later, my parents told me what happened: she had taken me from my mother's arms and whisked me into the chapel, where she laid me on the altar of our Blessed Mother. Then she had knelt and looked up at her. "This one," she had whispered, "is totally yours."

I can remember only one meeting with her, before she died. She was very tiny, very frail, and very old—the oldest person I had ever seen. In a voice that was scarcely more than a whisper, she said to me: "You know, child, you were dedicated to the Blessed Mother." She peered at me, to see if I understood, and when I solemnly nodded, she smiled. "Good!" Then her voice grew even quieter. "They tell me you want to be a sister. Is that true?"

"Yes, Sister."

She took my hand in both of hers, and I noticed that they were as small as mine, and the light seemed to go right through them. She spoke one more time, and I could barely hear her. "You will be one," she nodded. "I will be praying for you."

The Sisters of Mercy came from Ireland, as did all of my dad's family—McLaughlins from County Mayo.

We were Black Irish, I was told; it had something to do with our having Spanish blood in our ancestry, as a result of the Spanish Armada. (In 1588, the Spanish had assembled the greatest fleet ever seen and sailed north to conquer England. They were stopped by the British Navy and a hurricane, the combination of which resulted in many shipwrecks along the coast of Ireland and Wales.) Black Irish had dark eyes and dark hair (which often later turned completely white, as mine has). As families, they were extremely close.

On my mother's side, the ancestry was Bohemian and German; her name was Arletta, and she was a convert to Catholicism. My father was Russell J. McLaughlin, a devout Irish Catholic; together they were "Russ and Letty" to all their friends who were too numerous to count. Dad was a salesman for General Mills, which meant that in my early years we moved around a lot in the state of Iowa. From Dubuque on the state's eastern border, we moved to Cedar Rapids, where I attended St. Patrick's School. A bright kid, I started first grade a year early—and my teacher, seeing I had a quick mind, encouraged me to use it. I loved school, every minute of it.

But then in April of my second year, my father took a new job working for a coffee distributor, and we moved again—to Sioux City on the banks of the Missouri River at the opposite end of the state.

Suddenly, I was a displaced person, going to a new school called Blessed Sacrament, where all the kids would know each other, and be a year older than me. At breakfast that morning, my mother had warned me that the first day was going to be difficult, but after that, she assured me, it would be fine.

The teachers at Blessed Sacrament were Dominicans; their habits were all white and were, I thought, quite beautiful. But that first morning I could not have felt more awkward or self-conscious, as the principal took me into the second-grade classroom and left me there.

The second-grade teacher introduced herself to me as Sister Bede, and then introduced me to the thirty-five other kids—a sea of faces, all staring at me. She directed me to my seat, and then, looking down the rows of desks, announced: "Everybody, sit straight in the middle of your seats." The other kids already were, but at St. Patrick's we had been taught to sit to the side, to make room for our guardian angels to share our seats with us. "Rita? I asked you to sit in the middle of your seat."

"I can't, Sister."

"And why not?"

"Because I have to leave room for my angel next to me."

"Your angel is a spirit; it doesn't need any place to sit." She fixed me with her gaze. "And I have told you to sit in the middle of your seat."

Begrudgingly I finally moved over, inwardly apologizing to my angel: Sorry to knock you off the seat, but she's making me do it.

After lunch came reading, and now she asked us to come forward and sit on little chairs. In my previous school, we were all taught to read as a class, but here it would be done individually, with each of us taking a turn reading aloud, while the others followed.

"Rita, why don't you go first."

It was a simple book; I read it right off.

"Close your books, children," said Sister Bede. "Rita, you read that story very well."

Great, I thought, I can do this! I'm going to be real smart in this school! Mom's going to love me for this! In my relief, I failed to notice that Sister was not smiling.

"Rita," she now said, "what is a blend?"

"A what?"

"A blend." I looked at her, nonplussed; I'd never heard the word before.

"I don't know," I finally said.

"What is a digraph?" Her voice had grown icy, and she was definitely not smiling.

I felt panic now.

She opened the reader, read from it, and then asked: "Is that a blend or a digraph?"

"I—I don't know," I murmured, looking at the floor so she wouldn't see the tears starting to come. (What I didn't know was that in my previous school they taught reading by the look-see method; here, they taught by phonetics.)

"Don't tell me you don't know! You read that beautifully, and you're obviously very intelligent."

She waited, but I didn't know what to say—and could no longer hide the tears.

"You really are a headstrong little girl, aren't you?"

She glared at me. "Are we going to have to put up with this all year long?" I cried harder. "I think not!" she exclaimed, getting up and coming out from behind her desk.

She grabbed me by the hand, crying, "You don't belong in this classroom! Or in the first grade, either! You belong in kindergarten!" And with that, she marched me out of the room.

For the rest of my life I will remember the high-ceilinged corridor down to the kindergarten, with the paintings on both sides, and the little lights hanging down from long cords and reflecting in the polished, dark wood floor.

"I'll put you where you belong," she kept saying, and I kept pleading, "Please, don't do this." In the end she was dragging me, with my heels making scuff-marks on the floor.

When we reached the kindergarten, the kids, including my brother Ron, were all lying on rugs on the floor, taking their naps. Putting one of their little chairs in the middle of the napping kids, she commanded me to sit on it. Then she told the kindergarten teacher: "This girl does not belong in my classroom. Until she learns to do what the other children do, here is where she belongs."

I just sat there, staring at my shoes.

On the walk home that afternoon, my brother asked me: "Why were you in our room? And why were you crying?"

"I—I don't know," and then I grabbed his arm. "But don't you dare tell Mom and Dad!"

We walked on aways, me staring down at my shoes. After awhile I said: "Someday, I'm going to be a teacher. And children are going to love being in my classroom, because I am going to listen to them and love them, and I will never humiliate them."

"You're going to be a teacher?" asked Ron.

"Yes. And my classroom will be a happy place; no one will ever be afraid to come there."

There was no question that I was afraid to go back to Sister Bede's room. When I woke up the following morning, the first thing I did was throw up. I went to school, to Sister Bede's classroom, but was so afraid of being taken back to kindergarten that I never raised my hand, never volunteered for anything, never participated in class discussion. For the remainder of that year, I did nothing—and every morning I woke up with a stomach ache and a headache.

At the parent-teacher conference, Sister Bede told my mother and father that I was extremely immature. She thought it had been a great mistake to have entered me in school a year early, and informed them that she was going to recommend my being held back a year.

When my mother told me of the conference, she warned me that I would probably be held back, but I didn't really believe it. So, when we received our report cards at the end of the school year, and everyone was jumping around, shouting, "I passed! I passed!" I was stunned: my report card said "Retained in Second Grade."

I drew off by myself, tears flooding my eyes. Mom had tried to prepare me, but still. . . my whole world fell apart. And then I felt a little arm go around my shoulder. It was Sheila Ryan, one of the girls in my class—*their* class, now. "Don't cry, Rita," she said gently. "You're a very smart kid; I just know you're going to do really well next year. Remember: you're going to know all the stuff, and the other kids coming up—they won't know anything! You'll be the best in the class!"

"Oh, Sheila!" and I turned and sobbed on her shoulder. (To this day, I have never known such compassion in a seven-year-old—God sends us exactly the people we need, when we most need them.)

As summer drew to a close, I grew more and more depressed at the thought of repeating second grade under Sister Bede. When the first day of school came, I was probably the only kid in Sioux City who wasn't excited about seeing their old friends and starting the new year. I dreaded this day and could hardly drag myself into the second-grade classroom—which was new to everyone else, but very old to me.

When I went in, the kids were hyper-happy —it seem more than first-day exuberance, and I soon found out why, as one sang: "Ding, dong, Sister Bede is gone!" I didn't dare believe it at first, but it *was* true! She had left the school, and we had a new teacher.

When you have only seven years as a reference base, any significant change seems astronomical. But in this case, it proved to be no less: in the twinkling of an eye, my life had turned from night to day.

2

Gateway to Heaven

Sister Simeon, our new second-grade teacher, was warm, compassionate, and extremely fair; I started to love school again.

And my third-grade teacher, Sister Beatrice, was a delight! She was old, even older than my great aunt had been. So old was she, in fact, that she had grown shorter, until she was no taller than we were. We decided she must be at least a hundred. (In today's system, she would probably have been forced into retirement many years before—which would have been a great loss, for if the mark of a good teacher is the ability to inspire, she was outstanding.)

Sister Beatrice was a grandmother to us. We all loved her and started bringing her treats or giving her our lunch desserts which we would line up on her desk. Soon there was far more than she could manage. "What am I going to do with all these lovely things?" she cried with delight. "I know: we'll have a party!"

From the long skirt of her habit she produced a penknife and started to cut up the apples and Twinkies and other goodies. She put the pieces in a pasteboard box which passed to each of us, saying, "Take whatever you like, dear."

After the party, she gave us a silent reading assignment, and then sitting down behind her desk, she read a book herself—and soon fell fast asleep. We read for awhile and would then tiptoe around, so as not to wake Sister. The goodie-party and the reading and Sister's nap became a daily ritual. But we always completed our assignments, there and at home, because we loved her and did not want her to get in any trouble.

Perhaps because she was aware of what had happened when I had first come to Blessed Sacrament, she took a special interest in me. After the first day, she took me aside and said: "Rita, you are a very smart little girl. You are going to have a wonderful year!" So of course I did my absolute best to prove her right.

One day, not long after, in art class she came over to see my drawing and said: "So, you're not only very intelligent; you're an artist! I want you to draw me a picture every day, and I will put it on the front of my desk." And she did.

At the end of that year, as excited as I was to be going on to fourth, I was sad to be leaving Sister Beatrice. It was thanks to her that I developed my life-long passion for reading. It would consume me, and I practically lived at the library. I read *Mary Poppins* and *Grimm's Fairy Tales;* in fact, I must have read every fairy tale ever written. One of my favorite books was *Susanna, the Pioneer Cow,* the story of a pioneer family. Mom had started us on that one. Every night she used to read to my brothers and sisters and me. There were five of us by then—Ron and Ruthanne and Russ Junior, known to all as RJ, and Ricky. Ruthanne and I would leave our bedroom door open and our brothers would do the same, while Mom sat on the top step and read aloud. When she started *Susanna,* I got so caught up in the adventures of that family that I found the book and finished it on my own, before Mom could.

Books became the incentive for me to finish my chores quickly and well: Mom would put them out of reach on top of the refrigerator, until my work passed her inspection. And she was tough! The bed did not merely have to be made, it had to be made correctly and perfectly; she would have made a good Marine Drill Instructor performing barracks inspection. Whatever you were cleaning, it had better be *clean,* or you would do it over, until it was. As far as Mom was concerned, the number one enemy of "Best" was "Good." Only when your housework measured up to her standards, were you permitted to dive back into your latest beloved volume. (I resented her perfectionism, of course—and now, according to my kids, have wound up exactly like her.)

That was also the year I became aware of how seriously we McLaughlins took our faith. My parents went to Mass every morning, as we did at school. On Sundays, not only did we all go together to Mass, but we went back in the afternoon for Vespers and Benediction! We were also a family that prayed together—morning prayers after breakfast, and the rosary after dinner. No one was allowed to miss any of these, nor did my father tolerate anything less than a properly worshipful attitude, and my mother supported him with all the zeal of a new convert.

Fourth Grade was another wonderful year—though it, too, had initially seemed headed for disaster. There were to be two sections of the fourth grade: one would have nice, gentle Sister Angela; the other would have Sister Ephraim who was extremely strict and reputed to be the meanest ogre on the face of the earth. Naturally everyone prayed to be in Sister Angela's class, and I was devastated when the room assignments came out: I was to be with Sister Ephraim.

"Please, Mom," I agonized, "You've got to call Father Kelly and tell him I don't want to be in Sister Ephraim's room! I'm going to hate it! I'm going to die this year!"

"Rita," she said calmly, "I will do no such thing! You will go to the room you've been assigned to, and you will do everything you're asked to do, and everything will be fine."

"But Mom—" I wailed.

She just shook her head, wiped her hands on her apron, and turned back to the stove.

The next morning, as I filed head down into Sister Ephraim's room, you would have thought I was going to the executioner's block. I thought so, too.

Another thing that had caused the kids who didn't know her, to fear Sister Ephraim was her handicap: she had no fingers on her right hand, only a thumb. Now, as she entered the room for the first time, you couldn't help looking at her right hand.

She did not look at us, but went straight to the blackboard, where, holding a piece of chalk with her right thumb and the knob on the end of her fingerless palm, she wrote her name. We did not notice how beautiful her penmanship was; all we could see was her deformity. We winced—and some of us audibly gasped.

Sister Ephraim turned around. "Is this what's bothering you?" she asked, holding up her right hand for all to see. "Let me tell you about this stump," she said, not unkindly. "When I was a little girl, we lived on a farm. My mother had told me very carefully: 'Do not ever climb up on the windmill; it is extremely dangerous.' But," she sighed, "as little girls occasionally do, I thought I knew better than my mother. Surely she was exaggerating, and what a wonderful view there would be from up there! So one day, not long after my fourth birthday, I climbed it."

She paused, and all of us remembered the last time we had decided we knew better than our mothers. "There had been no wind when I started to climb, but now, once I had reached the top, the wind came up. The windmill started to turn, shaking the tower. I lost my balance, and as I started to fall, in desperation I reached out to grab something. What I grabbed was one of the moving parts that connected the windmill to the pump; it instantly cut off all my fingers."

She paused again. I looked down at my own right hand with all its fingers, then back up at her. "I fell off the tower, screaming," she went on, "and my parents rushed me to the hospital. My thumb was hanging by a thread, and my mother held it in place, while my father drove. When we got there, they begged the doctors to try to save at least the thumb."

She smiled and wiggled the thumb. "They did—and I am so grateful I have this thumb! It enables me to do almost everything that anybody else can do." She beamed at us, one at a time. "So don't ever feel sorry for me; join me in thanking God for this thumb!"

From that moment on, I loved Sister Ephraim. She *was* strict—in the same way my mother was: she never allowed me to do less than the best I was capable of. And she was holy. She would tell us the most wonderful stories about Jesus, bringing Him vividly alive for us, and helping us to know Him as a person, as no one ever had before.

She brought the saints alive for us, too—heroes of the faith, whose examples we yearned to follow. When my mother told me that my great aunt had died, I went to Sister Ephraim. "She always used to pray for me, and now she can't pray for me anymore," I concluded, my voice breaking.

"Nonsense, child," said Sister Ephraim gently. "Don't you believe in the Communion of the Saints?"

"I—I guess so."

"Well, now she can pray for you even better. Before, she prayed for you when she thought of you. Now, from up there she can see you, and turn and see God; she can pray for you all the time, before His throne!"

I threw my arms around her and thanked her.

All told, Sister Ephraim was the most remarkable teacher I ever had.

And that was the sum of my life—which did not flash before my eyes that sunny morning in July, 1950, as I sank ever deeper into the deep end of the swimming pool. . . .

As I went down and down, slowly turning in the water, I was terrified: all I could think was, I'm going to die now. Then all at once this immense peace came over me, as I thought: but I'm going to heaven! I'm going to see Jesus and Mary and the angels and the saints! And I was so incredibly happy. . . .

When I reached bottom, I opened my eyes. Off in the distance I could make out a ladder, and I thought: I'll just walk over there pull myself up and out.

I started towards it, but it was like moving through wet cement. Then all of a sudden, a whiteness enveloped me. And now in front of me, I could see Mary and Jesus and St Joseph. They were all seated in a row, with Mary closest to me, and it seemed I was looking at them from the end of the row. They were looking straight ahead and didn't see me. I yelled to them: "I'm over here! I'm over here!" But they wouldn't look. Several times I called to them, but they just kept ignoring me. I didn't care; I was just so happy and excited to see them all.

Then Mary did turn her head and look at me. She just smiled and shook her head, no.

The next thing I knew, I was lying on my stomach by the side of the pool. Someone who was rhythmically pushing down on my back, seeing my eyelids flutter, said,

"How much have you swallowed?"

"About a pint, I think." I was a very bright kid.

On the way home, I took Ruthanne aside and said, "Don't you dare tell Mom and Dad what happened!"

"Why not?"

"Because they won't let me go swimming anymore! Mom won't even let me out of the house."

"Well, I think I'm going to tell them, anyway."

And so I had to resort to the method that older siblings have always used to keep kid brothers and sisters in line: blackmail. "If you do that, I'll tell them about the gum I saw you take out of Mom's purse a week ago."

"You better not!" she said menacingly.

"Oh, yes I would," I nodded slowly, confide
that my submarine escapade would escape detection.

Just before we got home, she said, "You're awfully quiet—were you scared? What was it like down there?"

"I *was* scared, at first. But then I saw Mary and Jesus and Joseph, and after that—"

"You *what?*"

"I saw Mary and Jesus and—"

Before I could finish, she roared with laughter, doubling over and holding her sides. And at that moment, I learned to be very quiet about certain things. There were some things you just couldn't tell anyone about.

That experience at the bottom of the pool had a profound effect on me. I had always believed what grown-ups had told me about the existence of heaven, but from that time on I *knew* it was true.

And gradually I realized that I didn't really care what happened to me in life. There was only one thing I wanted: to go to heaven. I wanted to experience again that wonderful, unbelievable peace and happiness.

I would never be afraid again of dying. Death was nothing—just the gateway to heaven.

3

The McLaughlin Kids

The only person I ever told about what happened in the swimming pool was my sixth-grade teacher, Sister Winifred. She was the sort of person you could tell anything to, and she would understand. Sisters seem to have been guideposts in my life, and she was one of the incredible ones—teachers who required me to perform to the peak of my ability, and who had a profound effect on the course of my life. But before I met her, I had a year in public school. Between fourth and fifth grades, we had moved again, to a suburb of Sioux City known as Leeds. Our new home was miles and miles away from Blessed Sacrament School, and so our parents decided we would attend the nearby public school which their taxes were helping support.

Public School was a *lot* different than parochial school. It started off all right: in those days before the ban on prayer in public schools, our teacher, Miss Ring, began the school day (as so many teachers had for so many generations) with a reading from Scripture and a class prayer. That part was great, but the rest. . . .

In that school they practiced what someone once referred to as the "convoy system of education"—with everything geared to the learning rate of the slowest student in the class. As a result, I discovered that I already knew all the math we were being taught. And during reading one day, Ray Calhoun who sat behind me (and whose lifeguard older brother had fished me out of the pool) raised his hand: "Miss Ring? Rita already knows all this stuff."

Not long after that, we were given a diagnostic reading test, at the end of which Miss Ring announced: "Before I read your scores, I must tell you: I have one perfect test, by someone who is reading at the twelfth-grade, twelfth-month level." Everyone groaned. "That person is Rita McLaughlin!"

When I told my parents that night, I thought they would be pleased; instead, they were gravely concerned. "That school is not helping them," my father said. "In fact, they're all wasting their time there. We can't just leave them there; we're going to have to do something about it."

Lower academic standards were not the only thing which disturbed them. My brothers and sisters were coming home with language and attitudes which were absolutely forbidden in our household. I will never forget the last day of the school year: the kids ran out of school, throwing their books in the air and screaming, "School's out! School's out! Teacher let the fools out! No more teachers, no more books! No more teachers' dirty looks!"

Ron and I looked at one another, shocked: How did these kids dare say things like that? But pretty soon my two little brothers were chanting right along with the older kids. I said to them: "You don't say things like that about teachers!" But all the other kids were doing it, and they just looked at me and laughed, and shouted all the louder.

RJ kept it up all the way home, and even into our house. "No more teachers' dirty looks—"

My mother looked at him, her eyes narrowing, and said, "What did you say? Would you like to repeat that?"

He shook his head and got very quiet.

That evening, we had a "family talk." Normally I dreaded our family talks; they were usually occasioned by behavior sufficiently reprehensible that it could not be dealt with in the usual manner: swift summary court martial, followed by instantly-administered corporal punishment or incarceration. Family talks were for really serious breaches in the McLaughlin code of ethical conduct. And as I was the oldest, the onus of responsibility invariably fell upon me: "Rita, we are especially disappointed in you. You *know* better than to (fill in blank). At your age, you should be setting an example for *good,* not leading your brothers and sisters in the opposite direction!" If we all wound up in Sing-Sing, it would be my fault, and I would be serving the longest sentence.

But despite RJ's apprehension, this family talk was not to deal with misconduct. It was to inform us that, starting in the fall, we would be returning to Blessed Sacrament.

"But Mom, Dad," pleaded Ron, "I *like* my teacher!"

"Me, too!" I chimed in. "Miss Ring is nice."

"That may well be," conceded my father, "but you're not learning anything useful there. And some of the things your brothers are learning," he threw a glance at RJ, "they are going to have to unlearn in a hurry."

But, I thought, Blessed Sacrament was so far away—they didn't have any school buses that came this far; how were we going to get there?

I sensed it was not a propitious time to ask, and my parents did not volunteer that information. But my mind kept working on it: we had only the one car from Dad's company, and he was always away in it, except on weekends. Besides which, Mom didn't even know how to drive.

All that changed two weeks later, when Dad brought home a car that was so old you could see the road through the holes in the floorboards. But it ran, and Mom started learning how to drive.

Meanwhile, summers were made for fun, and if there was one thing the McLaughlin kids knew how to do, it was have fun. We never sat around; if we had a spare moment, we organized something. We lived close by a minor-league baseball field (*very* minor league, though it did have bleachers). Whenever there wasn't a game, I would get on the phone and call up enough neighborhood kids for a game of "work-up"—one-team baseball, where each time you made an out, you worked your way up through the different positions, until it was your turn to bat. We would play after supper until it got dark (in the summertime around 9:00), and we even got some glow-in-the-dark paint for the ball, so we could play later— until my mother told us we were crazy and had to come in.

If there was a league game, on the morning after, we would scour under the bleachers for any coins that might have fallen out of fans' pockets, or empty pop bottles which were worth two cents apiece—significant money in those days. "Dibs on that one!" one would cry, only to be challenged: "No! I had first dibs on that one!"

On really hot and humid summer nights, as a special treat we would be allowed to sleep out under the stars (and under our parents' window). And in the wintertime, when the city flooded the ball field for ice-skating, we would skate until our legs dropped off. Whatever the season, we were always doing, rather than sitting. Even when it rained, we were active: the boys building models, the girls baking. And while my own favorite indoor sport was curling up with a good book, at least my mind was fully engaged, creating the scenes which the author was evoking. (Unlike TV-watching, where all the creating has been done for us, and its smoothly-packaged attitudes and opinions are poured into our passive minds, while our emotional responses are played like a keyboard).

When it came to pranks or adventures, I may have been the oldest, but Ron was usually the instigator. The all-time best (or worst) prank was The Great Hand. Ron had gotten a new Batman flashlight from a cereal box offer, and Dad had gotten him batteries. To me, it was no big deal, just a flashlight which happened to have a Batman insignia on it, but to Ron it was almost magical.

"C'mon!" he whispered to me and Ruthanne one evening, when we were being baby-sat, "RJ and Ricky are asleep. Let's scare 'em with the Bat Light!"

We crept upstairs and into the boys' room. We were being as quiet as we could, but RJ woke up anyway. "What—are you doing?"

"Shh!" admonished Ron. "We're going to scare Ricky. But you've got to promise not to tell Mom and Dad." He agreed; even so, I made him double-promise, because RJ always told Mom and Dad everything. My own brother was the worst tattle-tale in the neighborhood.

The rest of us hid behind the bunk bed, and very softly Ron started making a low, unworldly moan, *"Uuunngh. . . ."* He held his hand above the flashlight, so that the silhouette of a huge hand appeared on the ceiling over Ricky's bed. *"Uuunngh—"*

Ricky woke up. "Huh?"

"I. . . am. . . the. . . Great. . . Hand," intoned Ron, sounding as sepulchral as he could. "I have come for you. Raise your eyes and look above you."

Ricky, age five, did—and froze. There indeed was the

Great Hand—and now its fingers began to move. Ricky's eyes widened. The Great Hand formed slowly into a claw—a reaching claw!

Ricky screamed. Leaping out of bed, he ran out of the room, yelling, "It's going to get me! It's going to get me!"

Meanwhile, Jeanine, our baby-sitter, came roaring up to see what all the commotion was about. "It's the *hand!*" gasped Ricky, when he could talk.

"What hand?" Jeanine demanded.

"The Great Hand! It's come for me!" he wailed hysterically.

Jeanine may have suspected a prank, but her first job was to calm Ricky down, which took about fifteen minutes, while under the beds we bit our knuckles to keep from laughing out loud. When the coast was clear, we snuck into our beds—and never told anyone what we had done. (Thirty years later, we did tell Ricky's wife, who was astonished. "You mean, that really happened? Everyone remembers their worst nightmare, and your brother was convinced that was his.")

When I said we never told anyone, I did not include priests; our father made us go to confession every Saturday, and we were never at a loss for things to confess.

The most memorable—and frightening—of all our escapades happened that same summer. Mom and Dad had gone away for the weekend, to my Aunt Helen's wedding in Philadelphia, and we were being looked after by two elderly spinster sisters from church, who had arrived in a Model A.

We had gotten up early that Saturday morning, because Ron had a plan. "I know a real neat place to go!" he confided to me, when we realized we could probably get away with a whole lot more under these sisters than when Mom and Dad were home. "You know that housing development going up near South Ravine Park?" I nodded. "Well, they're putting in the storm sewers now—great big round pipes, big enough to walk in!" He dropped his voice to a whisper. "Me and a couple of the guys have been in them; you can go *way* in—like caves!"

I was as excited as he was. "We'll take Ruthanne and—"

"Not RJ," Ron said, shaking his head, "he's too little."

"Well if we don't take him, he'll tell."

Ron thought about that and agreed. "You're right; he'll have to come."

In the morning, the four of us pulled on our T-shirts and jeans and sneakers, and went down in the kitchen to make our lunches. Noting that Ron had his trusty Bat Light in his hip pocket, I said, "What's that for?"

"Because sometimes it gets dark in there," then catching my expression, he added, "but don't worry; it's really fun!"

As we made our lunches, we informed the sisters that we would be going for a picnic in the park that day— all day.

"All day?" one sister asked.

"Oh, yes," I assured her, "on Saturdays Mom and Dad always let us do what we want," which was a complete lie.

"Are you sure?" asked the other sister. "Your parents didn't say anything to us about that."

"Yup," confirmed Ron, "we just pack our lunches in our knapsacks, and off we go."

And off we went. The first pipes we came to were above ground, in huge cement sections—we hollered into them for the echo and banged on them with sticks. Great fun— but just an appetizer; the main course was still to come.

"C'mon," said Ron, "I know where we can get into the ones that are in the ground!"

He led us down a hill, to where a storm sewer emptied

into a wide gully. Soon it would have a heavy padlocked grate over it, but for the moment, while they were still putting new sections of the system in place, it was accessible.

In Iowa, severe thunderstorms can create an enormous volume of run-off in no time at all—which was why such huge sewers were needed. I looked up at the sky: it was sunny and bright, not a cloud in sight. Nevertheless, as I peered into the vast, dark mouth gaping open before us like a yawning abyss, I felt my first niggling fear.

4
Lost—and Found

To RJ, going into the storm sewer was definitely a bad idea. "It's awfully dark in there," he declared, stating the obvious.

"C'mon," said Ron, and without looking back he marched into the darkness, before the doubt assailing the youngest member of his squad could infect the others. Ruthanne, who was never afraid of anything, was right behind him.

But RJ still hung back, searching my face to see if he could find anything in my expression to confirm what he was feeling. "Let's go," I said, before he could find it, and taking a deep breath, I went in smiling, as if this were the most fun in the world.

We had hardly gone a hundred feet when Ruthanne started singing a current hit parade favorite at the top of her lungs: "Tra-la-la, twiddle-dee-dee-dee, it gives me a thrill, to wake up in the morning on Mockingbird Hill!"

Hill-Hill-Hill-Hill. . . . as the reverberation echoed and re-echoed up and down the system, she broke into gales of laughter.

"Ruthanne, shut up!" Ron demanded. "If anyone up there hears you, we'll be in *real* trouble!"

Reluctantly Ruthanne curtailed the second Tra-la-la,

and from then on, we spoke in lowered tones, as we walked further—and further and further.

At first, the light from the mouth of the sewer enabled us to see reasonably well, and as our eyes adjusted to the darkness, we continued to make out where we were going. But there was no question that it was getting really dark. I kept looking behind us: each time the entry was smaller and fainter, until it was little more than a pinhole. And inevitably, there came a time when I could not see it at all.

We were feeling our way now, frequently reaching out to make sure the person in front of us was still right there. It was the blackest black I had ever known, even darker than when Ron had locked me in the coat closet the year before. Then, when my eyes had adjusted, the sliver of light beneath the door allowed me to discern shapes. But our eyes were as adjusted as they were going to get, and there were no shapes down here—nothing.

"It's too dark down here!" RJ whimpered.

"Are you afraid of a little dark?" Ruthanne snapped at him. "Don't be such a baby! Nothing's going to happen to you!" Then she laughed. "You don't want to spoil the fun, do you?" The rest of us laughed with her, partly to convince ourselves that we *were* having fun.

"Halt!" commanded Ron, and switched on the Bat Light. Suddenly the darkness was banished, and now our laughter was genuine, as we squinted in the sudden brightness.

"Juncture," he explained, and sure enough, we had come to a place where the pipe we were in split into a Y. Taking out a piece of chalk, he made a large arrow on the left side of the entry to our pipe, pointing back the way we had come. "See that?" he said, tapping a similar, older mark under the one he had just made. "That's the way we do it. Nothing to worry about!"

We could feel chill, clammy air coming down the left

arm. I found myself wishing we'd worn sweatshirts, instead of T-shirts.

"I'm cold!" RJ complained.

"Will you stop whining?" Ruthanne whirled on him. "Bringing you was a big mistake!"

"It was not!"

"It was so! You've been nothing but trouble!"

"Ruthanne," I said soothingly, "leave him alone. It *is* cold down here."

"C'mon," said Ron, exasperated. "The way to keep warm is to keep moving." And with that, he strode up the right arm of the Y, taking the light with him, and leaving the bickering Ruthanne and RJ behind, with me attempting to restore peace. In our scramble to catch up with him and the light, none of us noticed that we had just passed another juncture, in the shape of an inverted Y.

What I did notice was that the Bat Light seemed less bright than it had when he'd first turned it on a few minutes before. It was just my imagination, I told myself, and Mom had said that the only problem with reading so much was that it over-exercised the imagination. For awhile I was actually able to believe that the light had always been a bit yellowish.

Then reality interposed itself: the Bat Light was definitely turning yellow.

"How fresh are those batteries?" I demanded.

"I—I don't know," Ron admitted. He tapped the flashlight's head against the heel of his palm, like he had seen Dad do, and for a moment the light seemed brighter. Then it grew yellow again, even weaker than before.

RJ began to cry, and Ruthanne was uncharacteristically quiet.

"All right," I said, assuming the authority that came with being the eldest, "we're turning around and going back. *Now.*"

Ron did not protest, and took the lead. He had not gone ten steps, before the light went out.

We froze, in total shock. No one said anything, then in a small voice, RJ asked: "Are we lost?"

"No," I assured him, forcing conviction into my voice. "All we have to do is go is just go back the way we came." I could feel RJ's hand groping for mine, but I didn't want to take it, until my own had stopped trembling.

"That's right," added Ron cheerily, "and when we come to the Y, we just bear left."

We started out. Ron again took the lead, with Ruthanne right behind. Then came me, holding RJ's hand. I needn't have worried about him feeling me tremble; he was shaking like a leaf.

We walked—and walked and walked. The only sound was the *squatch, squatch* of our sneakers in the ooze at the bottom of the pipe, which in places was ankle deep. But that was strange, because the pipe we had come up was dry. And come to think of it, it smelled different in here— older, and kind of rotten. And there was a draft now, where there hadn't been one before. Also, by now, even moving more slowly in the pitch black, we had come a whole lot farther than the arm we had come up. . . .

"Ron, stop," I said, trying to sound calm. "This isn't the way we came."

"I know," he sighed.

RJ started to bawl, and when Ruthanne told him to shut up, there was an edge of hysteria in her own voice.

"All right," I declared, trying to sound like a grown-up, "somehow we've gone down a wrong arm. But all we have to do is just re-trace our steps, feeling the walls, until we come to an opening. Then we go down it. That will be the way out." It sounded so logical, so convincing, I almost believed it myself.

At least it was a plan, and we could take definite action.

The others settled down, and Ron and Ruthanne felt for the left side of the pipe, while I, still holding RJ, took the right. We walked—and walked and walked. Nothing.

And now I was genuinely scared. What if coming up, we had missed *two* openings? Then the directions I'd just given would get us even further lost. What if we got confused on which turns we had made and got so lost, we wandered around down here for hours? For the whole rest of the day? We still had our lunches but—

"I'm hungry!" groaned RJ, as if he could read my mind.

"You know, you're really giving me a pain!" Ruthanne yelled at him. "You couldn't be hungry! You had four pancakes for breakfast!"

"I don't care; I *am* hungry! And cold! And I want Mom!" He started to cry again.

"Oh, great!" taunted Ruthanne, "Little baby wants his mommy!"

"That's enough, both of you!" I shouted, trying to sound like a sister, and I clapped my hands sharply, which startled everyone.

It worked, sort of: RJ, grateful to have my hand back, stopped complaining, and Ruthanne left him alone.

But nothing could stop my mind from working. The poor sisters back home hadn't a clue where we were; for all they knew, we might have hopped a bus and gone to a movie. Even if they called the police, they wouldn't have the faintest idea of where to suggest they look. And of course, they would have to call our parents, and the whole thing would come out. Meanwhile, we would still be down here, wandering through the blackest black I had ever seen. . . .

And then another thought bedeviled me: even if all the available police went out looking for us, and Mom and Dad flew home early, no one would ever think of looking down here. And the workmen would not be back on the site until Monday morning—two more days! And even when they returned, there was no guaranteeing that they would be working anywhere near where we were—wherever that was.

That did it: I felt like calling out for Mom, myself.

"Rita?" whispered RJ up to me.

"What," I almost didn't want to ask.

"Are we ever going to get out of here?"

That was downright spooky: I would just have to stop thinking near him. "Of course we are," I whispered back. "Don't be silly!"

"I just wondered."

But now I had another thought that I *really* didn't want him picking up: this might not end with our starving to death or going crazy. What if it rained? They made these pipes this big, to handle flash flooding which completely filled them like a garden hose. . . .

If this were your usual faith-building testimony, right about here the protagonist would finally remember to pray. Not me: I was just too scared. It was all I could do to fight back tears and fight down panic.

And then, when I could not fight any longer and was about to give in, I saw that tiny pinhole of light.

I screamed for joy! So did the others, and we ran out of there, slipping and falling and laughing. When we burst out into the daylight, we pointed at each other, convulsed with mirth: all of us were covered with black muck!

But the sun was still shining, and the day was still warm—and we were still alive!

A creek flowed through the park, and we went to where it had thick underbrush on both sides.

Stripping down to our underwear, we did our best to wash the muck off. Then, while our clothes dried under the sun, we huddled under the bushes and ate our lunch. If anyone asked us when we got home, where we'd been (and they did ask, for there was no way we could wash out the permeating stench of that ooze), we could truthfully say we had done exactly what we had said: gone for a picnic in the park.

Looking back on that episode, I marvel at God's mercy: we may think we are lost and alone, wandering in the dark, but He is always there—whether we call out to Him, or not. And so is the angel He has assigned to look after us. If any child in my classroom ever sits off-center in his or her seat, to leave room for their guardian angel, they are welcome to sit that way all year long.

5

Upside-down Pieces

I cannot remember when I first wanted to become a sister—
probably the first time a teacher asked: "Which of you
is going to be a priest or sister, when you grow up?" A
lot of us raised our hands in those early years, but somehow
I knew that I wasn't doing it just because everyone else
was, or because it would please the teacher. Or because
it was an Irish tradition that one boy and one girl from
each family would give themselves to the Lord in religious
life, and I was the oldest girl in the McLaughlin family.
For me, it was real.

So every time I saw a sister from a different order,
I studied her habit: would I like to wear one like that?
For the rest of my life? So far, my favorite was the all-
white habits of the Dominican sisters. And because Mom
and Dad had decided that we would be going back to
Blessed Sacrament when school began in the fall, I would
soon be seeing a lot of them again.

To get us to that school, Mom had to drive ten miles
over an old dirt road barely wide enough for two cars that
wound through hills and fields—after which, she had to
go to work. (Kids are by nature totally self-centered; it almost
never occurs to them what enormous sacrifices their parents
might be making on their behalf, be it accepting a

diminished lifestyle in order that their children might go to college, or absorbing their children's hurtful wrath and lasting enmity by crossing their wills when other parents were unwilling to do so with their own children. Or by learning to drive over dirt roads before dawn and then working a full day, so their children might have the best education available. A generation later, as they raise their own children, their offspring might realize what had been done for them—hopefully not too late to say thank you.)

Because Mom was working, we had to come home alone. It took two transfers on the city bus system, then a mile walk and another bus and another mile home. When the buses were on time, and the roads weren't icy, it took an hour and a half. In the wintertime, we froze. Iowa winters were like that: by the time we got home, we could not feel our hands or feet.

But how I loved being back at Blessed Sacrament! My teacher was Sister Winifred, another ancient, beautiful sister. On the first day, she said to me: "I'm kind of old, and it's hard for me to walk; would you be willing to carry my books for me this year?"

"Certainly!" I exclaimed, honored.

So every day, when Sister had to go back and forth to the convent, I would carry her things, and she would talk with me along the way. One day, she asked me: "Have you ever thought what you're going to do with your life?"

"Sure, I'm going to be a sister."

"How long have you known that?"

"I don't know—a long time." Then I remembered the pool. "I guess I knew it for certain, summer before last."

Ever since seeing the Holy Family in the bottom of the pool, I had known that I wanted to be holy, too, so I could go straight to heaven and be with them. The only really holy people were sisters. Other people were just moms and dads, and moms and dads weren't holy, because they yelled at you and made you do your work, and made your life miserable; they couldn't be holy. So I had to become a sister.

That was when I told Sister Winifred what I had seen, when I had almost drowned.

Having never told anyone about it, I was a bit apprehensive—but she wasn't surprised or skeptical; she just smiled.

Then she asked: "What kind of sister do you want to be?"

"I—I never thought about that."

So I started thinking about it. And each day I would share my latest thinking with Sister. At first, I thought I might want to be a Carmelite, like St. Theresa of Lisieux. Sister Ephraim had made her sound so special—"The Little Flower," so faithful in her prayers for missionaries that she became their patron saint.

But then I thought I might like to be a missionary myself; then I could be a martyr and die for Jesus.

Sister Winifred frowned, when I told her that. "Child, are you sincere? Do you have any idea what you are talking about?"

I told her that Sister Ephraim had made martyrdom sound like the most wonderful thing God could ask you to do. My favorite of her stories was the one about St. Tarcisius, the little boy who carried the Sacrament to the early Christians being held in prison, before they were fed to the lions. Other Christians, caught trying to smuggle Communion into them, were thrown into prison with them. Finally, their friends decided to risk sending a boy, reasoning that the guards would not bother him. When they asked for volunteers, Tarcisius, the youngest, pleaded so urgently that they gave him the Eucharist to take, warning him not to stop or talk to anyone on the way.

Some Roman boys who knew him called out, "Tarcisius,

come and play!" When he refused, they jumped on him and tore open his cloak. Finding the Eucharist, and realizing that he must be a Christian, they stoned him to death.

That a boy no older than me would rather die than betray the Eucharist to unbelievers, had made a profound impression on me.

Well," said Sister Winifred thoughtfully, "if you are ever called to martyrdom, God will provide you the grace to fulfill that assignment. But I should remember, if I were you, that even the Lord Himself would have preferred to let that cup pass His lips."

One day she asked me: "Have you ever thought of becoming a Dominican?"

"Oh, yes; I love the way you dress, all in white; it looks so pretty!"

She shook her head. "Child, that is hardly a criterion for choosing an order." She was silent for the rest of the walk to school.

Then, as I held the door for her, she said: "I think you should start asking Jesus, what *He* wants you to do. Whatever He tells you, it will be exactly right for you, and you will be happy in it. But let *Him* decide."

So I started praying every day: Jesus, what do you want me to do?

Meanwhile, my parents decided that our commute to Blessed Sacrament was simply too much; in the winter we were leaving well before sun-up and getting home long after dark. So Dad found us another home, just five blocks from the Church (and school) of the Immaculate Conception. My seventh-grade teacher was Sister Camilla, and she was great, despite her black habit. Our teachers

were Servite Sisters—Servants of Mary, dedicated to Our
Lady of Sorrows.

Other than their white wimples, the only part of their
habits which was not black was the Eucharistic emblem
worn on their scapulars over their hearts. Made of gold-
plated metal, it was a circle surrounding three cut-out
initials, IHS, and it was worn on their scapulars over their
hearts.

Soon after school began, Sister Camilla explained the
meaning of this insignia to the class. "Does anyone know
what IHS stands for?"

"I Hate School!" shouted a boy in the back.

Sister did not get annoyed; she just shook her head,
a little disappointed. "The Greek letters IHS stand for Jesus
Christ, Saviour of Mankind," she said. "They're also on
the Eucharist." And then she told us why they wore them.

When St. Julianna of Falconarie (Italy), the niece of
one of the seven founders of the Servite Order, was on
her deathbed, she very much wanted to receive the
Eucharist one more time. Unable to swallow, she asked
the chaplain of the convent to at least lay the consecrated
Eucharist over her heart, so she might be as near to Jesus
as possible. At first the priest did not want to, but when
she pleaded, he finally draped the altar cloth over her,
then placed the host on top of the white linen. Right in
front of everyone's eyes, it disappeared! Later, when they
were preparing her body for burial, there, right in the
skin over her heart was the imprint of the host, with the
initials IHS clearly visible.

When she finished, the classroom was perfectly still.
And no one ever joked about the meaning of IHS again.

I loved Sister Camilla and the whole school; my only
problem was the other girls in my class. As girls enter
adolescence, they become extremely cliquish, and if you're
not in, you're out! New to the parish and the school, I

was about as out as it was possible to get—and no one invited me in.

Rejection is never fun at any time, but when one is twelve and peer relationships are the most important thing in life, it can be devastating! (A fact many parents do not appreciate.)

Sometimes the other girls would say things like: "We'd like to invite you to the party, but—well, we just don't have room." More often, they wouldn't say anything. Two or three of them might be talking in front of their lockers, and when they saw me coming, they would turn away and lower their voices. Or at lunch, a group might wave a friend over to join them—in the chair I was about to sit in.

Aware of what I was going through, Sister Camilla went out of her way to make me feel welcome. So did the other sisters, and not having anyone to talk to, I found myself spending more and more time with them. I also found myself spending more time with Jesus.

I knew that I was being labeled an apple-polisher, but at least the sisters would talk to me. It didn't help when our first grades came out, and I was at the top of the class. Or when my artwork was praised, and I was asked to make the posters for our parish's new building campaign.

But the worst was when Sister Camilla heard me sing. My parents had always put special emphasis on the creative arts, encouraging us wherever we showed talent or interest. On Saturdays, for instance, I went to the Art Institute for lessons. But music was the most important expression: both Mom and Dad sang in quartets, and my father had been selected for the Bishop's Choir, made up of the finest voices in the diocese. So I also took voice lessons—and piano lessons and clarinet lessons. I even learned to play the church organ.

One day, getting us ready for the diocesan children's

choir festival, Sister Camilla asked each of us to sing a few lines by ourselves. Afterwards, she took me aside. "You have a good voice," she smiled, "and you like to pray, too, don't you?" I nodded. "How would you like to sing daily Mass for us in the morning?"

I was nonplussed. In those days, Catholic parishioners joined in the congregational singing with reluctance, if at all; on Sundays, therefore, the burden fell to the choir to lead and carry the singing, and during the week it fell to appointed singers. I, a mere seventh-grader, had just been appointed! I was thrilled.

Each morning, my dog Ginger would walk me to church in time for 7:30 Mass. She was supposed to be our family's dog, but she had adopted me, and I her. At least half English Springer Spaniel, she had a reddish coat, which was why we'd named her Ginger.

She would wait outside during the service and then escort me over to school, before going home. In the afternoon, a little after two (according to Mom), she would get up and stretch and yawn, and trot off to school, to accompany us home.

And so, quite without intending to, I became a daily communicant. Something was happening to my life— something which I had not planned, and over which I had little, if any control. All I wanted was to be exactly like the other kids my age; in fact, I would have given anything, if I could just have been one of them. But that, apparently, was not to be.

What did happen was that my prayer life deepened. It was not intentional; it just happened. With no friends, I turned more and more to Him. But those times more than compensated for my loneliness; they were wonderful, and so was the fellowship with the sisters and Monsignor Smith, our pastor. He was an ex-Marine chaplain, really gruff on the outside—but not on the inside, I came to discover. On Saturday mornings after Mass, Ginger and I would go over to the rectory, where I answered the phone and fixed him breakfast, since it was his housekeeper's day off. (Ginger waited patiently outside.)

The first Saturday, after I'd served him, he said, "Well, where's yours? Do I have to get up and serve you, too?"

Delighted, I got a plate for myself, and that began a tradition which made Saturday mornings one of my favorite times of the week.

One day Sister Camilla asked me: "Have you ever thought of becoming a sister?"

I laughed. "Sister Winifred asked me the same thing at Blessed Sacrament."

"What did you tell her?"

"That I wanted to be one; I really loved their white habits."

"And ours?"

I made scrunched-up expression. "They're *black*, Sister. To wear nothing but black would be terrible; it's so ugly!" She recoiled as if I had slapped her, and instantly I wished I could take the words back. "Sister, I'm sorry! I didn't mean—"

"It's all right," she smiled, "it doesn't matter." But I could see the disappointment lingering in her face. I felt awful; she and her sisters had been so kind to me.

It is a testimony to the grace residing in Sister Camilla's heart that she never let my thoughtlessness affect our friendship. After that, I loved all those sisters so much that—well, I could not honestly say that I thought black was beautiful. But it certainly was not terrible.

Looking back now, I can see that all of this was God, gently, gradually, separating me unto Himself, preparing me for the life to which he had called me, and which I so wanted. But I didn't see it at the time; all I was aware of then, was the ongoing pain of being left out.

Matters came to a head the following year. May was Mary's month, and the highest honor in the parish was to be the eighth-grader chosen to be May Queen and crown the Blessed Mother. At Blessed Sacrament, all the eighth-grade girls had been eligible, and the class had voted for which would be May Queen. I had assumed it would be the same way here.

It wasn't. At Immaculate Conception, unbeknownst to me, the May Queen was chosen from among those with the best attendance at Mass. I learned that the hard way, when a girl named Phyllis who was also a regular at Mass, and her friend, Sally, confronted me one morning: "You think *you're* going to be chosen?" Phyllis demanded. "I've been in this parish since kindergarten! I can't imagine why they even put your name on the ballot!"

I was speechless.

"If you think that your going to Mass every day is going to get you to be May Queen, you've got another think coming!" declared Sally.

"But—I don't know anything about a ballot," I tried to explain.

"Like heck you don't! You expect us to believe that?"

I was unable to answer—which only made them angrier.

"My mother is so upset about this," Phyllis shouted, "that she is going to Monsignor Smith!" And with that, they stormed off, leaving me trembling and fighting back tears.

The day before the final vote, there were two names on the ballot, mine and Phyllis's. I went to our eighth-grade teacher, Sister Mary Cleopha who was also principal of the school, and pleaded, "Please, take my name off. Let Phyllis be May Queen."

She looked at me sternly. "No, Rita, your name is staying on there. This is the way we do it, and your name will stay on."

"Please, Sister," I begged, "I don't want to be May Queen! You don't know what I'm going through!"

But perhaps she did. Smiling, she said, "Why don't you let God decide who will be May Queen? Just let Him take care of it."

So I went straight to the church, to the end of the last pew on the right, my major-problem prayer-place, and kneeling down, I poured my heart out to Him.

I did not pray: Be it be done unto me, according to Thy word. I did not even pray: Nevertheless, not my will, but Thine be done. I prayed: "Please, dear God, don't make me be May Queen! Don't let it happen!"

When the vote was counted, and I was one vote short, I thanked Him from the bottom of my heart! Never had I been so grateful for anything that He had (or had not) done! The other girls didn't believe me, of course, when they asked me if I was upset, and I said, no, I was really happy Phyllis got it. Just before the end of school, her friend Sally came up to me and said, "Why don't you admit it: you could just die that you didn't get it!"

That summer I applied for early acceptance into a convent.

Years later on a retreat, a priest named Monsignor Berube would say: "Our lives are like a giant jigsaw puzzle dumped out on the table, with all the pieces upside down. There are two ways we can assemble that upside-down puzzle: We can do it ourselves, fitting the pieces together the way we think they ought to go. Sometimes they do seem to fit, but more often we have to force them together, making them fit where we think they should. The other way, is to let the Lord show us which pieces go with which, the order in which to connect them, and then how that group attaches to the next.

"At the end of your life, you turn the puzzle over. If you have done it yourself, a few parts may be recognizable, but most of it will be a chaotic mess. But if you have surrendered yourself entirely to the Lord—if you have let *Him* assemble the pieces—then it will be the most beautiful picture you have ever seen. You will see why He put which pieces together when—and how what seemed to make no sense whatever, makes perfect sense in the end."

6

To be a Saint

As soon as I saw the ad, I ran to the convent to show Sister Camilla. A Carmelite community in Rhode Island that had a prep school which would accept fourteen-year-olds! It was a boarding school for young girls who felt they had vocations, where they could complete their high-school education in a spiritual environment and then decide. Part of the convent was cloistered, which meant the sisters had no contact with the outside world. That would be all right, I thought; I could spend all my time praying for missionaries, like The Little Flower. But the other part actually sent out missionaries, and that sounded like more fun. I could go to South America and work in the jungle, helping the poor Indians. When it came to missionaries, I decided as I ran, I would rather be one than pray for one.

Sister Camilla was not as excited as I was. "Why would you want to be a Carmelite?" she asked.

"Because St. Theresa was one, and I like their white habit."

She smiled. "Actually, they wear white and brown."

"But it's still not black," I replied, and we both laughed.

She told me that I ought to go see Monsignor Smith; I would need a letter from him, as my pastor, for the

Mother Superior to even consider me.

Now in his sixties, Monsignor Smith, the former Marine chaplain, was inclined to be a bit gruff. The other kids were afraid of him, but we'd had so many cornflakes together, I was long past being intimidated by him.

He took a pitcher of iced tea from his refrigerator, and poured us each a glass. Then we took our customary places at the breakfast table, and in a rush I began my prepared speech.

"How old are you, Rita?" he asked, cutting in, before I was half-way through.

"Fourteen—fourteen and a half," I added, sensing that he must think I was too young.

He did. "Why on earth would a fourteen-year-old girl want to go into a convent?"

"Fourteen and a half."

"And why so far away? What's wrong with the sisters right here?"

"I don't like their habits."

That surprised him. "Whatever is wrong with them?"

"They're black."

He smiled. "I think you'd look really good in black."

What does he know, I thought, but I didn't say anything.

He shook his head. "You're so young to be making such a major decision!" Then he frowned and studied me. "Has anyone been influencing you?"

"No, sir. Well, yes—Jesus has."

His eyebrows raised. "He has?" I nodded. "You pray a lot, don't you," he mused, and I nodded again.

With a sigh, he got up. "I'm going to have a talk with your parents."

I was afraid he was going to try to get them to talk me out of it, but to my surprise, he took my side. He told them that he had never met a child so young with such a prayer life, and that while the final decision must be theirs, he did feel that it was the will of God. His only reservation was that Rhode Island seemed too far away.

When my mother related that to me, I could not believe it. Finally I figured that Monsignor must have prayed, and that Jesus must have told him it was okay.

But now I had my parents to deal with. While they had known of my desire to become a sister someday, they were shocked that I wanted to do so right now—and hurt that I had not confided this to them. Especially my mom. "I know the reason you want to go: it's me," she said, starting to cry. "I'm sorry I've been such a bad mother to you."

"Mom, it's not you; you've been a great mom!" I felt terrible.

"No, I made you work too hard, and I was all the time nagging you. I shouldn't have been, but I was only doing what I thought was good for you."

"Mom, please!" and now I started to cry, too. "I love you so much! Please don't go on this way!" and I gave her a hug.

After she calmed down, she told me something she had never mentioned before. "When I was growing up, I never had a lot of love." She paused. "So it's been difficult for me to know what to do with you children. I really— I didn't know how to love."

With a sob, I flung my arms around her. "You did great, Mom, really! My wanting to be a sister has nothing to do with you; I've wanted to, ever since I can remember." I smiled and dabbed away her tears, and mine, too. "I may have gotten mad at you, but I always knew you loved me. And besides, the other girls' mothers were yelling at them all the time, too; I never thought you were any different."

After that, we were okay. But then she started going out and buying me all kinds of expensive clothes, and

I knew finances were tight, especially with a new baby on the way.

"Mom," I finally said, as gently as I could, "I don't need all these clothes. I'm going to the convent. They'll give me whatever I need, probably just a black dress."

She started crying again. "They're not going to take off all your hair, are they?"

"No, Mom, of course not," I assured her.

With my parents' approval, Monsignor Smith had written to the Mother Superior of the convent in Omaha, the motherhouse of all the Servite Sisters in America, requesting that I be considered as a postulant candidate for their novitiate, and I had received an invitation to come for a visit. So, on a cool, overcast day in August, Sister Camilla and another sister drove me the hundred miles from Sioux City to Omaha.

The Servites' motherhouse was actually a working farm on one of the hills overlooking the city. As we drove up the long drive flanked by evergreens, I looked up at the old brick edifice and thought that it might be a little ominous-looking if I weren't so glad to be coming here.

We were shown into the guest parlor, and were served some tea by some young sisters, and then the Mother Superior, who was also Vice-Provincial of the order, came in. She was of medium build, about sixty, with a serene countenance. Her eyes were bright blue, and there were reading spectacles perched on her nose. I liked her.

No sooner had we sat down, than she addressed me: "Monsignor Smith has written me this letter," she said, holding it open and tapping it with her other hand. "He has asked me to admit you to our convent, but we have no program for anyone so young." She sighed and shook her head. "You would have no friends your own age, none of the things that must be of interest to you."

She put the letter on the tea table and peered at me over her reading glasses. "Young women coming here need to have completed high school and preferably to have had some college." She smiled. "Now suppose you tell me why a fourteen-year-old would want to enter a convent."

By that point I could not remember any of the logical reasons I had thought of, since first receiving the invitation. Instead, I heard myself blurting out the heart-of-hearts truth: "I want to be a saint."

The Mother Superior was taken aback. "There are other ways of becoming a saint."

"Not that I know of," I replied, then realizing that might be taken as rudeness, I quickly added, "It's all I ever wanted to be, since I was little."

She looked at me, as if she was thinking: you are still little right now. But she just nodded and stood up. She thanked me for coming, and the sisters drove me back to Omaha.

Two weeks later, a letter arrived. In it, the Mother Superior said that after submitting my application to the Servite Council (made up of five Mothers Superior from other convents, plus the Mother Provincial, the Vice-Provincial, and the Novice Mistress), it was felt that the convent would not be a good and healthy environment for a person my age, and that I should stay home with my parents, where, it was understood, there would soon be a new baby. It was felt that my help would be much needed at home. I should continue to pray, and after a few years, if I still felt as I did, I might apply again.

Tears were blurring my vision, as I finished the letter.

I went out and sat on the front steps and put my head down in my arms and wept.

I mentioned how often God sends the right person when we most need them. Sometimes they came on four legs, instead of two. . . .

Ginger was a little spaniel with a big heart. I loved that dog, and she loved me, and it really bothered her whenever I cried. Now she came up to me and whimpered and shoved her nose under my arm and licked my face, so that I had to stop crying and pay attention to her.

I hugged her—and all at once I stared at her. "Ginger! If I'd gone into that convent, I never would have seen you again!"

I gave her another hug—and suddenly I felt a lot better about being home.

7

Home, Sweet Home

Ginger was a great encouragement during that next year, my first in high school—and it was almost as if she knew she was helping. Actually, everyone was helping; dear Monsignor Smith asked me to also play the organ at morning Mass. Just before the service one blistering cold December morning, Monsignor saw poor Ginger shaking in the dark outside the church, waiting for me to come out. "Rita," he said gruffly, "that dog is going to freeze out there! You can let her into the vestibule. Just make her stay on that little rug over there, where people take their goulashes off. Will she stay? She must never, ever come into the church!"

"Yes, Monsignor. She'll stay."

And she did—for the first week. The choir loft and organ were at the far end of the church, above the vestibule and the front doors. Ginger had seen me going up and down the stairs, and one morning in the second week, as I came down from the choir loft for Communion, there she was, on the stair landing. The look on her face said: "I know I'm not supposed to be up here, but please, if I'm really small and quiet, can I stay?" Scowling, I shook my head at her—but did not drag her down to the rug.

Ginger's tail, however, was neither small nor quiet. When

I went back up to the loft, it went *wap, wap, wap* on the polished tile floor. And two days later, returning from taking Communion I found that she had crept all the way up to the loft. The instant she saw me coming—*wap, wap, wap.*

That was too much! Summoning all the silent authority I could muster, I glared and pointed at her to *go down to the rug*. She slunk down—but would go no further than the landing. She seemed to know that I was in no position to scold her, let alone force her to be obedient. We wound up in an undeclared truce—and for a few days the cease-fire held.

In the meantime, I was becoming familiar with the organ (which was hardly what kids today would term "user-friendly"). I was learning what the various stops would do, and beginning to use them during the service. But the foot pedals were another story; I had to learn them by feel, and spent a week practicing, first with no shoes, then with the special thin-soled ones I would actually play in.

The morning came for my foot-pedal debut, playing the Communion Psalm. I took off my school shoes, slipped on the special ones, pulled out the stops that activated the pedals, and—*Wohm, Wohm, Wohm!* The organ emitted the most horrible noises, as I felt something frightened and furry between my feet.

Ginger, having seen me take off my shoes, had come running up to play with my feet—and had stepped on the live pedals. With a yelp, she high-tailed it down out of the loft, while everyone down in the congregation craned around to see the young organist. I knew what they were thinking: Poor girl, she's never used the pedals before, and now look at the mess she's made! I could have killed that dog.

After that, Ginger never ventured up to the choir loft

again. She stayed meekly on the landing, a model of canine obedience—until the Sunday that I would never forget for the rest of my life.

It was ten o'clock solemn Mass—a thousand people, including my parents, were in the congregation, and I was singing in the choir. Our associate pastor, Father Wingart, a young and serious priest (who was a favorite of Ginger's, as he always stopped to pet her), was to give the sermon.

My first inkling that something was wrong came when I heard muffled snickering from below. I glanced over the edge of the choir loft—and was horrified to see Ginger coming down the aisle. Tail wagging as she looked up at Father Wingart, she lay down directly in front of the pulpit.

I stopped singing and just stood there in frozen horror. This could not be happening! It was worse than my worst nightmare—and there was nothing, absolutely nothing, I could do!

Busy arranging his Bible markers and sermon text, Father Wingart had not seen Ginger approach. But now, hearing the whispering and stifled laughter, and aware that something was distracting the congregation, he peered over the pulpit.

I didn't want to see his expression, but I didn't dare look away. He was not amused. "Rita?" he called up to me. "Would you please come down here and get your dog?"

No one said a word. I hurried down as quickly and quietly as I could, slipping out the front door and going around to the side door which was open for fresh air. "Ginger!" I said in a loud whisper, "Come here!"

She looked over at me—and then put her head down between her paws, to let me know she was staying. She liked this church, and also assumed that once again I was powerless to enforce my command.

"*Rita.*" Father Wingart's patience was at an end.

"*Ginger.*" So was mine.

Not Ginger's—*wap, wap, wap.*

Anger overcame mortification; I went in and dragged her out by the collar, her nails scraping on the marble floor. That sound, that awful moment, was seared into my memory. Ginger knew she had done a really bad thing, and for the rest of that day she went around with her tail between her legs. But I could not forgive her trespass— until the next time I said the Our Father.

I loved Catholic high school and threw myself into everything I could possibly get involved in—Swimming, Band, and Junior Chorus. In addition, I was still taking private voice lessons, as well as art lessons at the Institute on Saturday mornings, progressing from pastels to watercolors to oils and ultimately portraiture.

As for the schoolwork itself, I would get interested in the textbooks and read them all the way through, the way I did novels. After that, I found that if I concentrated in class, I could get it all, right there. Which was a good thing, because my study halls were taken up with extra-curricular activities, and any spare time after school I spent at the pool. That left the bus for homework—but by keeping my attention focussed, I was able to get all of it done en route, even the Latin and Algebra, which were a challenge.

In swimming, I was working hard to become qualified

as a Junior Water Safety Instructor. Looking back, it may
be that I was subconsciously compensating for the accident,
determined to conquer the thing which had nearly
conquered me. I don't know—all I knew then was that
I adored swimming. I was a big girl and growing bigger,
but in the water I never felt awkward; what I felt was—
graceful.

In my swimsuit I looked older than my fifteen years,
and boys began striking up conversations with me. But
the only boy I dated that year—well, sort of dated—was
someone I met at the drugstore, not the pool.

Vern was a bright, nice-looking boy, with a lot of
confidence. A junior in the local high school, he played
on their football team, and after we had talked a bit, he
asked: "Look, can we go out sometime?"

"Are you Catholic?"

He was taken aback. "What's that got to do with it?
Are you Jewish, or something?"

"No," I said, "but I *am* Catholic."

"Well, I'm not really any religion," he said, shaking
his head. "I'm not into that stuff." He looked at me and
smiled. "Is that a problem?"

"Yes," I replied, not meeting his gaze. "My dad is not
going to like you." Instantly I thought: why am I always
so blunt? I could have said that more tactfully—though
I could not think how.

It didn't seem to faze him. "Well, why don't you let
me meet your parents first? Maybe when they meet me,
they'll like me." Vern really had a lot of confidence.

"Well—"

"When is a good time?"

"No time."

"C'mon," he laughed, "give me a chance!" He paused.
"How about Tuesday night? There's no football practice
on Tuesdays."

I couldn't believe this: he was actually inviting himself!
But Tuesday was not good; that was the night we went
to Novena. "I'm busy Tuesday," I said, hoping that would
end it.

"How about next Tuesday?"

"I'm busy every Tuesday."

"What do you do on Tuesdays—do you have a job,
or something?" Vern was also not easily discouraged.

"No, I go to church."

"Boy!" he smiled, "You're really into that church
business, aren't you! Is your whole family?" I nodded. "Do
they all go on Tuesday nights?"

"No, just me."

"You go by yourself?" I nodded again. "Well," he
chuckled, "if that's the only way I'm going to get to see
you, I'll go with you!"

I was speechless.

Seeing my startled expression, he added, "Or is that
forbidden, or something?"

"No," I managed, "you can come with me."

"Fine!" he beamed. "What time should I pick you up?"

"Well, the service begins at 7:30."

"How far is it from your home?"

"It's only five blocks."

"Great! I'll be there at 7:15."

I shook my head. "If you were serious about meeting
my parents, you'd better come a little earlier. Fulton Sheen
comes on at 7:00, and they won't leave the TV set while
he's on."

We left it that he would come at 6:30.

Now that the arrangement had been made, part of
me began to get excited: my first date! But the other part
said: He'll never come! Someone going to Novena, when
he isn't even Catholic? Forget it! And if he does come,
what's Dad going to say? I suppose I've got to tell them

that he might come—but what a lovely supper that will be! I could imagine my father exploding, and my mother silently pleading with him, and the kids too fascinated to eat. . . .

In the end, rationalizing that since there was next-to-zero chance that he actually would come, I decided not to tell them. No point in needlessly upsetting them.

Tuesday supper, it seemed to me like everyone was dawdling through their meal. And we had to do the Rosary afterwards—I could just imagine Vern arriving, as we were all fingering our beads.

Looking at Ricky playing with his mashed potatoes, I would gladly have taken a funnel and stuffed them into his mouth! But if I said anything that gave away my impatience, my lovely brothers would undoubtedly want to know why I was in such a hurry. I compromised by clearing the dishes, though it wasn't my turn; I knew Ruthanne and RJ wouldn't object. Ricky did, though: "Hey! I'm not through with my potatoes!" Oh, yes, you are, you little creep!

During the Rosary, as usual we kids took turns doing the mysteries. This night we were doing the Sorrowful Mysteries, and it was Ron's turn to do the last one. As he started, I snuck a glance at the mantel clock: 6:23. Very good, Ron, very holy—hurry up!

During the final decade, I kept looking from the clock to the remaining beads—it was going to be close.

"— is now and ever shall be, world without end, Amen."

My mother looked over at me, her eyebrows raised at the vehemence with which I pronounced the last amen. But not my father; he was looking out the front window. "There's someone out there," he announced.

"I'll get it," I exclaimed, jumping to my feet and going to the front door.

"They haven't rung the bell yet," my father wryly observed.

The moment it did ring, I jerked open the door, and there was Vern, looking terrific in white bucks, white trousers, and a bright red shirt. Parked at the curb behind him was a gleaming white convertible. Standing behind me was my father.

"Hello, Mr. McLaughlin," Vern said, looking him square in the eye and holding out his hand, "I'm Vernon Rogers." I smiled, impressed at his maturity.

"Hello," my father replied, coming out on the front porch and shaking his hand—and waiting.

"I'm here to take Rita—"

"Son," my father cut him off, "how old are you?" He, too, was impressed with Vern's maturity, but not quite the same way I was.

"Seventeen."

"Rita's only 15; why do you want to take her out?"

"Actually, sir," said Vern still smiling, "my birthday's in June, so we're only 18 months apart—that's not really that big an age difference."

He must be his team's quarterback, I thought; he certainly handles himself well under pressure.

My father frowned. "What church do you go to?"

"Well, right now I'm going to church with your daughter—well, actually, she's taking me. But afterwards, I'd like to take her for a soda at Curran's Drug, if that's all right."

Dad turned to me. "You mean, you've already worked this all out?"

"Yes," I murmured, trembling, unable to meet his gaze. I was definitely not quarterback material.

Now my father was looking past Vern, at the car. "What does your father do, son?"

"He's in construction, Mr. McLaughlin. That's his car. He lets me use it, as long as my grades are up, and I haven't gotten out of line."

"Ever had any accidents?"

"No, sir."

"Ever been stopped by the police?"

"Daddy!" I whispered, but he ignored me.

"No, sir. Clean record, so far."

My father was silent, and I realized he must have run out of questions. "Well," he said, "I guess, if you're going to church. . . "

Seeing a gap in the defensive line and the goal line right there, Vern called an audible: "Mr. McLaughlin, I promise to have Rita back by 9:30, if it's all right."

For the first time since the doorbell rang, my father smiled. "That'll be fine; have a good time."

"Whew!" exhaled Vern, when we were in the car, "Your dad's tough!" He was careful to pull away from the curb slowly.

On the way to church, I though I'd better prepare him for what he was getting into. But where to begin? "Vern, when was the last time you were in church?"

"I don't remember," he shrugged, glancing at me. "To tell you the truth, I don't remember *ever* going to church."

"Well, do you believe in God?"

He looked out the windshield. "Yeah," he said after a moment, "I guess I do. I mean, somebody had to do all this stuff," and he gestured at the trees and the night sky.

Good, I thought, that was a beginning. "What about Jesus?"

"Who?"

"Jesus Christ."

"Well," he chuckled, "I use his name a lot on the football field; all the guys do." He saw that I was serious. "Who is he?"

"Jesus is God's Son. He is God incarnate." I could see that I'd lost him there, and tried again: "He became a little baby like us, so He could live with us, and so we couldn't say, 'Hey, God, You don't know what it's like down here!' And when He found out what it was like, He died for us."

Vern was listening, but it was hard to tell how much he was understanding. I plunged on: "He healed people, He made people happy, and then He died on the Cross, and He rose from the dead, and He went back to heaven."

Vern looked at me, eyes wide. "He did all that?"

I nodded and pointed out the entrance for the church parking lot. He turned in and found a place, but made no move to get out. He wanted to finish. So did I, and we had a little time; the clock on the dash said 7:10.

"But if he *was* God, why did He do all that? I mean, isn't God supposed to be this magic person who throws stars out in space and makes the flowers bloom?" I nodded. "Well, why would he want to do all that stuff?"

"Because He loves us."

Gently he hit the steering wheel with the palm of his hand. "I never even thought he cared," he murmured.

"He does—more than you can possibly know." I nodded at the clock. "We'd better go in."

"What are we going to be doing in there?" he said, getting out and coming around to open my door. Seeing his expression, I had to smile; for the first time since I'd met him, Vern looked a little unsure of himself.

"Well," I said, getting out, "it's very quiet in there, so we won't be able to talk. People will be singing and giving praise to God and His mother."

"His mother? Who's she?"

"Her name is Mary."

"You mean, you worship her, too?"

"Oh, no," I said hurriedly, "we worship only God. We *honor* His mother, for her perfect obedience when she gave birth to Jesus, God the Son." I could see I was losing him again. "It's a little complicated; I'll explain it to you later."

But as we went up the steps, he whispered: "This Mary—how do you honor her?"

"Well, one way is in song."

He shook his head. "That's really strange."

"Not really," I said, trying to be patient. "You must have heard the song, 'Mother McCree'—well, the Irish sing songs like that, because they love their mothers! So if 'Mother McCree'—why not the Mother of God?"

He pondered that and then nodded, as we went up the steps and into the church. "That makes sense."

After we had slipped into a side pew at the back, I whispered to him: "This isn't our regular worship service; this is what we call a Novena."

"What does that mean?" he whispered back.

"It comes from the Latin for nine and means Nine Days."

"You mean, you do this for nine Tuesdays?"

"Actually, it's a Perpetual Novena: we do it nine Tuesdays, and then we start over again. So it's all year, every Tuesday night. We pray for the sick and for people to be healed, and we ask the Blessed Mother—God's Mother, and this novena is to Our Lady of Perpetual Help, which means she's always—"

An old woman across the aisle from us, turned and scowled at me.

I nodded sheepishly and remained silent for awhile. During the singing, I shared the hymnal, and Vern made a real effort to join in. Then during the Magnificat, I tried to explain, in a barely audible whisper: "She's always with us, always ready to intercede on our behalf, to ask Jesus to help us."

"*Shh!*" The old woman was glaring at me.

I shrugged and decided the rest would have to wait until Curran's.

"That wasn't half bad!" Vern commented, as we came out of the church. "Not exactly how I usually spend Tuesday nights, but okay."

When we got to Curran's, a couple was just leaving my favorite booth, and we slid into it. We ordered two cherry Coke floats, and then he said, "Let's see if I've got this straight: Mary's main thing is to go to Jesus, and ask him to help us, right?"

I nodded. "It's one of the things she does. But she also—" I stopped and looked at him. "You really don't know anything about Jesus, do you?"

He smiled and held his hands open, palms up. "So— teach me."

I thought for a moment, then told him about the first time His mother had come to Him on behalf of someone else—which was what started His ministry on earth. "Mary and Joseph lived in the town of Nazareth, not far from the Sea of Galilee, and that's where Jesus grew up. In Galilee, everyone seemed to know everyone else, so when there was this wedding in another Galilean town called Cana, they were all invited."

I took a sip of Coke, but Vern forgot to drink his. "Go on," he said.

"Well, a lot more people must have come than they'd planned on, or else they were having more fun than they expected, or both. Anyway, they ran out of wine."

"Empty keg," Vern chuckled; he and few of his teammates had recently been introduced to the wonders of draft beer at an older brother's college fraternity.

I ignored the knowing look. "When Jesus' mother came to Him and explained the situation, knowing that He could fix it, He told her she was a little ahead of schedule; it wasn't the time for Him to start doing miracles. At which point she simply took charge—" I smiled. "She was a real Jewish mother!"

From his expression, I could see he didn't see the connection. "You don't know any Jewish people, do you," I asked.

He shook his head. "Nope. And until you, I didn't know any Catholics, either. My parents always kept me away from those kinds of people." Then he laughed. "They'd die, if they knew I'd been to a Catholic church tonight!" He quickly got serious again. "Go on with what you were telling me."

"Well," I said, first taking a deep sip, "totally ignoring what He'd said to her, she went up to the stewards—those were like the caterers—and said, 'You're out of wine? Fill those big stone jugs with water, and then, you see that tall man over there? That's my Son. Take them to Him, and do whatever He tells you.'"

With my straw I pointed to his nearly untouched Coke; the ice cream was melting in it.

"Then what happened?" he said, ignoring me. "Well, they did what she told them and brought him the water jugs. He said a blessing over them, and when they tasted it, they were astonished: it wasn't water; it was wine!"

"And then they got smashed!" he exclaimed. "What a great guy to have at a party!"

I slid out of the booth. "I think it's time I went home."

"Wait!" he said, hurrying after me. "Look, I'm really sorry." He tried to open the door for me, but I opened it for myself, and the car door, too.

We drove to my house in silence. When we stopped, he said quietly, "That was really stupid, what I said back there."

I nodded, but still didn't feel like talking to him. I did let him open the door for me and walk me to the front door.

"Can I come with you next Tuesday?" he asked.

"Sure," I smiled, "you can come with me again."

After that next Novena—and soda and Bible story—as we said goodnight on the porch, he asked, "What about Sunday?"

"Well, we go as a family on Sunday—Mom and Dad, and all my brothers and sisters. We go to what we call Mass, and we have Communion. . . ." my voice trailed off; there wasn't time to explain what all of those things meant.

"You mean, I can't come, because it's just for families, and I'm not part of your family?"

I shook my head. "No, it's not that—" I smiled at him. "I'll tell my mom and dad. I'm sure it will be all right if you sit with us."

But now *he* was having second thoughts. "No, I don't think it would be such a good idea; I really don't think your dad likes me very much."

I looked him in the eye. "Vern, if you come to church with us, and you kneel with us, my dad will like you just fine!" Not very tactful, but true.

So, on Sunday when we arrived at church, he was there waiting, dressed in a suit and tie. And he sang, and he knelt, and I could tell that my mother was pleased, and my father was not displeased.

But afterwards, out in front of the church as my parents were visiting with friends, he said, "I've got to ask you something."

It was obviously serious, so we moved a little away from the others. "I heard something about you yesterday," he said.

"Oh? What?"

"That you were going to be a nun."

"Yes, I am."

"Like one of those Sisters in there?" He nodded towards the church.

"Yes."

"Then you've been leading me on, haven't you."

He was angry, but behind the anger I could see that he was very hurt. "Vern," I said as gently as possible, "I've regarded you as a friend. I thought you felt that way about me, too."

He looked in my eyes, and could see I was telling the truth. "Well," he said brightening, "I don't know exactly what a nun is, but I can tell you this: you are going to be one beautiful nun."

8

A Proper Environment

The white glare of the gym's floodlights had been replaced by islands of soft, warm illumination from standing lamps borrowed from the faculty lounge and placed strategically around the perimeter. Over the loudspeaker system came the mellow strains of the Four Aces singing "Sentimental Journey," while directly above center court, one of those thousand-mirror revolving balls cast tiny specks of light in slow, clockwise orbits. In our sock feet, we shuffled in approximately the same direction, dancing close—but not too close; Father Lafferty, my homeroom teacher, and the other chaperones were watching.

It was my first sock-hop, and I was thrilled; each time they put another record on, another boy cut in. I'd never paid much attention to boys, but suddenly they were paying quite a bit of attention to me. And I found that I liked it. . . .

When God places a call on someone's life, when He gives them a vocation to the religious life, and that person responds with a desire to fulfill that calling, He allows the enemy to test them. He also provides enough grace to withstand temptation—that is, normal temptation. Should the temptation threaten to become too great, He will often either remove it—or the person.

At the end of the school year, I again applied for early admission to the Servite Sisters' novitiate. And this time, to my surprise, the council reversed their decision: I was invited to report to the convent on August 21, to join the new class of postulants.

At fifteen, I would be by far the youngest they had ever accepted. I regarded it as a miracle—and in a way, it was: God had intervened to preserve my vocation. For the boys were getting more attractive—had I waited one more year, I would never have applied again.

Years later, I learned what had changed the council's mind: Monsignor Smith had written the Mother Superior another letter. This one, however, was hardly diplomatic. What he said, in effect, was: Every year I ask you for sisters for my school, and every year you tell me you cannot give me another one, because you have so few. Well, now I am sending you one; do not tell me you are not going to take her! If you do not have enough as it is, why on earth should you refuse this one?

Soon after that letter was received, I received mine: "Dear Rita: It is my pleasure to inform you that the council has decided. . . ."

In January of that year, my baby sister was born, and since 1955 was a Marian year, as well as the year of Elizabeth II's coronation, my parents named her Regina Elizabeth (more for the Queen of Heaven than the Queen of England). She was the sweetest baby! She made everyone happy, and I loved her. I got to take care of her a lot; in fact, Mom and Ruthanne and I sort of shared her. Mom was the happiest I had ever seen her, except that she kept buying me clothes. I did sense that it was no longer out of guilt; I think she just didn't want me to leave. But that was not the sort of thing we could ever talk about.

Before I knew it, it was August! Each year, on the Feast

of the Assumption of Our Lady, the Servite Sisters renewed their vows, and those novices who were ready, made their formal professions and received their habits. The following Sunday, the candidates for the new postulant class arrived. That year, they would include a 15-year-old who wanted to be a saint.

My mother had a tea-party for me, to which she invited my best friends from school. She didn't know what to call it (a going-away party sounded sad), so she called it a convent shower—and she went all the way, making little frosted cakes and petits fours, and using her grandmother's china and doilies which almost never came out.

What a beautiful tea! We had a ball, laughing the hardest when it came time to open the presents, and there was one pair of black stockings after another! Then it came time to say good-bye, and we all cried, and I promised Ginny Lertz I would write her every day.

Whenever a person is about to take a major step towards God, it seems that the evil one throws up a major obstacle— and the greater the step, the more daunting the road-block. As long as we stay where we are, we pose no great threat to him. But once we set foot on the Way of the Cross, we become a real problem for him, because God will begin to use our lives to draw others to His Son.

So—if the enemy sees us planning to go on a retreat which he knows will change our lives, he stirs up a fight, or gives us serious car trouble, or foments a business emergency—anything to make it 'impossible' for us to attend. Similarly, if we determine to break a relationship which we know in our spirit is wrong, he will pull every heart-tugging rabbit out of the hat. Or, if we finally resolve to stand with Christ against our self-love (in the area of food, TV, gossip, fantasizing—whatever), the enemy will run temptations past us that we could not even imagine!

And God allows it. It is part of the testing, and it is

also love: in the long run, it is infinitely more merciful that the less-than-resolute turn away at this point, than later on, when it could be emotionally shattering.

Saturday morning, the day before I was due to leave, I was holding Regina in my arms. She was seven months old now, and she seemed strangely listless and sleepy. And *hot;* in fact, she was burning up! "Mom?" I called, "Something's wrong with Regina."

My mother's eyes widened, as she read the thermometer: 105 degrees!

"Russ!" she cried, "Get the car! We've got to get Regina to St. Vincent's!" I wanted to come, but I had to stay home and sit the kids. So I prayed and got them to pray, also.

It seemed like forever, before we heard the car returning in the drive. When our parents came in the kitchen, I searched their faces. "She's got double pneumonia," said Dad matter-of-factly. "They've got her on a bed of ice, and if it brings her temperature down, she'll be okay."

If? Suddenly I realized that—I might never see Regina again.

"Mom! Please! I can't go to the convent now! Let me stay home and help care for her!"

I sensed that with all her heart, my mother wanted to give in. But instead, she said: "No, you go. God will take care of her. You have to go."

I know something now: The hardest thing for a mother to do is to cut across her own love for her child, to put God's loving will for that child first.

If that ever seems too much, we have only to look at the example of Mary, and what it cost her, to release her Son to go to the Cross.

And so, the next day my mother and father and all us kids got in the family car (which began to resemble that car in the Ringling Bros. Circus—Ricky would sit up front in the middle, and the four of us in back would fight over who got the windows). We set off for Omaha, but first, at my request, we went by the hospital, because it really might be the last time I would ever see Regina.

When they took me up to the children's ward, I was not prepared for the sight of her little body with tubes running out of it, lying on a bed of ice. I just buried my head in my mom's shoulder and sobbed and sobbed.

Nor did it get any better in the car. It was a grey, dreary day, and no one felt like talking. Inside, I listened to the voice of reason telling me that I was throwing my life away. And doing it selfishly, because my mother desperately needed me. Part of me knew where that voice was coming from—but the other part was pointing out how much sense it was making.

The closer we got, the more agitated I became. Finally we pulled in the driveway, and the old brick edifice loomed ahead. I was wrong last year: it was definitely ominous-looking. *Why was I doing this?*

All of a sudden, I wanted to scream out with all my might: "Dad! Stop the car! I don't want to go through with this! Turn around! I want to go home!"

Do it! Do it! Say something—hurry!

"Mom, I—"

She knew. "We're here," she smiled, as my father parked the car near the main steps.

"Dad—" But a sister had come out on the front steps and was smiling a greeting.

It is said that one's imminent demise wonderfully concentrates the mind—all I know is that on that long walk down the hall to the guest parlor I was noting the minutest details.

On the dark, paneled walls were large paintings hanging by wires from the wainscotting far above, and the terrazzo floor was spotless. Marveling at its shine, I wondered: who cleans these floors?

The guest parlor was furnished with stiff, high-backed Victorian chairs—which even Queen Victoria would have found uncomfortable. There was an oriental rug, and again I noticed the wood floor around it: I had never seen such a high polish—who did that? For that matter, everything was immaculate—and austere: what we would term "a proper environment." But there were no flowers, no plants—nothing to make the room feel the least bit warm or cosy. I got the impression that while guests were welcome, they were not encouraged to linger.

The Novice Mistress entered, accompanied by another sister who asked if anyone would like something to eat or drink. It had been a long drive on a hot day, and our car did not have air-conditioning. The kids were hungry, and everyone was thirsty. In a few moments, the other sister returned with a tray filled with cookies, and five frosty glasses of lemonade. Only five? As the tray was passed, and my family began gratefully helping themselves, I whispered, "Sister? I think we're a glass short."

The Novice Mistress overheard me. "No," she said quietly but firmly, "we're not."

"But—"

I then received my first instruction as a new postulant: in a low voice meant only for me, she said, "We do not eat or drink with people from the outside world, only with our sisters in community, and since you are here, you are now one of us."

Catching the drift of what was going on, my father smiled and said, "They're probably planning a welcoming party for you downstairs."

The Mother Superior came in then, and everyone stood up. "I'm Mother Loyola," she smiled, greeting each of them. When she came to me, she gave me a real hug and a kiss on the cheek. I was surprised: it was the softest cheek I had ever felt! In that instant, I knew she loved me and really cared for me. It was a graced moment—saving grace, that I would remember more than once, later. But with all that happened next, it was instantly forgotten.

As my family finished their lemonade and cookies and chatted with Mother Loyola, I watched them in a daze. It was as if I was somewhere up above, looking down on all of them. Dad, Mom, Ron, Ruthanne, RJ, and Ricky—I carefully photographed each in my mind and tucked them away in my memory-book.

And then it was time to say good-bye. I gave each of them a *long* hug, starting with the littlest first—dear, sweet Ricky, then RJ, with his big innocent eyes behind those big thick glasses. . . . He started to cry, and I was trying so hard not to, that my head hurt, and my eyes ached. Then came Ruthanne and Ron—and poor Mom, so desolate that she couldn't speak. Now I did start to cry.

By the time I got to Dad, I was crying uncontrollably. All the others were crying, too; even Dad had tears in his eyes. "Well," he said to Mother Loyola with an embarrassed smile, "it's not as if we won't be seeing her for Thanksgiving and Christmas."

"No," said the Novice Mistress, not returning his smile, "you won't."

"What do you mean?" asked my father, alarmed.

Now the Novice Mistress did smile, but it was not a warm smile. "Our sisters do not go to their former homes on holidays. They do not return to their families at all, except in the event of death, until three years after they have made their final professions. At that time, they may pay a visit, accompanied by another sister." She paused. "The first year in the novitiate is the postulant year, after which the number of years one spends in the novitiate depends on the maturity of the novice." She looked at me. "Since your daughter is only fifteen, I would imagine that she would not be visiting you for another eight to ten years."

My father was dumbfounded—we all were, as the reality of what she had just said, sank in. No one had told us! In the ensuing silence I added ten years to my sister and brothers—and realized they would all be in their late teens by the time I would visit home again. And little Regina, if she lived—I was too shocked to cry.

Sometimes, when we take a major step of obedience in response to the call of God, in His infinite mercy and wisdom He will withhold from us some of the specifics of our vocation. In our heads we know that any vocation, if we serve Him faithfully, is bound to entail suffering. But our hearts would recoil from the pain. . . . Once they have accepted His call, they will learn the eternal truth: that there is *always* grace commensurate to any pain, enabling us to endure any suffering for His sake, and grow even closer to Him in the process. But there is no way of knowing this in advance; the only way a heart learns this is by walking through it.

That my family and I had no idea what I was getting into, was not the fault of the convent, or anyone else. I could have easily asked my friend, Sister Camilla, any number of questions about the life of a sister, and she would have gladly told me. But it never occurred to me to ask— and that, too, may have been the mercy of God. . . .

Mother Loyola, seeing how close we were and how unprepared, now moved mercifully to conclude our parting before it became unbearable.

"Well," she said, getting to her feet and gently putting am arm around me, "I think it's time for Rita to go up to the novitiate."

The Novice Mistress took me upstairs to the novices' dormitory—a long room with about twenty beds in it, each separated by white curtains into a little cubicle. In each cubicle was a cupboard and a washstand with a basin and pitcher on it. I was told to put my suitcase on the bed, open it, and remove its contents.

"You won't be needing these," said the Novice Mistress, re-packing most of the clothes I had brought with me. "We find that two outfits are quite enough." I just stared at her.

"You won't be needing that, either," she said, pointing to my wristwatch. I took it off and handed it to her. "Here, time belongs to God," she explained, putting it in an envelope and placing it on top of the clothes in the suitcase.

Next she scooped up the little statue of Mary which had stood on my bedside table, ever since I could remember. "Time to put away personal things." As the statue went in the suitcase, I was thankful I'd had the presence of mind to leave my teddy at home.

After the statue went the two small framed photos which had stood beside it—of Mom and Dad, and my brothers and sisters. "You can carry your family in your heart; you don't need to look at them. We have no mementoes from the past here."

All that remained on the bed were two sets of stockings and underclothes, and two dresses which I would wear until the postulant class received its black dresses and veils.

"You may put those away in there," she nodded towards the cupboard, "while I take this suitcase downstairs, so it can be stored for you. Then I will introduce you to the other novices and postulants and give you a tour."

I opened the cupboard and started to hang away my two dresses. As soon as I was sure the Novice Mistress was downstairs, I hurried over to the window, to see if I could catch one last glimpse of Mom and Dad.

I was too late; the car was gone.

Resting my forehead against the window frame, I closed my eyes. "I'm okay, Jesus," I assured Him, "I'm okay."

But we both knew it wasn't true.

The Novice Mistress returned.

"Come," she called me, the way I used to call Ginger, "the other novices are in the Community Room."

She showed me into a room with long dark tables and straight-backed chairs, in which sat perhaps two dozen young women. Most wore the white veils of novices; a few wore the little black postulant veils.

Recreation room? There's nothing here but tables and chairs—how do you recreate in a place like this? "Hi, everybody," I said nervously.

No one answered. They looked up from their handwork and went right back to it. I was more embarrassed than hurt, because I now realized that they weren't talking to each other, either.

"*Deo Gratias,*" said the Novice Mistress, coming in behind me.

"*Alleluia,*" they replied in cheerful unison.

"This is Rita, our newest—and youngest—postulant," she explained. "You may speak with her for a few minutes." She turned to me. "And Rita, if you have any questions, this would be a good time to ask them." She turned and left the room.

My mind was reeling! I'd had no idea that, other than recreation times and other special occasions, signalled by "*Deo Gratias,*" that the rule of silence was observed.

"How does this—" and I gestured in the air, "this no-talking thing work?"

The novices took turns answering. "You only speak when spoken to," one said.

"Or when the Mother Superior or the Novice Mistress give permission," another added.

"And then there are certain subjects which are forbidden," piped up a third, "like politics and nationalities, and—family. That's probably the biggest one."

"Nothing from your past life or the world," clarified a fourth.

Miss always-first-with-her-hand-up and always-ready-with-an-opinion (a *strong* opinion) was stunned. "Well," I finally asked, "what *do* you talk about?"

They looked at each other and began to giggle. "Well—we talk about God, and the little things that happen here, and—" she shrugged and smiled, and now, as they realized how this must sound to someone like me, they all began to chuckle. I laughed a little, too—it was so awful, I had to.

"What about mail?" I asked, desperate for some channel to reality.

"Oh, there's not much mail," replied the first novice, laughing. "You're allowed to write one letter a month, and it goes to your parents."

"And it's censored," another gleefully offered. "If the Mother Superior or the Novice Mistress don't like something that's in it, *snip, snip,*" she made the sound of gesture of scissors at work, "and it goes home in pieces."

Now all the novices were convulsed in mirth. I was laughing because they were, but inwardly I was appalled: "What about letters to friends?" I asked, recalling my promise to Ginny.

They shook their heads. "You only get to write one letter—if you write a friend, your parents don't get one."

"Do you get any mail?"

"One letter a month, from your parents."

"And that, too, is censored; if there's anything in it that might be 'unhelpful'—*snip, snip!*" They roared with laughter—until the door opened, and the Novice Mistress re-entered. The hilarity abruptly subsided.

"Well, Rita, I see you've made quite an impression on the other novices." She was not smiling. "Our rules may seem strange to you, but with time I think you'll see the wisdom of them."

She led me out and showed me the library, the refectory, the kitchen and laundry, concluding my tour in the chapel. "I will leave you alone with God now. I am sure you must have quite a bit to pray about."

As she left, she closed the large oak door behind her. It did not shut with a great hollow *clang,* like in those old prison movies. But there was the awful sound of finality to it, nonetheless.

9

Home

Clang-clang-clang! What—? My mind, striving to weave the intrusive sounds into a dream from which it did not want to awaken, deduced that it was a whole bunch of prison doors closing in rapid sequence. . . . But what was I doing frolicking with Ginger in a prison yard? Even for a mind willing to go to almost any lengths to suspend disbelief, that was too much.

I woke up.

The incessant clanging was an old-fashioned school bell I realized, rubbing my eyes and propping myself up on an elbow. I was in a strange bed, in a very strange, little white-curtained cubicle. . . . I could hear others up and about—moving quickly, from the sound of their feet on the polished wooden floor. I glanced at my watch— but it was missing. And slowly the events of the day before came back to me: this was my first day in the novitiate.

A bright face with cheerful brown eyes peered around the edge of my curtain. "You're still in bed?" she whispered, her eyes widening. "Get up—quick!" she urged, nodding towards the wall clock which could be seen above the curtain partitions: 5:12. I squinted: was that 5:12 in the morning?

"Hurry!" pleaded brown-eyes. "We've only got fifteen minutes to get to Chapel!"

"Why are we whispering?" I whispered, getting out of bed.

"The Great Silence! No one ever speaks, from the end of compline in the evening until after breakfast!"

"Well, you're speaking!" I whispered.

"Yes, and if I get caught, I'm in big trouble!" She smiled. "But I'm assigned to be your guardian angel, and if I don't look after you, who's going to?" She sighed. "I didn't realize you wouldn't know *anything!*"

"What's your name?"

"Sister Mary Carol."

"Do I call you *all* that?"

"Yes, in the convent we always use our full names. And because we are dedicated to Mary, her name comes before our religious name."

She frowned. "Listen, you've really *got* to get a move on! You've got to wash and get dressed and make that bed and get down to chapel in less than —" she glanced up at the clock, "twelve minutes!" She shook her head. "Otherwise, it'll be a penance for both of us!"

Her apprehension was contagious; I leapt out of bed, poured some water from the pitcher into the basin, splashed it on my face, doffed my long white nightgown, and practically jumped into my clothes. Fear of penance, I found, wonderfully concentrated the mind. But what was penance?

I had just finished making my bed, when Sister Mary Carol came around the curtain and inspected my bed. "Oh, Lord!—and that's a prayer, not a swear—this is terrible! Didn't anyone ever show you how to make a bed?"

"It was good enough for my mom," I retorted, forgetting to whisper, "and she's the toughest D.I. I know!"

"You don't know our Novice Mistress," whispered Sister Mary Carol, shaking her head. "Mother Carmelita is tougher than John Wayne!" She tore my bed apart and re-made it with triple-folded corners, stretching the top sheet and blanket till they were like a board. Over her shoulder she glanced at the clock—5:27.

"C'mon, we got to really run for it now, or it's penance on the floor! Keep your eyes down and don't look at anyone; that's part of the Great Silence, too."

"But—"

"Just follow me and do what I do; we're going to make it—by seconds!" She ran out on tip-toe, and I flew after her down the stairs to the basement and down the hall, wondering what penance on the floor was. Not until we actually entered the great oak doors did we slow to a measured, reverent pace.

Because I had not yet been assigned a seat, I could not sit in the choir with the sisters and other novices and postulants, of which, I saw now, there were 26 Sisters, 12 novices, and eight postulants. I sat in the first of the pews available for "others"—and was grateful, not having the foggiest notion of what was about to happen. This way, I could just follow whatever they did—and there was an awful lot of sitting, standing, bowing and kneeling that morning.

Traditionally (I was later informed) the monastic offices, called Hours, had been observed every three hours around the clock, beginning with Matins at 3:00 AM, followed by Lauds (and Mass) at 6:00, then Terce, Sext, None, Vespers, and Compline, and Vigils. Over the centuries, mainly for health reasons this rigorous schedule had been somewhat modified; in our community, for instance, our final night prayers were said at the end of Compline, and Matins and Lauds comprised our prayers before half an hour of meditation and Mass in the morning. Terce, Sext, and None occurred together, followed by the rosary just before lunch, and Vespers followed by half an hour of meditation and the Salve Procession came before supper.

When all this was explained to me, it seemed like an awful lot of prayer crammed into one day—indeed, it seemed like all we would ever do was pray. (The day would come when I would appreciate how much it was prayer that bonded us to Christ, and to each other.)

For a woman, a vocation to religious life is a call to be a handmaiden of the Lord. To pray and to serve—how these are worked out is unique to each order, but all have this in common: the religious no longer belong to themselves but have become brides of Christ. Thus, as Mother Carmelita had indicated, how their time is spent is immaterial—because it is not their time. In their life in community, if God would have them gather together in communion with Him frequently throughout the day, then so be it.

The services were chanted in Latin, exactly as they had been by various religious orders since the days of the Early Church. Each week two novices would take turns being the Antiphonarians, the cantors who led the Gregorian chant. The rest of us would follow in our large black "office books," so named for the Divine Office, the liturgical prayer of the Church which followed the calendar of the Saints.

That first morning, I found what penance on the floor was: two other novices came in about two minutes after us—which was about a minute and fifty seconds too late. To my shock, they came to the front of the center aisle, knelt down and kissed the floor, and then remained kneeling upright until the Mother Superior rang a little bell, signaling that their tardiness had been noted. Then they could get up and take their places with the other novices for the remainder of the service.

Please, dear God, I prayed, don't ever let me be late.

Mass followed immediately after, celebrated by the convent's chaplain, a little white-haired German priest named Father Zeiss. The way he said Mass was entirely different from what I had been used to: he seemed to roar onto the altar with Teutonic defiance, attacking every phrase with the same level of intensity; then he roared off the altar when the Mass was ended. Later, I would come to appreciate that he was actually a very good priest, though not given to warm feelings or trite conversation. But that morning his unique style left me breathless.

While he was subduing the liturgy, I had an opportunity to study the sisters' habits. They were the same as Sister Camilla and the other teachers had worn at Immaculate Conception—all black, with a leather belt cinched at the waist, to which was attached the Servite Rosary. Each habit was made entirely by hand with precise, quarter-inch hems. Over this was worn a black scapular, and then a wimple of starched white linen which covered the head and shoulders. Here, the handwork was quite artistic—knife pleats, about a quarter-inch wide.

The veil was also starched white linen, and professed sisters wore a second veil, in black, which allowed a half-inch of the white under-veil to show on either side. Like the wimples, these veils required a great deal of artistic handwork to achieve their exact shape—and they had to be re-shaped after each washing. As they soiled easily, it seemed that one was forever in the wash.

The laundry problem was exacerbated in the height of summer in Omaha, where the temperature not infrequently exceeded a hundred steamy degrees. The black material of the habits was French wool serge, and the convent did not have the luxury of air-conditioning. . . .

The Mass, Father Zeiss announced triumphantly, was ended. The sisters, bowing to the altar and to each other, filed out two by two in stately procession, their hands folded serenely under the long black mantles worn only for solemn occasions. They were followed by the novices who were followed by the postulants (who were followed by me), and thus we all processed to the refectory, where we filed down either side of the long narrow tables to our places. There were no chairs, I noticed, only stools, though very old or infirm sisters were given straight-backed chairs.

No one spoke; the Great Silence was still in effect. Mother Loyola began the Morning Prayer, which was followed by prayers for the departed faithful, and then we sat down on the stools and silently passed each other the different ingredients which made up breakfast that morning (and every morning): cereal, oatmeal, toast, hard-boiled eggs in the shell, and coffee with milk already mixed in it.

The oatmeal had large lumps in it, I noticed, my eyes on the bowl in front of me. (In addition to not conversing with one another, we were not to look at one another, but to keep our eyes downcast.) The toast was over-cooked—black, really—and served without butter or anything else to put on it. (There were these things, but with my eyes down, I didn't see them.) Never having drunk coffee, I passed on the *cafe au lait,* not realizing it would be the only liquid we would be offered. (A sister, noting my predicament, kindly brought me a glass of milk.)

When we all had our portions, the reader for that meal went to the reading stand and began to read aloud from the Roman Martyrology. The text assigned for August 22, 1955, described in grim and graphic detail what was done along the Apian Way to one captured Christian (whose name I shall not mention, lest I forever color someone else's recollection of that saint by my own—and also, because I cannot remember it).

As previously inferred, a vivid imagination was a mixed blessing, at best; that morning I experienced the worst side of that mixture. In my mind I could see every detail that the reading sister was relating, and whoever chronicled the ordeals of the early martyrs in Rome, omitted nothing. First, the poor soul was drawn—stretched out on a vertical torture rack, until his joints parted. Then, one by one, his fingers and toes were cut off and dropped into a vat of oil which was simmering in front of him. (I stared down at my lumpy oatmeal.) Next his tormentors slit open his stomach, and taking care that their victim not expire or lose consciousness, they removed his bowels and entrails, and deposited them, too, in the simmering oil. (At this point I became acutely aware that my own stomach was contemplating the imminent reversal of peristalsis.)

Now the torturers added sticks to the fire under the vat, bringing the oil to a high boil, so that the martyr could smell the aroma of his flesh cooking—

Clapping a hand to my mouth to keep from bringing up the contents of my own entrails, I leapt up from my stool and ran wide-eyed from the refectory to—with no idea where the bathroom was!

Weaving, I reached for the wall to steady myself—and then lost it.

If I could have died right then, I would have. I just stood there, shaking, weeping, aghast at what I had just done.

A sister came up and put her arm around my shoulders. "There, there, it's all right," she said soothingly, "you're new, and everything's so strange—these things happen—don't be afraid—we'll clean it up—but let's take care of you, first." And she led me to the washroom.

I cried the harder; that she was being so loving made me all the more ashamed. She left for a moment to get me some fresh clothes and soon returned. "What about that mess I made back there? Please, let me go back and clean it up—"

"Don't worry about it; someone will take care of it.

Mother Loyola wants to see you in her office."

Mortified, I let her lead me there. She opened the door for me, and then left us alone.

"Dear child!" Mother Loyola came to me and took me in her arms. "You must be so homesick."

I just sobbed and sobbed, unable to speak, as she held me. "It will be all right," she assured me gently, "I know how badly it hurts."

When I recovered, she had me sit down in a chair and sat down next to me. "I remember how I felt, when I first came here," she said, smiling. "I was so lost!" She shook her head at the memory. "All I wanted to do was call my parents and ask them to come and get me. I just wanted to go home."

I looked up at her, wiping the last tears from the corners of my eyes with the heel of my palm. "Did you?"

"Well, I probably would have, except that a sister said to me: 'Don't go home now. Give God a chance—and give yourself a chance, too. Try it for a few weeks. It gets better.' "

"What did you do?"

Mother Loyola smiled. "I'm still here."

I got up and hugged her. "Thank you, Mother."

I loved her so much that I vowed to pray for her every day after that—and I did.

10

The Way of the Cross

Give God a chance. . . . Mother Loyola's words echoed in my mind, as I sat down carefully on the end of my bed in the little curtained cubicle. I'll try, God, I told Him, my stomach still a little uneasy. And then I smiled: things *had* to get better—because they could not have started off any worse!

Sister Mary Carol's head popped around the curtain. "There you are! I've been looking all over for you! You're supposed to be in the Community Room for Instruction Time."

I sighed and got up. "I was just trying to catch my breath, after what happened at breakfast."

"Well, don't catch it here! We're not supposed to be back in here until bedtime. C'mon, Mother Carmelita's going to have a bird!" And with that, she departed at top quiet speed. I followed, thinking that at least I'd learned one new thing: how to run on tip-toe.

The long, L-shaped Community Room was bright and sunny, thanks to the tall windows along both walls, and all the new novices and postulants were in their places. There was a vacant chair at the far end of the long table, and without speaking, Mother Carmelita directed me to it.

"Sister Rita," she addressed me formally, "I am

disappointed that in less than twenty-four hours you seem to have forgotten what I told you about time. Here, we think of the bell that summons us to worship, to meals—to Instruction time—as the voice of God." She glanced up at the wall clock. "He summoned you here nine minutes ago."

"I'm sorry, Mother, I—" She raised her eyebrow, and I realized it would be wisdom not to continue.

"The chair in which you are sitting is assigned to number 302. That is your number; it will *be* your number for as long as you are here. In this room, as in chapel and at meals, we do not choose where we sit; we sit where we are assigned. You are assigned to sit there, next to 300, across from 301 and 303. If a novice or a postulant leaves, you may move up a chair, but you will still be 302."

I shuddered; her voice seemed to have a hollow *clang* to it.

She discerned what was on my mind. "There is a reason for this, just as there is for everything we do. In community, we are a family of sisters; we cannot have particular friends. In the world, to prefer one and not prefer another—indeed, any relationship without the purifying filter of Christ at its center—can be destructive. Any of you who have ever been left out of a clique, know how hurtful that can be."

I remembered, and nodded; looking at it that way, I could see the sense in it—God's sense.

Consulting her clipboard, Mother Carmelita now introduced the twelve new postulants, and she was obviously quite pleased with nearly all of them. She began with a retired executive secretary, who would be "a great asset to our family." Next on her list was a former educator who had taught at university level and had a string of degrees behind her name.

Next came a professional cook who was going to work

in the kitchen. The rest were either college sophomores or freshmen, or graduates of the Servite High School, in Detroit—except for Sisters Rita and Margaret, who were both fifteen.

Another fifteen-year-old?

I looked more carefully at 303, sitting across from me: yes, she *was* my age!

Mother Carmelita did not share my enthusiasm. "I want to welcome all of you to your first year in our community. This year is going to be different than any previously, because this year we are going to do something I never thought we would: we are going to have a nursery." The others looked at one another, bewildered, but I knew what she was inferring; she was glaring at our end of the table.

In case anyone had missed her meaning, she now made it abundantly clear: "I was opposed to your coming," she declared to the two of us, "but I was out-voted. So here you are." She fixed us with her gaze. "I want you to know: no exceptions will be made for you. If you are old enough to enter the novitiate, then you will do what everyone else does, and you will comply with all the novitiate rules."

I felt my face burning. I knew that public humiliation seemed to go with a saint's call, and that future saints accepted it with equanimity, offering it up to Jesus. At the moment, however, I was being excruciatingly reminded just how far I was from being cut out for sainthood. All I wanted to do was disappear under the table!

This was unbearable! Maybe I should just call Mother to come get me—

"Personally," concluded Mother Carmelita, smiling and shaking her head, "I don't believe either one of you will ever make it."

I felt my jaw harden. I might be only fifteen, but I was Irish. God had called me here, and nobody—*nobody*—

was going to drive me out! If she thought—well, she had another thing coming!

I concentrated now on the rules and observances she was introducing, determined to remember each perfectly:

In this Instruction Time, or in any gathering, until the *Deo Gratias* which permitted conversation, we were to remain silent and practice "custody of the eyes." That meant we were not to look at one another, or at anything else, but to keep our eyes down cast, sitting with our hands folded in our laps. Thus were we to remain in a state of repose, practicing the presence of God and not allowing any distraction to interfere with our contemplation.

All work was to be done to the glory of God. That meant, if it was not done as well as it could possibly be done, it would be re-done. (I smiled, for the first time grateful for what I once regarded as my mother's obsessive perfectionism.) We were to work, as if God Himself were observing each stroke of the paintbrush, each sweep of the broom—which He was. Recently, during the renovation of Canterbury Cathedral, an angelic face was discovered on the *upper* side of one of the great stone arches that supported the roof. It was invisible from below; the Twelfth-century artisan who had carved it, had wielded his chisel for God, not man.

We were now separated from the world, set apart by God for His purposes. That meant, not only were we never to speak of politics or world affairs or our past social and family lives; we were not to allow our minds to dwell on them. The here-and-now of reality might not always be pleasant; indeed, there would be times when it was exceedingly painful. But it was Truth—to be lived in, walked through, or borne with prayer and with grace— and it was infinitely preferable to escaping into unreality. Fantasizing was of the devil. Before God, we were accountable for our thought-life, and were to bring all truant thoughts captive unto Christ—II Corinthians 10:2. (At that, I had to smile: I had already tried this custody of the mind—and found my mind to be as difficult to discipline, as my dog Ginger.)

"I realize that this, all of this, may seem impossible to some of you (she had an uncanny way of anticipating my thoughts), but I want to assure you: *nothing* is impossible to God. He has sent His Holy Spirit to help conform you to the image of His Son, and if you will cooperate, He will provide the necessary grace. Here, a leopard *can* change its spots: I've seen it happen here, year after year. But I give you fair warning: it is never easy, and I have never known it not to involve suffering." She paused. "And why should it? He has called you to deny yourself, pick up your cross daily, and follow Him—Luke, 9:23. Well, sisters, the Way of the Cross leads to Calvary. But if you're faithful, if you'll persevere, you'll discover that the Cross is not a post but a door; when you go through it, you'll leave self behind and enter into the Resurrection Life with Him."

She *was* a little like John Wayne, I mused. And in a way, we were a little like a busload of raw recruits, newly arrived at spiritual boot camp. Moreover, there was an urgency to get us shaped up quickly, for there was a spiritual war on, and every soldier of the Cross was needed.

"You are in training to take vows of poverty, chastity, and obedience," Mother Carmelita was saying. . . .

Poverty—meant that no longer were we to use the word "mine;" we were henceforth to think in terms of "ours." She warned us that it would not be nearly as difficult to relinquish ownership of things, as it would be to let go of personal time and space—and opinions.

Chastity—we all had womanly needs; they were to be taken care of in an attitude of prayer. We were never to be alone with a man, under any circumstances, not even our fathers or brothers. We were to practice custody of the mind, where any former relationship was concerned. And we were to have no special friends here; we were to love everyone equally. (Impossible, I thought; I loved people and thrived on friendships!)

"Jesus loves all of us equally, doesn't He?" she asked. "And are we not called to become like Him?"

Obedience—meant that whenever a superior asked us to do something, we were to obey at once, without argument and without expressing our opinion. There would be things we were asked to do which would make no sense to us, which might even seem ridiculous. But if we loved Jesus, we would do them without question. "Remember: the opposite of obedience is rebellion." She paused and smiled. "Did you ever wonder why God prefers obedience to sacrifice, as it says in II Samuel 15:22? Because obedience is someone else's idea of what we should sacrifice."

While we reflected on that, she left for a moment and returned with another sister who was short and rotund and had huge thick eyeglasses. "This is Sister Mary Joanna, our assistant Novice Mistress. I have asked her to tell you the story of the Obedient Nun, because I think it sums up all I have tried to say on the subject. We tell it at the beginning of each postulant year, as it offers a model for all of you," and with that, she left Sister Mary Joanna with us.

As Sister began the story, I noticed that when she spoke, her nose twitched—like a rabbit's. She was unaware of it, and certainly unaware that in combination with her greatly magnified eyes, this twitching was—quite funny. Sensing that train of thought could be headed for serious trouble, I made a determined effort to avert my gaze from her nose, as she got into the story.

There once was a young nun in the convent of an abbey, who was having a struggle with obedience. In her heart she wanted to obey, because she knew that obedience was as a pleasing fragrance in God's nostrils. . . . (Nostrils? I couldn't help looking at Sister's nose; it gave a big twitch, and biting my lip I quickly looked away.)

But the young nun was strong-willed and had come to the convent having been well-educated; too often, she thought she knew best.

The Mother Abbess cared for her, so did the other sisters, but nothing seemed to help. (Sister Mary Joanna paused for us to consider this, and I could not resist considering her nose: did it also twitch when she wasn't speaking? It did. Sneaking a side-long glance, I noted that a few of the younger postulants were apparently considering the same thing. I furrowed my brow in concentration.)

One Easter, she resumed, the Mother Abbess called the young nun to her study. "In the service this morning, you did not seem to have the same joy as the others—a shame, since this is the Lord's day of victory. Is something the matter?"

The young nun sighed. "Nothing new, Mother. My quick tongue has gotten me in trouble with Sister Agnes in the kitchen—again." She sighed. "I'm sorry." And she meant it, for she loved this wise old friend and knew that she was loved in return.

The Mother Abbess bade her come over to the study window which looked down on the convent's garden. Handing the young nun a sick about two feet long, she said, "I want you to take this stick and plant it in the ground over there, under the apple tree."

"But Mother, this stick is dead."

"Do as you are instructed—for when you obey me, you obey the voice of God."

So the young nun took the stick, and with the Mother Abbess watching from the study window, she went out and planted it under the apple tree.

When she returned, the Mother Abbess said: "Now each morning at ten o'clock, you are to pour one quart of water on that stick."

"But Mother—" she fell silent. I am an obedient nun, she thought, and you speak for God; I will do it.

So, each morning, precisely at ten, she went out and using one of the pitchers from the kitchen she poured exactly one quart of water on that stick. She did it all summer and all fall. She did it even in the driving rain, when the stick and the ground around it were already drenched.

One winter morning a fierce blizzard raged around the convent, and the young nun went to the Mother Abbess, to draw her attention to the conditions outside. The latter, knowing what she was about to say, simply looked at her, and the young nun turned without speaking and went to don her cloak.

All through the spring, she continued to water the stick, until as Easter approached she found herself actually enjoying this little task. That surprised her, for she had resented it so mightily in the beginning. But now, as she greeted the stick each morning, it was almost as if she were bringing a drink of water to a friend. It made her happy to do this, because she knew it pleased the Mother Abbess—and more important, it pleased the One for whom the Mother Abbess spoke.

Finally, it was Easter Sunday morning. And when the young nun went out, her heart was full of joy; the celebration loaves which she had helped Sister Agnes bake, had come out of the oven better than either of them had dared hope; their sisters would be delighted. But there was another, deeper reason for the joy: she felt that morning as if she were standing with Mary, staring at the empty tomb.

Approaching the stick, she noticed that there was something red on the end of it, and as she drew closer, here eyes widened, and the pitcher fell from her hand. Growing from the end of the stick was one perfect rose.

Sister Mary Joanna smiled as she concluded, expecting silent appreciation of this story which she obviously loved so much.

Instead, there were muffled snickers. I could hear them around me, people snorting and trying to hide it. I was determined not to laugh—but it was so funny! Flowering sticks—were these people for real? Where had they been buried? What kind of lunatic asylum had we gotten into?

If only I hadn't looked up to see what Margaret's reaction was—but I did: she was beet red, her lips were pressed together, her cheeks full of air. She looked like she was about to explode! That did it—I burst out laughing.

Instantly, everyone else sobered up. And so did I, as I heard my laughter echoing all alone in that long room.

Peering down the table at us through her thick glasses, Sister Mary Joanna was not angry; she was hurt. "I thought you would be edified by that story," she said softly.

I am ashamed now, of my reaction. It *was*—and *is*—an edifying story. I know first-hand that God does far greater miracles than causing dead sticks to bloom. And for that matter, how many people today must perform daily tasks that seem to make even less sense than watering a dead stick? Yet, out of sheer obedience, they do it. They can take solace in the fact that God knows what their obedience is costing them, and how pleasing it is to Him.

But, as my students would say, that was then, and this is now. And back then, too often I was an arrogant, smart-cracking fifteen-year-old who thought she knew everything.

I was about to learn how much I didn't know.

11

A Day in the Life

Sister Mary Joanna now gave out our work assignments which, she informed us, we were to regard as ours for as long as we lived there. "Each of your responsibilities will be carried out thoroughly and spotlessly. This is God's house, a gateway to Heaven, and we expect it to look like it. Each work area will be inspected frequently, at times which will not be announced." So *that* was how the front hall came to be so polished, I mused.

The motherhouse was a working farm with 160 acres under cultivation, so there was more than enough work to go around. Their main cash crops were corn and potatoes, with some wheat—and alfalfa to feed the livestock, for they also had a dairy herd. And chickens.

I shuddered; chickens were my worst nightmare. Well, I assured myself, it was a big farm—so big that they had to have a couple of hired hands to do the heaviest work. Since there was so much to do, the chances of my getting stuck with the chickens was next to zero. . . .

"You will be shown exactly how to do each job," Sister Mary Joanna was saying, "and you will do it exactly as you are shown. And if you think you know better, just erase that thought from your mind." She smiled. "There are convolutions in your brain—behavior patterns and responses that have been there since childhood; these, no matter how deeply ingrained, are to be erased."

She did not say how this would be accomplished, and so I imagined little Munchkins with Brillo pads: "Scrub-scrub here, and a scrub-scrub there, and couple of tra-la-la's; that's how we scrub our brains away in the merry old land of Oz!"

But Sister Mary Joanna was quite in earnest. "You all are starting a new life, one which should be mentally and spiritually new, as well as physically. You must imagine yourself as a clean slate, on which the hand of God will write and design your life."

She read off the work assignments, and eventually came to mine. "Sister Rita? You will be responsible for the novitiate stairs down to the professed sisters' hallway." (Good! They want spotless? They haven't begun to see spotless! Talk about a gateway to Heaven—I'll show them a stairway to Paradise!) But she was not finished: "You will also help Sister Anna with the chickens."

I went cold. Numb. When I was six, visiting my Grand-mother Mizner on her farm, she made me accompany her, as she killed the two chickens we were going to have for Sunday dinner. One minute, they were scurrying around the hen yard; the next, thanks to her swift, sure cleaver, they were headless corpses. But not lifeless—the carcasses were still flopping and wriggling, when she handed them to me. "Here," she had said, "hold these."

Horrified, I gingerly took them by the legs, and then noticed that the feet were covered with chicken manure. Wrinkling up my nose, I dropped them on the ground.

Grandmother looked at me sternly. "You just dropped our Sunday dinner in the dirt."

"They were gucky!"

"Pick them up."

I just stood there.

"I said: *pick them up.*"

I still did not move.

"You are an ungrateful child," she said softly but with controlled anger. "That's one thing you learn on a farm: to be grateful. Now pick those chickens up, or you will not be invited to the dinner table."

I set my jaw and refused to move.

I went without dinner that day, and never ate another bite of chicken. I hated them—so much that it may have had something to do with the allergy I developed to their feathers. . . .

Now I raised my hand: "Sister? I'm allergic to feathers."

"I'm sure that if you pray hard enough, the allergy will be taken from you."

So I prayed: Dear God, help! Please don't make me go into that henhouse and start sneezing and rubbing my eyeballs.

After Instruction Time, we had about half an hour before the combined offices of Terce, Sext, and None at 11:00. This time, we were told, was for indoor recreation. Good, I thought; I could use a rest. But how we recreated was not up to us; the time was to be spent in the Community Room, doing handwork.

Assigning me a section of shelf in the large cupboard at the end the room, above which she wrote 302 on a piece of tape, Mother Carmelita asked me if I could do anything.

"I can embroider and crochet," I said matter-of-factly. Actually I was quite good at it, thanks to my rip-that-out-and-do-it-over mother.

Mother Carmelita looked at me, mildly surprised. "So your mother did teach you something—we don't get many girls anymore who are trained to work with their hands. I'll get you a set of pillow slips to crochet for our annual bazaar."

While she was gone, I thought back to the first pillow slips I ever had to do. They were for Grandma McLaughlin, and I thought I had done a really good job. "Look, Mom, all done!"

She had taken them and immediately turned them over, to see the back sides, which had threads going every which way. "This a mess!" she declared.

"But, Mom! You didn't even look at the good side!"

"It's the back I look at, not the front. If you are doing it the way you should, the back will be as neat as the front. That means you have to cut your threads; you don't just stretch them or string them across. You go the extra mile, which means cutting and knotting each time you move to another area." Well, Mom, I may have hated you then, but I sure am grateful for you now. You and Mother Carmelita are exactly alike; I'll bet she checks the backs first, too.

Mother Carmelita returned then with the pillow slips, and handed them to me, along with needle, thread, and hoop-frame. I smiled; I could hardly wait till they checked my work. They'll think the Blessed Mother herself did it!

"Thank you, Mother," I said, trying to sound humble. "I'll do the best job I can."

"I expect it," she said, turning away—which brought me back down to earth in a hurry.

The bell rang—God's voice was calling us to the Chapel. Sitting in the front pews for Terce/Sext/None, we postulants tried to follow the Latin service, but were soon floundering and looking at each other's books, to see if anyone had a clue where we were. Well, we would start finding our way soon enough—right after lunch, in fact, as we began our study of Church Latin.

At lunch, we had a special treat: *Deo Gratias!* Conversation at meals was usually reserved for high holy days (whence the word, holiday) and the feast days of the different sisters' saints (which we celebrated in lieu of their worldly birthdays). Today *was* a festive occasion, of sorts—and the refectory was soon filled with the cheerful chatter of postulants comparing notes.

The refectory tables were long and narrow, with the head table facing an open U, around which sat the sisters, according to seniority—which meant that the postulants were at the bottom of the U. What a peculiar arrangement, I thought; it made no sense whatever. Then the older novices got up and began to serve. Moving inside the U, they were quickly able to place serving dishes within reach of everyone. Now, of course, it made eminently good sense, and moreover, I soon discovered that it was possible to converse comfortably with someone across the U, and easily hear someone speaking from the head table. Wondering why the world hadn't picked up on this excellent and functional way to serve forty or fifty people and make it feel—intimate, I decided that henceforth I would not be so quick to rush to judgment.

The younger novices and postulants were responsible for clearing and doing the dishes, and in the kitchen, as everywhere else, cleanliness was next to godliness. That, too, reminded me of home, and I made a mental note to tease Mom in my first letter, by speculating that she had been raised in a convent and never told us.

Latin was Latin, and in this one instance I felt fortunate to be the youngest: only three months had passed since I had been studying it. New Testament Studies was fascinating, made the more so by Sister Mary Joanna, who reminded us that what we were reading was not literature or mythology; it was history. She proceeded to make it so alive for us, it was as if we were walking with Jesus and the Disciples by the Sea of Galilee. (I really loved learning, I realized—and now once again, I was being blessed, by having a really gifted teacher.)

But the Bible was even more than history, Sister Mary Joanna emphasized: it was the Word of God. That meant it had supernatural properties. Any problem we might ever face in life had already been faced by the people of God, whom we would find in these pages, if not in the New Testament, then in the Old. All we had to do was ask the Holy Spirit to direct us, and He would lead us to the particular Scriptures which would illuminate whatever dark corner in which we might find ourselves.

The moment she said it, I knew in my heart it was true—and I could hardly wait for us to be given some reading time.

The bell rang, and Sister Mary Joanna announced that Tea would be at 3:30; until then, there would be outdoor recreation. Now that's more like it, I thought, wondering if they knew how to play work-up.

We went out on the back lawn, and there was Mother Carmelita, waiting for us. "Well," she said to me with a smile, "how are things going?"

I was taken by surprise; it was the first time she had been the least bit warm to me. "I *love* New Testament Studies!" I exclaimed. "Sister Mary Joanna is wonderful: I could *see* Peter getting out of the boat and walking over the water towards Jesus—and then remembering that he couldn't do what he was doing!"

She chuckled. "Well, how would you and Sister Margaret like to join me for a walk?"

"A walk?" It was too late to hide the disappointment.

She looked at me. "What sort of outdoor recreation did you have in mind?"

Oh, no, here we go again. . . But she was still smiling, and she did ask—I decided to risk it: "Don't you all ever play?"

"Play? You mean—games?"

"Sure!"

"What sort of games do you play?"

"Well, ball games, mostly. Especially work-up."

Mother Carmelita thought for a moment. I think we could do that occasionally," she mused, nodding. "In fact, I think it would be a good thing. But I've never heard of work-up; you'll have to teach us how."

My mouth fell open, and I stared at her. Mental note, #2: Don't rush to judgment about people, either.

"Where are we going on our walk, Mother?"

"I thought you and Sister Margaret might enjoy seeing our cemetery," she said, waving to Margaret to come over.

Cemetery! Our recreation, our *only* recreation, was going to be a walk to a cemetery? It was hard not to judge something that was so obviously kooky.

The motherhouse itself was on the crest of a hill, from which could be seen the skyline of Omaha in the distance. Behind it was another rise, crowned by pine trees, and now Mother Carmelita led us up there, along a curving drive lined with pines. As we walked up between them, a breeze sighed through their needles, and it was as if they were whispering to one another. At the top of the hill, there was a clearing, and in it was the convent's cemetery—with simple stone crosses marking each grave. On each was carved the name of the sister, and the dates of her birth and death.

My impatience vanished. I sensed the presence and the peace of God here. Even the whispering of the pines seemed hushed, reverent. "This is holy ground," I murmured.

Now it was Mother Carmelita's turn to be surprised. "Yes, it is," she nodded. Her voice trailed off, as if she were speaking more to herself than to us. "I come here sometimes—when I need to be reminded of my vocation, and all that it entails." She indicated the gravestones. "The sisters pray with me. And then it's better." She smiled now, a little embarrassed at having let her heart show.

"Well," she said, drawing formality back around her like a protective cloak, "as you know, ours is an English order. Our founding motherhouse is St. Mary's Priory, in London, and that's where our Mother General is. But there are also Provincial houses like this one in Canada and Italy. The first sisters came over in the 1920's." She gazed over the cemetery. "As a young novice, I knew most of them. . . Mother Julianna. . . Sister Mary Elizabeth. . . Sister Mary Clair. . ." She named each with fondness, as we walked from stone cross to the next. "They were— they are—good friends."

We came to an open space where there were no crosses yet. "And here—" she paused at a site I guessed to be about forty future stones from the most recent, "here is where you will be one day, if you persevere."

We stared down at the ground in front of us, speechless.

"I must go now," she said, excusing herself, "to make sure the others are not late for tea." She smiled. "Being an English order, Afternoon Tea is really quite important to us, actually." She spoke the last phrase with an exaggerated British accent, and I laughed.

When she was gone, I whispered to Margaret: "I'm standing on my own grave."

"Me, too. Kinda weird, isn't it?"

"Do you suppose postulants 1247 and 1248 are one day going to be standing here, looking down at us?"

Margaret shivered. "Don't do that."

"But seriously, this is us, a hundred years from now."

"Rita, if we don't shape up, this is us tomorrow!"

Tea made me homesick, because it reminded me of Mom's farewell tea for me. Yet as painful as that was, it was over way too soon. For as soon as we finished, I was to accompany Sister Mary Anna, to learn the details of my assignment.

There were more chickens than I ever dreamed of: *five hundred* laying hens in the hen house, and about the same number of roosters in the rooster house. The eggs brought in a steady income for the convent, and the roosters provided an inexpensive source of meat. My job: feeding the roosters, and then collecting their manure and spreading it as fertilizer over the vegetable gardens.

First came the feeding. This should be a piece of cake, I thought; from working with my grandmother, I already knew about all there was to know about feeding chickens: you shoveled in the cracked corn, the mash, the oyster shells, and that was all there was to it.

But—that was not the way they did it at the convent. (So, what else was new?) In each hand Sister Mary Anna had a bag of old stale loaves. "These are for the roosters," she explained. "They're pretty aggressive; they seem to think they're attack birds. So you go into those bushes over there," she pointed to underbrush next to the fence, "and you throw a loaf over the fence, as close to their house and far away from the gate as you can get it. Then, while they're pre-occupied with that loaf, we can slip in with the others and put them by the gate, to draw them out here, while we go into the house to get the manure."

I looked at where she was pointing: "Those bushes are brambles, Sister. Why do we have to throw it all the way down at the other end? Wouldn't it be easier to just open the gate and throw it in from there?"

Sister Mary Anna shrugged and smiled. "Well, we've always done it that way, but—why don't we try it your way? Go ahead, open the gate and throw it in from there."

Finally! A sister who was open-minded! Funny how sometimes it just takes a fresh perspective to see how an old thing can be done so much more simply—I opened the gate and walked in, and got ready to throw the first loaf. . .

Instantly, five hundred furious roosters were assaulting this intruder! They were all over me, tearing at the loaf, at me, at everything! Screaming, I ran for the gate which Sister Mary Anna, convulsed with laughter, slammed behind me.

I was angry—mainly because I was scared, but also because I was humiliated. "I don't see what's so funny! I could have been hurt in there!"

"Sometimes," she replied, when she stopped laughing and could catch her breath, "old ways are the best ways. I'm sure I'm not the first one to tell you that there's usually a reason for why we do things the way we do."

I glared at her—and then had to smile. "No, it does seem to me that I've heard that before," and I, too, laughed.

She handed me a hoe. "You ready for your next lesson?"

"Lead me to it." She did.

While the roosters were busy attacking the loaves at the other end of the yard, we slipped into their house. I gagged: the smell was so strong I thought my brains were going to come out my nose!

"You get used to it," Sister Mary Anna said. She showed me how to scrape the manure from the boards under the roosts into large baskets, being careful to get it all.

Suddenly I was that little child of six again, whose grandmother was asking her to handle something disgusting. And unfortunately I was no more ready to do it now, than I had been nine years before. If my mother knew what they were making me do, I thought, she'd drive the hundred miles in a shot! But then, darn it, that would make Mother Carmelita right!

Sensing my revulsion, and seeing my knuckles whitening on the handle of the hoe, Sister Mary Anna simply suggested: "Do it for Jesus."

So, I started in. "Dear Jesus," *scrape,* "this is for You," *scrape.* "Dear Jesus," *scrape,* "this of for you," *scrape.* Before long, I was laughing.

We had another *Deo Gratias* at supper, and now we had so much to talk about that Mother Loyola, sitting at the center of the head table, had to stand up. "Sisters! I'm glad everyone has had such a wonderful day! But please: have mercy on the some of the older eardrums in this place!"

We all laughed, and I felt really happy to be there.

After supper, we "newies" were told to get our aprons on and report to the kitchen. My first impression of that vast, gleaming place, was that I had never seen so many pots! Some of them were big enough to put my baby brother in, and all of them were dirty! But they were nothing compared to the dirty dishes which were stacked—everywhere!

I looked around the kitchen. I could see huge tub sinks, but—

"Sister," I asked the person who seemed to be in charge, "where are the dishwashers?" I figured there had to be more than one, since there were so many dishes.

Sister Mary Archangela was a great big woman with a great big smile. She just smiled that smile at me now. . . . and gradually I realized that *we* were the dishwashers.

We washed and washed and washed—and after about an hour, the last dish and the last pot were done. But we weren't. "Now you scrub the counters and mop the floor," said Sister Mary Archangela jovially, "and if I find one spot anywhere, you do it over. You'll leave this kitchen shining."

"We'll be here till midnight!" I burst out in what was

supposed to be a whisper, but which carried over the tile floors. Sister chose to ignore it.

But she could not ignore my next observation: "I don't see why they have to use so many pots and pans!"

"What are we supposed to do, cook in air?" she asked. "How long have you been here—has it been 24 hours yet?"

"I'm sorry, Sister," I replied, meaning it.

"You should be. If you had kept silence, as you're supposed to, you would never have had the opportunity to say what you did." I nodded, and then she chuckled. "But who can do dishes without talking? Only from now on, keep it down! I'm the one who gets in trouble, when the Mothers come by and hear talking."

We finished by 8:00—well before Compline. There was even some time for reading. I decided I would start with the Gospel of Luke, and I devoured it like a novel, being startled when the bell called us to Chapel.

Compline was my favorite service of the day. The chapel was darkened when we arrived, lit only by the candles on either side of the altar, and the sanctuary lamp which always glowed there, signifying the presence of the Lord in the Tabernacle. As we filed in, the lights were turned on, but the spirit of hushed reverence remained. And as the Gregorian Chant began, there was, I realized, a great serenity in my soul.

Listening to the sisters chant the Nunc Dimitis, I thought of my family back home, and how Mom used to make sure we all said our prayers, before she tucked us in. I wasn't homesick; I felt united with them. Because that's what we were doing here—saying our prayers, before we tucked the church in for the night.

At the end of Compline, Mother Loyola began the night prayers for the community, praying for the sick, for those in prison, for the lonely, for all the deceased members of the community, for the deceased and living members of our families. . . .

When she was finished, she rapped once on the pew with her book, signaling the beginning of the Great Silence. We were not to speak again, until after breakfast.

Just before I fell asleep that night, I thought back to what Mother Loyola had said that morning. (Could it have been only that morning? It seemed like weeks ago!) *Give God a chance.* . . .

Well, dear Jesus, I guess You really didn't need as much of a chance as we thought. I may change my mind tomorrow, and this may be just beginner's grace, but I think (say it, Rita)—I think I'm going to love this place. Only please: I'm going to need some help with Mother Carmelita; she's tough. But nothing's too tough for You—not even, apparently, a know-it-all like me.

12

The White Veil

The following morning, the homesickness returned in full force: I was so homesick I was nearly physically sick. In fact, I dared not eat anything. That happened morning after morning, and throughout the day, as long as I kept my mind on my work, or on what the others were saying during Deo Gratias, I was all right. But the moment my thoughts turned to home, I began to cry.

One morning, after another breakfast in which I did not break my fast, Mother Loyola called me to her office. "You're really having a hard time, aren't you?" she asked gently. I burst into tears and just sobbed. "That's all right," she said, "just go ahead."

She kept handing me tissues, and I kept blowing my nose and sobbing. Then she said, "You *are* very young to be here." She paused. "But I truly believe God has a plan for you here. Now, I can call your parents and ask them to come and get you, and I will right now, if you want me to."

Part of me wanted to say yes, but the other part shook my head. "No, I'll be okay. It'll take awhile, but I'm going to make it."

"Well, you're going to have to eat something." She opened a drawer and took out a box of chocolates.

"Someone gave me these; let's have some," and she sent downstairs for some cookies and tea to go with them.

As we enjoyed this treat, she asked me to tell her about my family, and then she said, "By the way, I have some very good news: I had a call from your mother last night: your baby sister is out of danger now, and is home. She's going to be fine, and your mother said for you not to worry."

Mother Loyola smiled. "That was the other reason I called you in: I sensed you were grieving for her."

I nodded. "I was afraid I might never see her again, and—I think I felt guilty about not being home to help."

"Well," she said getting up and putting an arm around me, "I think the homesickness will be better now."

It was—and one morning in chapel three weeks later, it simply lifted and disappeared. I *was* home.

Poverty, Chastity, and Obedience—those were the vows for which we postulants were in training, the vows we would make on the day we became professed sisters and took the black veil. But first we had to convince the powers that be—the Mother Provincial and Vice-Provincial and the other members of the Council—that we deserved to take the white veil, the veil of a formal novice. Did we have the makings of one day becoming a sister? Was the maturity there? The perseverance? The spirituality?

The main thing was attitude—and that was my main problem: too much pride. In schoolwork, for instance: starting in September, I took high-school equivalency courses at the convent and was able to complete three years' work in two, so that I completed high school a year early, at age 16.

The quickness of my mind and my ability to concentrate were both gifts from God—but I didn't see them that way. They enabled me to absorb abstract equations and mathematical theorems like a sponge, to answer a teacher's question almost before she could ask it, to grasp philosophical points on several levels at once. And while I gave lip service to these gifts being from God, and being grateful to be able to use them for His glory (I could sound humble), the truth was, too often I used them to glorify me. Top grades, record scores—too often they justified my feeling equal (or superior) to most of my teachers, and nearly all of my elders.

As for my singing ability and my artwork, I did use them to glorify God—but my ego certainly enjoyed the recognition and approval they brought me.

I was aware that I had a problem with pride—how could I not? I had to excel at everything. I kept my stairway to paradise gleaming, and even raced the elevator that the really old sisters had to ride. I would greet them casually just as the elevator doors were closing on the first floor, then take the stairs two at a time and be there when the doors opened on the second floor, greeting them casually without even breathing hard.

But my quick tongue was my worst enemy; it was constantly getting me in trouble. To see a thing was to speak it—and often for a laugh. I had not yet learned the twin values of silence and patience—though I was grateful to God for having called me to an order where they were encouraged. Time after time, I would be convicted that my most recent quip was nothing but pride, or my ego using humor to be the center of attention. Or that I didn't need to answer the third question in a row.

One of the old hymns spoke of pouring contempt on all one's pride—I always seemed to be reaching for the bucket after the fact, rather than before.

I was struggling, but it was mostly an inner struggle; there really wasn't anyone to talk to about it. Different priests would come in to hear our confessions, and that helped, but it was only once a week; I needed it about once an hour.

Meanwhile, I was not getting the constant approval that my ego craved. In the world, if you did a good job, you got praised for it, and if you did an exceptional job, you got a lot of praise. (I didn't realize it then, but I was addicted to approval.)

In our community, however, the Mothers and senior sisters were hardly lavish with praise. When one did excellent or even outstanding work, it was no more than was expected. When one showed dramatic improvement, that was admirable, but it, too, was expected. And if they ever suspected that anyone was giving anything less than the utmost of which they were capable. . . .

No wonder I occasionally dreamed of being home— with the family that loved me just as I was and approved of practically everything I did. But only occasionally; most of the time, I was happy here, and knew it was where I was supposed to be, and so was not harassed by thoughts of home.

Poverty—in terms of material things, it was no great problem. Ah, but poverty of spirit! To choose to believe that you did not know everything, that you did not always have the right answer, that the project or the discussion could get along fine without your contribution—that was where it got hard!

Chastity—again, no big deal, where men were concerned. Had I come to the convent a year later, it might have been another story. (I would probably not have come at all.) But this business of having no special friends—it was impossible for me to pretend I didn't feel closer to people like Margaret or Sister Mary Carol— So, I made a determined effort to feel close to *everyone*. That seemed to work; at least, I didn't get corrected in that area.

Obedience—here was where I was having the greatest struggle. Someone once described rebellion as: "reserving the right to make the final decision," and too often, that was me: outwardly conforming, but inwardly questioning and challenging. In the Gospel of Luke, I was deeply moved by the example of the centurion who was able to recognize Jesus as a man under authority—because he was under authority himself. That was not me.

But I wanted it to be me, and each night before I fell asleep, I would plead with God to give me a submissive spirit. I would ask Him to forgive me for the places where I had not submitted, and to show me any other places I had not seen. (Invariably, there were more of the latter than the former.)

At times, I was tempted to despair, convinced that I could never change—and pretty sure that the Mothers and elder sisters were sadly in agreement. The only thing that kept me going, was that Jesus had said that for Him, nothing was impossible—not even me.

Before I knew it, it was August. In two weeks it would be the Feast of the Assumption of Our Lady, which would be preceded by our annual eight-day Great Retreat. The entire community anticipated it, as one might look forward to a wedding in the family. For on this day, professed sisters took their final vows, senior novices took their first vows (and the black veil that went with them), and postulants took the white veil of novices and received their religious names. At least, those postulants whom the Council deemed worthy, did.

In my case, that was far from a sure thing: when I had arrived a year before, Mother Carmelita had been appalled at my extreme youth and immaturity, and I had seen little in her attitude towards me which would indicate a change of heart. I could still remember how it felt, when I had not been allowed to advance to the third grade with the rest of my class—was that going to happen again? Please, dear Jesus, let me become a novice.

He didn't.

Just before the list of new novices was posted on the bulletin board, Mother Carmelita called me to her office. "Sister," she said gently, "you are not going to receive the habit. You have made remarkable strides in the past year—far more than I would have imagined. But the Council and I feel that you need another year as a Postulant. I know how much you were counting on it, but someday you will appreciate God's wisdom in this decision."

"Thank you, Mother, for telling me," I managed, and left.

As soon as I was outside her office, I stomped off down the hall in a fit of anger. How dare they call me immature! How dare they do this to me! I busted my back trying to please those people, and show them I was just as good as any of those novices, and—

The hard side of me interrupted now and said, Why don't you just give it up and go home? They don't want you here; just go on home.

But my pride or spirit or whatever came right back: They're not going to win! *I'm* going to win! I'm going to show them!

When I saw Margaret and realized she hadn't been accepted either, we cried on each others shoulders. Oh well, at least we would have each other.

At the beginning of my second year as a postulant, Mother Loyola called me into her office. "I want to give you a Reflection for the coming year. It's from St. John's Gospel." She looked down at the open Bible in front of her: "Unless the grain of wheat falls into the earth and dies, it remains just a grain of wheat. But if it dies, it produces much fruit."

I frowned, not sure of its meaning, or how it applied to me.

"I am pleased with your first year here," Mother Loyola said. "I have seen many things that I like: you're compassionate and talented; you love animals and beautiful things. . . you're going to be an asset to the community. But—"

(Why, I thought, did there always have to be a but?)

"—as part of your Irish heritage, you are extremely strong-willed and opinionated. When you think you're right, you're right. And everyone else is wrong. So I want you to take John 12:24 as your motto, because you have a lot of dying to self to do."

Seeing that I was still frowning, she went on. "You need to die to your own opinions and start listening to the opinions of others. It's not that your opinions are bad, but you can learn from listening to others. If you will do this, you will learn from what others have gleaned from life. And then you will grow in maturity, and you will produce much better fruit."

I was nodding, but sensing that I still did not get its full implication, she made it unmistakably clear:

"Community means coming together—each of us knowing we are planted here by God. We're not meant to be an entity unto ourselves. You cannot bake a loaf of bread with one grain of wheat. But Rita, you want to bake the whole loaf with one grain: yourself."

Now I got it.

"You need to open yourself up to others in the community, take their ideas and let them color your own. That will form good bread."

I thanked her and said I would try—but in my heart I was still not convinced she was right.

The next year proceeded much as before, only faster. The main difference being that we were now the senior postulants, if there was such a thing, and made no bones about letting the five "newies" from Servite High School know it.

When August came around again, and the list of new novices was posted, my name was there.

The day we received the white veil and our religious name was called our Investiture Day, but it was an awful lot like a wedding day. To symbolize our becoming brides of Christ, we would wear real bridal gowns, and our fathers would escort us down the aisle and give us away at the altar! Certainly no brides-to-be had ever been more nervous and excited than we postulants, as we waited for our day to come.

At last, it did. I was awake an hour before the bell went off, and I watched the sun come up over the apple orchard, like a great orange ball. It was going to be a beautiful day—a perfect day for a wedding!

The new chapel, a proper brick church, had a really high ceiling which allowed the Gregorian chant of the sisters to hover far above, like smoke from incense—and the rising and falling Latin phrases, like the ebb and flow of ocean surf, lingered in your mind long after you left.

Tall clerestory windows lined either side of the upper nave and emitted diagonal shafts of morning sunlight. There were flowers everywhere, mostly yellow roses backed with white gladioli. The church was packed. All our families were there, and mine took up at least two pews.

One by one, our fathers escorted us in our bridal gowns and veils down the aisle. When we got to the front, we took our places in the first pews, and our fathers joined our families in the congregation. Archbishop Bergen now signaled us to come forward for the Prostration. Each of us went up the steps and knelt before the altar, and then went fully prostrate on the marble floor with our arms outstretched in a symbol of our total surrender to Christ, while the choir chanted the *Veni Creator Spiritus.*

At the end of the chant, all of us rose to the kneeling position. The archbishop and Mother Loyola then came to each of us, and as Mother handed him each folded garment of our habit, he prayed aloud over it and placed it in our open arms.

When we had all received our habits, we processed one by one out of the chapel, where we were each met by a professed sister who accompanied us to the novitiate and helped us put on the habits which we had waited so long to wear.

When we all returned to the chapel, the professed sisters who were making their final vows that morning, were just leaving the altar. Once again, we processed down the aisle, one by one, this time radiantly beaming as everyone craned around to see what we looked like in our habits.

We all knelt together in a line at the bottom of the altar steps, and the archbishop came to each of us, to pray over us and give us our religious names.

As I knelt on the cold marble, I prayed my name would be one that I liked—or at least could live with.

"Rita McLaughlin: henceforth, you will be known in

religious life as—Sister Mary Raphael of the Immaculate Conception."

I was thrilled! Raphael, the archangel of healing, was my favorite! I could not have dreamed of hoping for such a name, which was so much better than any of the ones I had imagined!

Now, from behind me a sister affixed a crown of yellow roses to my white veil. I gazed up at the Cross. I am Yours now, my Jesus—now and forever.

13
The Black Veil

I looked at the other even-numbered novices and postulants huddled on the open hillside, shivering in the wind that was driving stinging needles of snow in our faces—and burst out laughing. This was supposed to be a *picnic!*

The others looked at me, startled. A few began to laugh, too, then more, but the majority were so miserable, all they could do was hug themselves and pray that it would soon be time to go in.

What a difference a day made! The previous day, the day after Thanksgiving, had been a balmy Indian Summer day, with a southerly breeze, the temperature in the 60's, and not a cloud in the sky. All the postulants who attended college during the day were home for the long weekend, and as there were still potatoes to be harvested, the novitiate went out to glean the fields, as it were. The potato-picking machine had gotten most of the potatoes, but it had missed some of the full-sized ones and all of the little ones. And being good stewards of the Lord's provision. . . .

We would take turns: the odd-numbered ones would go out on Friday, and we evens, would go out on Saturday. The thirteen odds had a gorgeous day! We had *Deo Gratias* whenever we were working in the fields, and so it was more like a picnic than work—in fact, they did have a picnic, complete with peanut butter-banana-marshmallow sandwiches and for dessert, chocolates! We could hardly believe them, when they returned, still exuberant from all the fun they'd had. We could have worked up some serious jealousy—except our turn was coming in the morning.

But that night an Alberta Clipper came through: the wind shifted around to the northeast and picked up sharply, the temperature dropped into the 20's, and it started to snow—fat, wet flakes at first, but then sharp, icy darts. No longer jealous, the evens now prayed that the two remaining potato fields could wait for more clement weather. The trouble was, there was no telling when that might come, and in the meantime, the cold and wet might ruin the remaining potatoes. . . .

So out we went, complete with our own picnic lunches. Leaning into the wind, I bent over and started digging potatoes out of the ground and dropping them into the burlap sack I clutched at my waist. As I worked along the row, my fingers grew numb with cold and gradually locked into the shape of a garden claw. God, why have You done this? I wondered. Why did You give the others such a lovely day, and us—this?

There was no answer—and I remembered what someone had once told me: in life, everything was either a lesson, a reward, or a test. And regardless of which, the main thing God was interested in was: how would we respond? In life, especially in a life of obedience, we might have no control over what happened to us—but we had total control over how we chose to respond to it.

That was why the prayer which got the second fastest answer was: "Lord, change my heart." (The fastest was: "Jesus, help me!" or just pleading His name.) If we were given an assignment which we detested—but which, out of obedience, we had to assume was God's will for us at that juncture—then if we asked Him to change our heart, He would. We might never reach the point of enjoying what we were doing, but He would grace us to at least tolerate it. And if we also asked for a grateful heart and a cheerful spirit, we might just find ourselves smiling, in spite of the awfulness of what we were doing (or eating, or. . . .) I prayed that prayer—and was actually surprised when, coming to the end of a row, I found there were no more rows to be picked.

As the wind blew up the hill from Omaha, we gathered for lunch, shaking and stamping our feet, blowing on our dirt-caked fingers. The sister in charge got out a large jug of water, so that we could wash our hands before eating—only it was frozen. When we went to eat our sandwiches, the marshmallow had hardened to the consistency of taffy; you could hardly get your teeth through it. And speaking of teeth, the *coup de grace* was delivered by the *piece de resistance:* the chocolates were like little brown rocks. I bit into one—and felt a molar on the left side of my lower jaw go *crunch.*

For the past couple of weeks, I'd had a tooth-ache back there on and off, but I had not mentioned it, because it was my canonical year. During our final year in the novitiate we were not to leave the convent, unless it was an absolute emergency. It did hurt, badly at times, but in true martyr-in-training fashion I had prayed for the Lord to remove the pain, and if not, to grant me the grace to suffer it as an offering to Jesus.

But now the pain was excruciating! As soon as we went in, I went to Mother Carmelita: "I think something is wrong with my tooth."

"That's too bad," she said, "Let's see if it will clear up in the next day or so."

By that evening, it had grown worse—unbearable (and I had a high threshold of pain). I went again to Mother Carmelita. "The pain has now gone up into my left eye; I cannot stand it."

She reached in her desk and pulled out a bottle of aspirin. "Here," she said, "take these," and she poured two into my palm.

"But Mother—"

"It's your canonical year," she said, cutting me off.

I wished she could feel what I was experiencing! If pain were blood, they'd have an ambulance here by now!

The aspirin did help, however, and I was able to get to sleep. And when I awoke in the morning, it had subsided somewhat. At breakfast, as long as I chewed on the other side of my mouth, it was bearable. Whenever it flared up, I offered it up: "Jesus, this is for all the lost souls, who don't know you. And Raphael," I said to my namesake, "since you *are* the archangel of healing, how about a little help down here?"

I got through the day that way, and the next, and the next. And then one morning about two weeks later, I was awakened by pain shooting into my brain. Somehow I stumbled into my clothes, but I was too dizzy to go to chapel or to breakfast. Finally, I went to Mother Carmelita. "Please," I begged her in tears, "I can't stand it." She made an emergency appointment for me, at 11:00.

Peering into my mouth, the young dentist who contributed his work to the convent, shook his head. "I don't see anything wrong with the tooth. Oh, there's a little cavity there," he added, "and I'll be happy to fill it, but I don't see how it could be the cause of all the pain you describe." And with that, without using expensive novocaine, he drilled and filled it.

"You should be okay, now," he said cheerfully, as I got out of the chair.

I nodded, hurting too much to speak. For the rest of the day and the whole sleepless night I endured it, but by morning it hurt so much I thought my brains were going to come out my ears. I went back to Mother Carmelita.

"He fixed your tooth," she said, annoyed. "You just want to go back out again."

"No," I wept, "I'm in such pain I can't pray; I can't even think. All I can do is experience pain!"

"All right!" she snapped. "You'll go again! But there had better be something the matter!"

When we arrived at his office, the dentist was perplexed. "I filled that tooth yesterday; there's nothing wrong with it."

"She insists that there is," said the sister who had driven me.

The dentist shrugged. "All right, I'll drill it again."

But this time, as soon as he touched the filling, the whole tooth disintegrated.

"Oh my God!" he exclaimed. "How could this happen? You must have been in so much pain! I am so sorry! This is awful! How long have you been in pain like this?"

I indicated a couple of weeks.

"I'm so sorry," he said again. "I can't save the tooth now," he added, shaking his head, "I'm afraid there's nothing left to save. Not enough left to put a crown on, or pin anything to—I'll just have to take out what's left."

This time he did use novocaine, and I went home with a great empty hole in my left lower jaw. By the time I reached the convent, the side of my face was all swollen, and they put me in bed with oil of cloves and an ice-pack to reduce the swelling.

That evening, shortly before lights out, Mother Carmelita came to see me. "I just talked to the dentist—why didn't you tell me it was that bad?"

"I tried to."

Filled with remorse, she shook her head. "I didn't believe you. I thought you just had a little tooth-ache, and were using it as an excuse for an adventure outside the convent." She sighed. "Other novices have done that— more than you might think. After awhile, they just get tired of being in here and want an outside view." She came over to the side of the bed and looked down at me. "I'm so sorry—will you forgive me?"

"Of course!" I exclaimed. "It's okay." At that moment, all I wanted to do was hug her. We looked at each other— and I knew that she knew what I was feeling. "Well, goodnight, Sister; I will pray that your mouth heals quickly and that you are free of pain."

"Good night, Mother and—thanks."

Everything was different, after that. When we passed in the hall, we smiled and meant it, and without showing favoritism, Mother Carmelita took a genuine interest in my academic progress, my artwork and singing—in my life. She became like a mother to me—not the kind *I* might have chosen, warm and loving and approving; the kind *God* knew I needed. He had given me a spiritual mother, who would not be satisfied with anything less than the absolute best I was capable of, and who would stretch me well beyond what I considered my limits. Who would not fail to remind me that the gifts He had given me were to be used for the Body of Christ, not for my ego's gratification, and who under no circumstances would feed that ego the praise and recognition it craved. In short,

Mother Carmelita *was* tough—but I was beginning to appreciate the value—and the necessity—of tough love.

The trick, of course, was being grateful for tough love at the time it was being administered. Like the time she informed me that I was going to be the reader in the Refectory for the following week. At each meal, unless there was a *Deo Gratias,* a reader would read through the entire meal. The antiphonarians would read the Roman Martyrology at breakfast, but at lunch and dinner a suitable spiritual volume was read. And if perchance we got a bad reader, which happened not infrequently, there was nothing we could do but listen and suffer through—all week, which sometimes was just sheer agony.

I was petrified, convinced that I would be worse than bad, the worst they had ever had. I would become part of the oral history of the motherhouse: "Do you remember the time when Sister Mary Raphael tried to read? Wasn't that the only time they ever had to change readers in the middle of the first reading?"

"I can't do it," I told Mother Carmelita.

"You will do it," Mother Carmelita told me. She took me over to the Refectory to practice, and all I did was cry. "Please, don't make me do this," I wailed.

"You will do it," she replied, unmoved.

So, I practiced. I got a copy of the biography of St. Theresa of Lisieux, the assigned reading, and I read it aloud—to the gravestones in the cemetery, to the pines, to the sinks in the bathroom late at night.

Monday noon, I was so nervous, I almost croaked, as I led the Latin prayer: *"Deus in audjutorium meum in nomine Domini."*

"Qui fecit caelum et terra," the sisters replied.

Mother Loyola rang the bell and gave me permission to read.

I began—and to my amazement, it went well. Very

well. So well that I began to think: Hey, I'm good at this! What was I so scared about? This is fun!

There was humor in The Little Flower's story, and I played to it; before long there was laughter. When I finished, Mother Loyola summoned me to the head table. "That was outstanding," she beamed. "Simply outstanding!"

I don't think I touched ground after that—until Mother Carmelita beckoned to me. "You did remarkably well for the first time," she said, not beaming. "But tomorrow we will need to work on your diction and your clarity."

I couldn't believe it! What I'd done was perfect! Mother Loyola said so!

But the next day, back in the refectory with Mother Carmelita, she sat in the farthest removed chair, while I read.

"I can't hear your T's" she would call out. And, "You're slurring your L's." And, "Read more slowly and distinctly." She drilled me for an hour, till I was practically in tears. But she did teach me how to read aloud. And years later, I saw that she had also kept my pride in my reading from ruining whatever the Spirit of God might do through it.

Pride, pride, pride—that was all I seemed to hear inwardly and outwardly during my canonical year. And finally, in the Pit (literally), it began to register.

Halfway through my canonical year, I was given an additional assignment: Chief of the Pit. The Pit was the small basement room where vegetables were prepared for dinner, and all postulants not attending school, were assigned there, under my supervision.

As I surveyed my new kingdom, my heart sank. I could not imagine a more dismal place to spend a morning shucking corn, or peeling potatoes or onions, or shelling peas or snapping beans or scraping carrots. The Pit was aptly named: there was an incinerator in there and an old rusted stove. The floor was ugly raw concrete, and a grey sink ran along the wall. The only windows were two little ones up at ground level, looking out on the equipment shed, and the main piece of furniture in the center of the room was a chipped and battered old butcher's block table which was used primarily for—you guessed it: dressing chickens. (God does have a wonderful sense of humor, though we seldom appreciate it at the time.)

Well—you could sit around cursing the darkness, or you could light a candle; I was definitely a candle person. Since I was now responsible for the work done in the Pit, I decided that no one could work in a place so dreary and depressing. . . .

So—no one was going to have to! I had just finished my morning chores, which meant I had about an hour before Chapel. Normally I would use this time to prepare for my afternoon classes—but today was no normal day! "This day," I announced aloud to the butcher block, "will go down in the convent's chronicles as: The Day the Pit was Transformed!"

Where to begin? Hands on hips, I took stock of the situation, evaluating what could be helped and what couldn't. I would start with those windows! Some curtains were needed—and I knew just where to get them.

Up in the Community Room, under the bottom shelf, was a large box of scrap material. I hurried up there and pulled it out, selecting a cheery blue-checked pattern. In less than twenty minutes I had hemmed up the sides of four small curtains, found two rods, and hung them. Hmm, much better—but now they made the rest of the room look unbearably drab—even worse than before, if possible. Now what?

The butcher block! I went out to the shed where the old paint was kept, selected a small can of green enamel, found an old brush, and as an afterthought scooped up a can of black enamel for the stove. I painted the butcher block's legs green, which looked rather bizarre—except that when it was covered by some sort of cloth, it would look perfect.

As long as the brush was in my hand, I started painting the stove a glistening black, and was just getting to the top, when Sister Mary Pelagrina, the octogenarian garden sister, happened by with her little dog Tootsie.

"Well, goodness!" she exclaimed, peering in, "What are we doing in here?"

Sister Mary Pelagrina was the darling of my heart, and so I took her into my confidence.

"Well," she whispered conspiratorially, "a few flowers wouldn't hurt, would they?" I shook my head with a big smile. "Why don't I just go and see what my garden might contribute."

In a little while, she came back with a bouquet of daisies and yellow snapdragons in a fruit jar, just as I was finishing the stove's feet. Putting the jar of flowers on the butcher's block, I knew what had to come next: a covering.

Up to the kitchen I went, to see what I could scrounge. An ex-army sergeant had once confided that scrounging, refined to its ultimate, was an art form (he was the most gifted "cumshaw artist" in his battalion). Art? I didn't know about that, but transforming the Pit *was* the greatest creative challenge I had faced since coming here.

"Sister Mary Archangela? You wouldn't happen to have an old tablecloth you're not using—something small?"

The big-boned sister wiped her flour-covered hands on her apron. "What do you want it for?" she asked in her plain-spoken way.

"A surprise."

She hesitated—and then smiled. "A messy surprise or a clean surprise?"

"More messy than clean," I replied, smiling back.

She dug out a large oil-cloth type covering with a bright orange pattern on it. "Will this do?"

"Perfect!" I exclaimed, thanking her and running down to the basement. And thrown over the block, with the flowers on top of it and the green legs showing underneath, it was!

Taking another look around the Pit, I grinned: the name seemed hardly appropriate anymore. Really, there was just one more thing to do: stored on shelves under the long sink were all the pots and pans we used. With the rest of the room now so warm and inviting, they were a particular eyesore. But my mother had shown me what to do.

I ran back up to the Community Room and pulled out the box of fabric scraps. There was still some of the blue-checked material left—just enough! Working feverishly, I hemmed up a two-piece skirt for the sink, raced back down, and tacked it in place. There!

But as I stood back, catching my breath and surveying my handiwork, I suddenly realized that I was late for Chapel—terribly late! I flew out of the Pit and over to the new chapel which had just been finished, slowing to approach speed just before quietly opening the door. Inwardly, I groaned; the service was half over. I was going to have to go up to the altar and do a penance. Taking a deep breath, I went forward, eyes down, posture contrite. There was no way of doing this unobtrusively, I thought; the only plus was that I had not seen either Mother Loyola (who was now our Mother Provincial) or Mother Carmelita in their customary places. Maybe I was going to luck out, after all. No, there was no such thing as luck, I reminded myself—but maybe God was so pleased with what I had accomplished that He would cover my tardiness. . . .

After the service, we processed out and went to lunch,

where we listened to a reading from the life of St. Aidan. I had grown to love these mealtime readings, especially when they told a story, and now I became totally engrossed in the saga of this unknown, seventh-century monk in the cold, fog-shrouded island monastery of Iona, off the west coast of Scotland. Aidan had expected to spend his whole life there in prayer and quiet contemplation, when suddenly he had been sent for by Oswald, King of Northumbria (later to become St. Oswald). Aidan's commission: to spread Christianity throughout Northumbria (in middle England). After years of faithful service, founding numerous churches, monasteries, and schools, at the close of his life he withdrew to another holy island, Lindisfarne, off the east coast of Scotland, where he spent his remaining years in prayer and quiet contemplation. Writing of him a generation later, the Anglo-Saxon theologian and chronicler known as the Venerable Bede (also canonized) drew attention to Aidan's generosity and simplicity of spirit; in sum, he evangelized more by the example of his life than by words.

As we filed out of the refectory, I was dreaming of becoming like St. Aidan, when Mother Beatrice, the new Vice-Provincial and Mother Superior, beckoned to me. "Weren't you a trifle late for service, my dear?"

"Yes, Mother—but you'd be so happy at what I was doing!"

"What were you doing?"

"Well," I took a deep breath, "you know the Pit?"

She nodded, and I burst out, "It's been transformed!"

"What do you mean, transformed?" she frowned, and before I could answer, she added, "Maybe I'd better take a look at this."

I followed her downstairs, imagining how surprised and delighted she was about to be.

But when she entered the Pit, there was no gasp, no

exclamation of joy. She said nothing, as she walked over to the new curtains and examined them. "These are good hems," she said, without smiling. Now she turned to the stove. "I hope that's stove enamel; if it isn't, it will burn up the next time we put a fire in that stove."

It wasn't stove enamel; I didn't know there was such a thing as a special enamel for stoves. I had assumed that since the stove was rusty, it wasn't being used any more. My own joy was beginning to curdle in my stomach.

Now Mother Beatrice turned to me. "Did it ever occur to you to ask permission to do this?"

Slowly I shook my head.

"I thought you were in training to take a vow of obedience."

I didn't answer; there was nothing to say.

Mother Beatrice sighed, more sad than angry. "I believe this," she made a gesture that took in all the changes, "was inspired by the Holy Spirit. If you had only come to us and asked, you would have found us more than happy to help you. In fact, it could have been a most enjoyable community project." She paused. "But then, of course, it would have been God's, not yours—your pride would have received nothing from it."

She straightened and prepared to leave. "By rights, I ought to have you strip this room and restore it to the way it was before. But too many novices have had to spend too many difficult hours down here. They deserve to have these changes. And so what you have done will remain— but for you, it will always be a reminder of the selfishness of your pride."

I was devastated. Not hurt, convicted. Because in my heart I was seeing for the first time how much my pride grieved God.

And a curious thing happened: from then on, I was more successful in my struggle with pride. More and more,

I found that I could defer, could keep silent, could obey without judging. It still seemed like I lost another battle every time I turned around. But I knew now that it *was* possible for me to change.

In fact, I was beginning to see everything in a different light—a sort of Copernican epiphany. For just as Medieval man had been convinced that the heavens revolved around the earth, I had been convinced that the world revolved around me. In the 16th century, the astronomer Copernicus had pointed out that the earth revolved around the sun, and in my 17th year, God through the Servite Sisters had begun pointing out to me that my world was to revolve around His Son.

It was difficult to see, because my soul—my will, intellect and emotions—wanted so badly to remain on the throne. But my spirit—the part which yearned to be united forever with the Spirit of God—wanted to yield the throne to its rightful Owner. My soul was so strong that, were it not for the Servite Sisters, it would never have stepped down. But the Word of God was as a two-edged sword, separating soul from spirit (Heb. 4:12), and thanks to God—and Mother Loyola and Mother Carmelita and all the others—I was beginning to catch glimpses of that reality.

I began to repent—not for what I had done, but for who I was.

With repentance came discernment: I began to see that I was not the innocent victim I had always assumed, the one to whom cruel and heartless treatment had been unfairly accorded. I saw I was like the boy Joseph, so pleased with the coat of many colors his Father had given him that he did not realize how offensive his behavior was. And God had *allowed* his brothers to sell him into slavery—because nothing less could have prepared him for what was to come.

Like Joseph, I was by nature so proud that I was often

an offense without realizing it, as I delighted in the many-colored gifts my Father had given me. And so, in His infinite mercy He had to allow extreme dealing to come to me—to free my spirit to come to Him.

That was a truth I caught only glimmers of, but knew at the bottom of my heart I must hold onto: *whatever befell me, God allowed.*

Almost imperceptibly, I found myself becoming more grateful for the daily will-crossings of this life to which He had called me (albeit never at the moment of being crossed). While I was unaware of any significant change in attitude, it was not lost on those responsible for my spiritual direction—who always seemed to know me better than I knew myself.

One warm Saturday afternoon in the spring of my canonical year, the novitiate was up in the alfalfa pasture, having a picnic which would be followed by a softball game (both Mother Carmelita's idea). The fair weather was a welcome harbinger of summer, and the peanut butter-banana-marshmallow sandwiches were delicious; savoring the final smooth bite, as I recalled the last time we had been up here, trying to eat the same fare: could it have been only five months ago?

Mother Carmelita, seated under an oak tree, waved me over, and I came and sat on the blanket next to her. "Would you like a chocolate?" she smiled, offering me the box.

"Um—no thanks," I smiled back.

She looked out to the distant Omaha skyline. "I am going to tell you something which, if you take it the wrong way, will slow you on your walk. But I believe God would have me give you this encouragement: I am impressed with the maturity you've shown in the past few months. You have convinced me that my original assessment was wrong: you are going to make a fine sister, Mary Raphael."

I was speechless. Tears came to my eyes. "Thank you, Mother," I managed.

Have you ever noticed, when you go back to a high-school or college reunion after ten or twenty years, it is invariably the teachers who were the toughest and most demanding that you seek out first? It's because in the intervening years we've have come to appreciate how valuable was their uncompromising stance, and how it forced us to become (at least in their courses) more than we were. We want to tell them how it paid off, or just show them we're finally grateful.

I had a sense of that, up on the hill that afternoon, sitting next to a nun whom I knew I would have as a friend for the rest of my life—one who had cared enough not to care about my feelings toward her.

The Assumption of Our Lady, 1958—ours would be the second ceremony, after the senior sisters had made their final vows. As we waited to process, I thought back to the last time I had waited here in the narthex, one year before. Then, it was to receive the white veil; now, it would be the black. Then, I had been alternately nervous and excited, and solemn. Now I was serene; when I came back up this aisle, there would be a plain gold band on the third finger of my left hand.

I gazed down the long aisle and up at the Cross above the altar; the Bridegroom awaited.

14

Sister Mary Raphael

A few days later, Mother Loyola called me into her office. "Sister Mary Raphael, I have some news for you, which I'm not sure you're going to like: I'm sending you to Detroit. Your first mission assignment will be as a second-grade teacher in St. John Berchman's School." She looked at me, to see what my reaction would be.

I was shocked. While I'd accumulated some sixty college credits from Duchesne College of the Sacred Heart, plus those in philosophy and theology that the Jesuits from Creighton University had provided at the convent during my canonical year, I had yet to complete a full year of college. I now started to point this out, even though my academic record was open on Mother Loyola's desk: "All my work has been just part-time studies, Mother; I don't—"

She nodded, smiling. "I feel you are ready," she paused. "And I also feel it will be good for you."

"But I'm not certified."

Mother Loyola shook her head. "You won't have to be, your first year. There's such a shortage of teachers, they're issuing emergency certification. You'll continue your studies, of course, while you're there."

She waited for a response, but I was nonplussed. "I know how difficult this must be for you," she finally said, "and how much you had counted on staying here." All I could do was nod. "At least until you had completed your degree at Duchesne." I nodded again.

She got up and went to the window. "I could tell you that Mother Church has great need of you in Detroit, and that, as much as we have become your family here, since you are moving in obedience you will find as strong a family there." She turned back. "But all you need to remember is this: being a bride of Christ means we go where He sends us, when He sends us, how He sends us; it is not for us to decide. But we have this consolation: He *always* comes with us."

And so, two weeks later, I arrived in Detroit, moving into St. John Berchman's new convent facilities, and putting away my two habits in my room—my own room, after living in a curtained cell for three years. It was a large room, with a desk and a work area and a closet—it even had a private bath! And it would be my mine for the foreseeable future. (For a Servite Sister, the maximum foreseeable future was five years in any one place. They were never assigned longer than that, lest they form attachments to an area and its people that would be difficult to break, when it came time to move.)

Yet in the midst of this unbelievable luxury, I was miserable. My old family was in Iowa; my new family was in Nebraska—all the people I loved in the world were hundreds of miles away! I knew no one here. I had no one to talk to, no one to share with or confide in. No one. Except Jesus.

He should be enough, I told myself; but as usual, my heart was lagging far behind my head.

I spent much of that first night, listening to the strange sounds of the city, mixed with the blowing and tooting of tugs and barges on the river. How I missed the comforting lullaby of frogs and peepers.

Fortunately, the first day of school took all my attention. The parish's school facilities were as ancient as the convent's living quarters were modern. The second-grade homeroom was down in the basement, next to the boiler-room, so that steampipes ran through it. There were fifty-four desks in there. They were the old kind on runners, and they were crammed in so tightly right up to my desk, that there was no room to turn around. A row of basement windows at ceiling level looked out on an alley, directly across from the back door of a funeral home.

At 8:20 the bell rang, and by 8:30 every one of the fifty-four desks were filled. These kids were beautiful—full of excitement and looking at me so expectantly. . . .

"Good morning, children. My name is Sister Mary Raphael, and I will be your teacher this year."

I could not get over how good they looked! Eyes up, hands folded on their desks—all except one little one whose hair was disheveled, his shirt filthy and his fingers grubby, including the one inserted deep into his left nostril.

Seeing where I was looking, a girl in the front row whispered: "Don't mind him; we just ignore him."

I looked down at the seating assignments—well, William Fowler, you are going to have a much better year than you expect.

At recess, I announced we would play dodge-ball, and I asked William to carry the ball out to the street. We filed after him (since there was no schoolyard, they blocked off the street for a playground), and I called for the children to make a big circle. Easier said than done—by the time they got done wrangling and pushing and arguing about who would be "it," and had formed a circle, the bell rang, and it was time to go in. We were obviously going to have to work out a system. . . .

Hardly were we back in the classroom than a horse clopped by the window. Have you ever tried to compete with a horse for a child's attention? On top of that, it was pulling a wagon, one of whose wheels was shrilly complaining of lack of grease—but not as loudly as its shabby driver was crying, "Bottles? Cans?"

It was the junkman, I was apprised by my first-row informant whose name—I checked the assignment sheet—was Dorothy. He and his wagon came by every Monday, Wednesday, and Friday about this time.

I shuddered as the clopping, squeaking, and crying receded in the distance, and brought the class's attention back to spelling. But now an even greater distraction loomed outside—in the shape of a very long, very black Cadillac which pulled up across the alley. Out from the funeral home came two men in dark suits who opened the back of the vehicle and eased out a wheeled stretcher with a blanket-covered form strapped on it. (I confess I was as fascinated as the children.) As they rolled it inside, Dorothy whispered: "About the only time they unload during school is on Mondays; you know how family weekends can be."

"All right, children," I said, clapping my hands, "in a minute I'm going to pass out papers and give you some words like these to spell," and I went to the blackboard and put up some familiar examples.

Then I summoned William Fowler to my desk. He came, head down and dawdling, certain he was in trouble, though unsure what for. I lowered my voice, so that only he could hear me. "Would you like to pass these papers out?"

His eyes widened; he wasn't in trouble? He nodded enthusiastically. "Good," I nodded and then added sadly, "But look at your hands—you'll get them all dirty." I paused, and we both gazed at them. "Look," I said, brightening, "why don't you go wash them in the lavatory; there's soap in there. Be sure to dry them—but hurry!"

He practically ran out of the room, returning a few

moments later with hands that fairly sparkled. "Do I get to pass them out now?"

"Yes! And as long as those hands are that clean, you can be my paper passer-outer every day."

I had not forgotten what a little special attention had meant to me when I was his age, and from then on I was alert for little tasks that would make William feel special about himself. Before long, he was coming to school with his face as clean as his hands, and he began to find other things about himself that he could clean up, too.

Meanwhile, I was learning as we went, trying to stay a week ahead of where we were and pouring over teachers' manuals, trying to figure out how best to reach these children and give individual attention to so many. Fortunately I had a wonderful principal, Sister Mary James, who knew I was floundering and who would stop by each afternoon after school, to help me sort things out and prepare my lessons for the next day. And Sister Mary Winifred, the first-grade teacher who'd had these children the year before, was a great help, giving me pointers on their different personalities.

But my biggest problem was not teaching; it was homesickness. At the beginning of my postulant year, I'd had a terrible time with that, and never expected to have to deal with it again. But this time around, it was even worse—and now it was the motherhouse I was homesick for! All I had to do was wonder what Margaret or Sister Mary Carol or Mother Loyola, or even Mother Carmelita, were doing, and I would get a lump in my throat. And if I didn't pray quickly, tears would soon follow.

Mother Liguori, who had been our Mother Provincial and was now my new convent's Mother Superior, was aware of my problem—though I had no idea how aware. One Friday afternoon she called me into her office. She was extremely tall, well over six feet, and as a child her face had been ravaged by small pox. It gave her a fierce demeanor, and when people first met her, they were terrified by her. That included me, for I had not yet gotten to know her. (You would have thought by now I would have learned *never* to judge a book by its cover.)

"Sister Mary Raphael," she said with a smile, bidding me sit down next to her desk, "tomorrow you're going over to St. Julianna's, our other convent in the city, to spend the day there."

She looked at me expectantly, but I just nodded. "Yes, Mother," I answered, trying to sound agreeable. I didn't have anything particularly planned for Saturday, but I knew it wasn't that.

She looked puzzled, and then she smiled: "You don't know who's over there, do you?" I shook my head. "Well, an old friend of yours would like to see you."

That piqued my curiosity. "Who?"

"Sister Mary Camilla."

"From Immaculate Conception in Sioux City? She's *there?*"

Mother Liguori nodded.

"Oh, that's *great!*" I hadn't seen Sister Camilla since her last Christmas visit to the motherhouse, but I loved her and thought of her as my big sister in the order. (As her student, I had never used her full name and didn't now.)

Mother beamed; this was the response she had expected. Now she put her hand on mine. "Child, I know how miserable you've been. We love you, and we want you to feel at home here." She smiled. "So tomorrow, I want you to feel free to tell Sister Mary Camilla everything that's on your heart. Don't hold back anything. And have a wonderful time!"

What a joy to see Sister Camilla again! She really was more like an older sister than a former teacher—and she was as delighted to see me, as I her. She had organized a party, complete with games and streamers, ice cream and cake. She and her sisters had practically stood on their heads to help this newly-professed sister get over her homesickness, and I *did* have a good time, a wonderful time—until Gloccamora.

Knowing my love of Irish music, Sister Camilla located a record of Irish songs and put them on. What fun to sing "Sweet Rosie O'Grady" and "When Irish eyes are smiling" and deliberately harmonize atrociously on the endings. But then came "How are Things in Gloccamora?" and you couldn't kid around with that winsome melody. When we came to the line, "Is that willow tree still weeping there," these Irish eyes were far from smiling. I started bawling, and nothing they could say or do helped; I was inconsolable. Finally, their Mother Superior, Mother Dolors whom I had known and been fond of at the motherhouse, came over to me. "Now stop that crying! Right now! Everyone here, and everyone at St. John Berchman's, loves you, the same as they do at the motherhouse. So there is no reason for you to carry on that way."

I did stop, and when I returned to my convent, I felt somewhat better—but only somewhat.

Late that night, I began to feel really awful, and it had nothing to do with homesickness; deep down inside my stomach, something was wrong. I threw up twice in the night, and by morning I was doubled over in pain, unable to get out of bed. When I did not appear for chapel, Mother Liguori came to see how I was.

"I think I have the flu," I managed.

She looked at me, her head tilted. "Where do you hurt?"

"All through my stomach."

"Press your left side—is that worse or better?"

I did as she requested, and was surprised. "That does help, a little."

Mother Liguori bore a look of grave concern. "I'm afraid it's a little more serious than flu."

"What is it?"

"It may be appendicitis; anyway, I'm getting the doctor right away."

He was there in half an hour, and five minutes later, I was on my way to the hospital. As soon as we arrived at the emergency ward, I was put on a rolling stretcher—just like the funeral home used, I recalled with a shudder—and wheeled right into an operating room. Having already contacted my parents for permission, they performed an emergency appendectomy.

I found out later that because I had waited all night and not told anyone, it was a fairly close thing; had Mother Liguori not acted as quickly and decisively as she had. . . .

I spent the rest of that day in a recovery room, heavily sedated, drifting in and out of consciousness. In the morning, I was moved into another room, and the charge nurse came in to obtain the admission details which there'd been no time to get when I arrived. She started filling in the blanks on a form she had on her clipboard: Name, address, age—

"Eighteen? You just said you were a sister at St. John Berchman's convent."

"I am."

"How can you be one, so young? Are you an orphan?"

"There's nothing that says you have to be old, to be a sister."

"D'you always want to be one?" she asked, her clipboard forgotten.

"Yup."

"Why?"

"I don't know; I guess because God wanted me to."

"How did you know He did?"

I looked at her; she wasn't a whole lot older than I was. "Are you—thinking about becoming a sister?"

She was startled. "Oh, no, I'm serving God right here in this job! I mean, He wouldn't want me to do *that!*" She stopped, embarrassed, but I just shrugged and smiled.

"Have you, um, ever regretted it?"

I shook my head.

"Ever been unhappy?"

"Sometimes—no one's happy all the time."

She shook her head. "I always envied you people; I thought you all were so close to God that nothing ever really bothered you."

I laughed, then had to stop, because it hurt my stitches. "Me, too," I nodded. "I used to think that nuns and priests were the only holy people; now that I am one, I know how little different we are from everyone else." I paused. "I guess it's like a girl thinking that getting married is going to solve all her problems."

Now it was her turn to laugh. "I almost did, and for that reason." She grew serious again. "But—you do feel closer to God, don't you?"

"Than before? Of course; I'm where He wants me, doing what He wants me to do. But it does help to have all the reminders in our daily life, and to be living with others who feel the same way."

She went over to the window. "That's what I miss," she mused, "having others around; and the reminders. too." She hesitated. "I stop in at the chapel each morning before check-in, and sometimes I go down there after lunch, but. . ." her voice trailed off.

"You know," I said softly, "if you *are* called to be a religious, you'll never be happy anywhere else." She kept looking out the window, but she nodded imperceptibly.

"Well," she said, briskly turning back, "I'd better finish this form."

After she had left, I remembered the part about being where God wanted me, doing what He wanted me to do. That was true. All that was needed now, was for my heart to catch up with my head.

That evening, I had two visitors—Sister Mary DeLourdes and Sister Mary James. "When we told your class what had happened to you, they all wanted to write you letters. These were ready by the end of school," Sister Mary DeLourdes said, handing me six. "I'm sure there will be many more."

I opened the top one: "Deer Sistr Rafeel, I hope the nrs takes gd kare of you—" I had to stop reading, for fear my laughter would pop a stitch.

That night, before I turned out the light, I tried again, reading just a bit at a time, like sipping tea too hot to drink. I saw something in the letters: those kids really missed me and loved me. Well, that went both ways; I couldn't wait to get back to them.

As the days passed, I had a lot of time to reflect on my life—and to realize how truly grateful I was. Dear Jesus, I often prayed, I love teaching! I can't imagine a better job than teaching and being with children all day long!

And as my body healed, so did my mind and my spirit.

One evening the nurse came in to say that a sister had come to visit.

"If it's Sister Mary DeLourdes," I chuckled, "have her leave the letters outside; I'm too sore!"

But it wasn't Sister Mary DeLourdes. As the nurse left, the silhouette framed in the doorway, so tall and imposing, could have been the angel of death. But it was just the opposite—Mother Liguori.

"How are you doing?"

"Fine, Mother. I have a new appreciation of the line: it only hurts when I laugh."

"Are they feeding you well?"

I smiled. "I get a little tired of yellow jello and mystery meat, but otherwise—" I shrugged.

"When I get home, we'll prepare a care package for you: chocolate and cookies and—the rest will be a surprise."

She looked around the room. "Hm, no telephone—you'll need one tomorrow. I've talked to your parents, and arranged for them to call you tomorrow evening. You'd like that, wouldn't you?"

"Oh yes! Thanks!"

Now she studied me. "You seem more at peace."

I nodded. "The upside-down puzzle pieces are fitting together again." I paused. "I can't tell you how glad I am to be a teacher! Those kids—" I indicated the homemade cards and refrigerator art which decorated my room, "are precious!" I could feel my eyes filling. "I'm so glad to be here!"

"Good!" she smiled. "You can't be any gladder than we are." She grew thoughtful. "You know, sometimes it takes something this drastic, to get us to stop and be still long enough to get a new perspective—His perspective—of our life."

She got up to leave. "Well goodnight, Sister. You'll be home soon."

2nd Grade, 1947

The McLaughlins, 1955

Postulant, 1955

Investiture Day, 1957

The white veil, 1957

The black veil, 1958

Rita with her sister Regina and her husband David, and Kristen, Ellen and Heidi, 1981. (Note deformed right leg and slipped kneecap.)

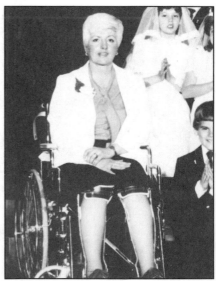

With First Communion class, 1985

Leading children's choir, April, 1986

Healed, July, 1986

The Klauses, 1990

Rita Klaus, today

15

Balance

One evening, not long after my return to the convent, we were in the Community Room after supper, doing handwork. As long we kept our eyes on our work, we were allowed to talk, and I was so busy visiting with the three younger sisters at our end of the table that I did not see Sister Mary James, the grammar school principal, approaching. I was startled when she said, "Sister Mary Raphael? I want you to come and play cards."

"Cards?" I said, wrinkling my nose. "I hate cards!" Then I bit my lip; when would I ever learn custody of the tongue?

"You hate cards," she replied with an even smile, "because you don't know how to play them. Now come on over to my table, and I'll teach you how to play."

"But I don't want to play."

"I didn't ask you if you wanted to."

I got up and followed her, thinking, I am going to hate this. I hate cards. Jesus, I offer this up to You.

If Sister Mary James had an inkling of what was going on in my mind, she remained resolutely cheerful. Sitting down at a table for four, she motioned for me to sit next to her, and from the folds of her habit she produced a deck of cards. "Do you know anything at all about cards?"

Like most kids, I had played go fish and slapjack when

I was little, but I was not about to admit to even that. I hated cards, and nothing was going to make me enjoy this! I shook my head.

"Well, you are a very bright girl who learns quickly, and you are going to learn cards quickly," she said cheerfully but firmly. "We are going to play a game called '500'—this evening."

She started turning over cards and explaining their face value and role: "This is the ace, the strongest. . . . this is the deuce—a wild card that can be substituted for any card in its suite."

"What's a suite?"

"Hearts are the strongest suite, then diamonds, then clubs, then spades." On and on she went, until all the deck had been explained.

"Now," she announced, "we will play 500." She signaled Sister Mary DeLourdes to join us. "Sister will be your angel; she will sit next to you and tell you every time you make a mistake."

Sister Mary DeLourdes was a math whiz, as well as being a math teacher, and was an ace at 500. We started to play. . . .

An hour later, Sister Mary James glanced up at the clock. "Goodness, look at the time! Sisters, we must get ready for compline."

"We might have time for one more hand," I grinned; I had won the last four—handily.

Sister Mary James shook her head. "I think I have created Frankenstein's monster."

After that, we played every night; cards were my new passion. Soon other sisters began to play, and before long the whole convent was playing.

Finally one night, Mother Liguori made an announcement: "I know we all love cards dearly. But we have handwork that's not getting done. So—we will limit our card-playing to Wednesdays, Saturdays, and Sundays. On the other evenings we will stick to our handwork."

Balance was restored.

And balance was Mother Liguori's primary concern, regarding her youngest charge, as I was about to discover. One morning she called me into her office and asked, "What do you read?"

"Let's see—right now I'm reading St. Louis de Montefort and St. Augustine—"

"No, I mean, for fun."

"For fun?"

"Yes."

I was shocked. "I don't read for fun."

"Not ever?"

"We're not allowed to," I added with a tinge of self-righteousness.

"That was at the motherhouse; this is here. I want you to start doing some reading for fun."

I didn't know what to make of that: the more I got to know Mother Liguori, the more I respected her, but she was constantly surprising me. With a jolt I realized I didn't know her nearly as well as I thought I did.

"Now I read Agatha Christie for fun," she was saying. "I adore her and read her every night before going to bed. I read Thomas a Kempis and Agatha Christie."

She picked up a well-thumbed volume on her desk and handed it to me. "Here's an anthology of hers; I want you start it this evening, and I want you to give it at least fifteen minutes a day. That's all you have to do, but I want you to do it. I'm not going to ask you for a book report, but I *will* ask you tomorrow how you like it."

I stared at her, scandalized.

"Don't look at me that way," she said, smiling. "They're light, there's nothing wrong with them, they're good and clean, and they make your mind work."

Her smile faded, as she added: "You need to be a well-balanced nun, Sister Mary Raphael, and you are not balanced. You are super-spiritual. Do not misunderstand me: I am not saying there's anything wrong with spirituality; in fact, we cannot live this life without it. But anything can be taken to extremes. When that happens, when someone starts seeing everything in super-spiritual terms, it can be a dangerous excursion into unreality—dangerous, because life becomes a spiritual fantasy. . . ."

Sensing (correctly) that I was only half hearing what she was saying, she suddenly slapped the desk hard. "And Jesus is found in reality! In the grit and grime and sin of everyday life! You walk through it with Him, and you are the better for it! You learn by going through reality, no matter how painful: that's where you find out who He truly is—and who *you* truly are, when you're not in Him."

She smiled grimly. "*That* is not a very pleasant sight! Which is why we turn so quickly from that mirror—and are tempted to escape into super-spirituality."

I was speechless; I had never heard her speak this way before.

Confident that she had my undivided attention now, she resumed a more conversational tone: "Jesus said: *I am the Way, the Truth, and the Life*—well, there are many evangelists showing that He is the Way, and many theologians showing that He is the Truth." She sighed. "There are not that many believers showing that He is the Life. Which is why He has called us here to live as we do, helping one another in our daily walk: to live the Life and show others that it is possible."

She got up and walked to the window, her hands clasped behind her. "It's not an easy assignment, this business of being in the world, but not of it. In many ways, it would be easier to be a cloistered order, with no contact with the outside world. But that's not our vocation, not what we're called to do."

She turned to me. "Sister Mary Raphael, you're going to have to meet with the parents of the children in your class, and parents who come to visit your sisters here, and tradesmen, and so many others." She smiled. "You told me once that when you first dreamed of becoming a sister, it was because you wanted to be a saint. Well, if you read the lives of the saints carefully, you'll find that with very few exceptions, most of them had to walk through reality, often pretty painful reality, to get there."

She chuckled. "And somehow, my dear, I don't think you're cut out to be a mystic hermit."

I laughed.

"So," she pointed to the volume in front of me, "I want to bring some balance into your life. I know you're convinced you won't like Agatha Christie, but—you felt that way about playing cards, too, before you tried them."

That evening I discovered that I loved Agatha Christie. Miss Marple and all those characters became real people in my life. I had always enjoyed a challenge to the intellect, and now I tried to see how quickly I could solve each mystery myself. Soon my problem was keeping my mystery-reading in balance!

From time to time, Mother Liguori would invite me into her office for a chat. They were fun times; we would talk about spiritual things and mystery stories, about how school was going, and about politics. But she soon discovered that when it came to politics and world affairs, though my opinions were just as strong there as everywhere else, I was not very well informed.

"Sister Mary Raphael, do you read the paper?"

"No. At the motherhouse, we weren't—"

"Never mind the motherhouse. You're a teacher now;

you have to know what is going on, because your children are going to be asking you questions—and so will their parents."

She leaned back in her chair. "When you were in the novitiate, God had separated you unto Himself for a season, because you needed a complete break from the world. He was creating a new life in you, a life in Him, and the world and the past could have prevented that life from putting down the tap root it would need later. But now you are well rooted, and now it is time for you to be re-introduced to the world—judiciously, just enough so that you can be an effective messenger."

"Messenger?"

"Carrying the message of this place—that He *is* the Life—to the world." She opened the center drawer of her desk and pulled out a copy of the Detroit *Free Press*. "So, here is another reading assignment," she said, putting it on the desk in front of me. "I want you to read this every day—thoroughly, especially the editorials and the columnists on the op-ed page."

"What's the op-ed page?"

"The page opposite the editorials," she smiled. "You really haven't read the paper much, have you?"

I shook my head. "Other than the comics when I was a kid, no."

"The pages to start with are usually the last two in the first section." She turned to the editorial page and scanned it. "You may not agree with a lot of this—I don't; but you need to know what they're saying."

So I started reading the paper—and now in my chats with Mother Liguori, we discussed the Cold War and the health of the local economy (the car-makers were having a banner year with their '59 models), and whether the Senator from Massachusetts would make a run for the Presidency. And from all of it I learned that it was all right to be interested in such things, as long as they never became the main thing you were interested in.

The year passed quickly; before I knew it, school was out, and it was time for me to return to the motherhouse for summer school (I still had a degree to earn). Before I left for the train station, I dropped by Mother Liguori's office for one last chat.

"I want to thank you for—" I hesitated, stuck for the right words. "Look at me," I stammered, "and you know, I'm hardly ever at a loss for words." We both laughed.

"You've grown a great deal, Sister Mary Raphael," she said warmly. "In many ways you were still a child, when you came here." She paused. "You've become a young woman."

"Well, I owe that to you."

She shook her head. "No, I merely gave you some direction. It was your love of Jesus and your perseverance that did it." She stood up, and I did, too. "You're a nun now, a real one. And a well-balanced one," she added, and we both laughed.

16

Massena

"One lump or two?" asked Mother Loyola from behind the gleaming silver tea service.

"Two, please," I replied.

Wielding the tiny silver tongs with a practiced touch, she extracted two cubes of sugar and deposited them one by one in my waiting cup.

Through the open window of her office, a warm summer breeze stirred the curtains, and brought the scent of roses from the garden below—and the distant sound of sisters' laughter at Afternoon Tea.

When it came to matters of ceremony, I reflected, be it crowning a monarch or observing a tradition, no one did it better than the English. . . and perhaps there was no more civilized—and civilizing—custom than Afternoon Tea. I used to smile at the thought of them donning dinner jackets on an African safari, or crooking a finger as they raised a cup of steaming Darjeeling (while a thin red line of Grenadiers was trying to hold the Khyber Pass less than an hour's ride away).

But now I could see the subtle benefit to mind and soul—how this gentle custom, polished by centuries, was both harmonizing and reassuring. It created a gracious setting in which the pieces of a fractured day could be drawn together, or the rough edges from an abrasive exchange could be smoothed and mended. And for us, it was an opportunity to recapture the equilibrium so necessary to our lives.

It was also about the only chance we had to visit with one another. People outside the convent assumed that because we lived together, we saw each other all the time; nothing could be further from the truth. Usually we were working under a deadline or praying, or eating or doing handwork alongside those who had come into the order when we had. But at tea, we had a chance to catch up with all the other sisters whom we knew but seldom saw.

Which is what I would be doing shortly, when Mother Loyola was finished with me. But for the moment, I was content to be here in her office, savoring what it was like to be home. That was something else that Afternoon Tea did: it blended the senses. The smell of freshly-cut grass, the sighing of the pines, the white clouds scudding across an azure sky, the feel of warm sunlight on cheek and brow—all mingled with the soothing taste of these delicate leaves.

I glanced out the window at the sisters on the lawn, chatting and sipping, taking tea or sampling cookies. . . the way the golden rays of the late afternoon sun behind them caught the white edges of their veils and seemed to give them halos. . . the rhythmic flow of their black habits, as they slowly gathered or dissolved. . . .

"Sister?" Mother Loyola called my attention back to the room. "Mother Liguori is quite pleased with your year in Detroit."

"I loved it, Mother. It was hard at first, but it got so much better; I can't wait to go back."

She looked at me. "That's why I wanted to talk to you: you won't be going back."

"I won't? *Why?*" Shock, hurt, anger—it was all out, before

I could stop it. Not that I would have, for I trusted Mother Loyola—to the point where I *wanted* her to know my innermost feelings.

"Because I feel that it is God's will for you now."

I felt like crying. Those kids— "Why, Mother? Why does He do that? Every time I get adjusted to a place and begin to love the people, He moves me! I mean, does He enjoy making me miserable?"

She smiled. "You know better than that." She looked out towards the city; already the shadows were creeping across the valley. "Sister Mary Raphael," she said thoughtfully, "you are a nesting person. Perhaps because of your strong family upbringing—and I wonder if you have any idea how fortunate you are to have had such parents, such a childhood—your heart's nature, which your head will often be unaware of, is to repeat that experience and re-create that environment as quickly and as deeply as possible."

I nodded. I had never seen that and didn't fully comprehend it, but my heart (ahead of my brain, as usual) was telling me that it was true.

"So," she went on, "you put down roots and open your heart to others and embrace everything around you and— make a nest."

She put an arm around me. "Some day, God may let you do that. But not yet. You've grown a great deal in a short time. But you still need to grow a little more."

The hurt and the anger were gone; I looked at her in gratitude—and a little awe. "Can you tell me where I will be going, Mother?"

"Yes," she smiled, "when I know myself." She thought for a moment. "Probably at the end of the Great Retreat. In the meantime, I want you to concentrate on your studies. I also want you to start taking voice lessons from Sister Teresita. God has given you a marvelous instrument; you must develop your singing to its full potential."

She stood back from me, seeing me as if for the first time. "God has gifted you in so many ways! But as Scripture says: to whom much is given, much is also required. You have a responsibility to utilize every one of your talents, for He will be expecting a great deal from you."

I groaned. "Mother, I really don't want that. All I want is to just be a sister."

She shook her head. "You really don't have a choice— any more than I do." Then she chuckled. "Mother Liguori tells me that you love to play cards: well, in this life, you play the hand you've been dealt; you don't turn in your cards for others." She turned serious. "If you will accept what He has given you and use it for His honor and glory, what you do will be blessed—and you will be blessed in doing it."

She looked out at the lawn and realized that everyone else had already gone in. "Come on," she said, "we'll be late for Vespers."

The summer passed quickly—time always did, when one was fully committed and fully scheduled. August arrived and with it our ten- day Ignatian retreat, to prepare us for the Feast of the Assumption. Most of the time I was able to concentrate on spiritual things, but like all the other sisters who were up for re-assignment, I couldn't help wondering where I would be going next, or if I would be staying at the motherhouse till I finished my degree.

That was invariably topic #1, whenever we had *Deo Gratias*. One afternoon at tea, Sister Mary Joachim and I were speculating on the future. She had entered the order during my canonical year, and having the same sense of humor, over the years we had become close friends. Now she asked: "Sister Rafe? (She was the only one who ever called me that.) If you could go anywhere you wanted—*anywhere* we had a convent—where would it be?"

"Massena," I said, without hesitation.

"Massena? You've got to be kidding! That mission's 1200 miles from here! The end of nowhere—the boonies! Why on earth would you ever want to go there?"

"I don't know," I answered truthfully. In fact, the only thing I did know about the little town in upstate New York was that it was about as far upstate as it was possible to get—on the St. Lawrence River, ten miles from the Quebec border. But I had a good feeling about it—a sense that there I could become the fuller person that Mother Loyola had indicated two months earlier.

So, when Mother invited me into her office for my annual review, before she could give me my next assignment, I said: "Can I tell you where I'd like to go? Where I've wanted to go, ever since I knew I wouldn't be going back to Detroit?"

"Yes, I think you should—but I should caution you: it isn't going to make a bit of difference."

"Massena."

"That's where you're going."

I clapped my hands in delight—and then looked at her, astonished—because she *wasn't* astonished. "Mother Loyola, doesn't *anything* ever surprise you?"

"Yes, but not that," she replied. "But it is reassuring, and it should reassure you, too: God had put that desire in your heart, long before He told me where you would be going." She chuckled. "Now get your bags ready; you'll be leaving Friday."

The gentle rocking of the sleeping car, the muffled *clickety-clack,* and the fact that we had sat up in coach the night before—all these things should have conspired to put me sound asleep. But the passing scene was simply too exciting. Of course, all I had to was pull down the shade. . . . But I would have missed the ancient clapboard stations with their steep-gabled roofs. Or the ancient baggage-handlers on their platforms, pulling big two-wheeled carts that balanced on either end through escaping steam that swirled about them, turning them into figures of mystery.

As I nestled my head in the Pullman pillow like that kitten in the ad, I did try closing my eyes—but I could still hear the dinging signals at grade crossings, rising in intensity as we approached, then quickly receding in pitch, once we'd passed. Forget sleep—and try to tell exactly when the train started to pull out of a station. Their departures were so incredibly smooth, you had to watch something stationary, to be sure you were actually moving. And if there was another train in the station alongside of you at the same time, you could never be certain it was you moving, or them, or both. It occurred to me that these graceful departures must be a source of tremendous pride to the engineers, like a farmer's ability to plow a perfectly straight furrow over a long field, or a sailor's skill at holding a course.

Ding-ding-ding-ding-ding—an old Ford pick-up was waiting at the crossing as we rushed past, and I wondered what it was doing out in the middle of the night in the middle of nowhere. Perhaps a child had come down with a terrible fever, and her father was driving for help. Then I remembered that it was Saturday night. . . .

When the train rounded a left-hand bend, I could sometimes catch a glimpse of the great steam engine up front, its headlight reaching out into the darkness. As we glided along beside the black ribbon of the St. Lawrence in the still night, mist figures were rising from the river's surface like the wraiths of ancient Algonquin warriors, and the reflection of the full moon seemed to draw a path directly to my window. It was all so beautiful—I grinned and hugged my pillow in the darkness of my berth.

It must have struck the engineer the same way, for suddenly, miles from any town or crossing, the locomotive emitted a long, haunting cry from its whistle. I imagined the fireman, his sweaty, grimy face red in the light of the open firebox, glaring over at the engineer: what was that for? That just cost him two shovelfuls of coal. But the engineer kept his eyes on the twin strands of silver racing into the night in front of them. He was grinning—the moon's reflection of the river was drawing a path straight to the cab's window.

Finally I did fall asleep—but not until the moon had gone down, and the sky was beginning to lighten with the coming of dawn.

My first view of Massena fulfilled all my expectations. It was a jewel of a town—a village, really, with streets lined with old maples that made green tunnels of shade and quaint shops that had been there for at least four generations. The heart of Sacred Heart parish was a grey stone Gothic church that must have been one of the first buildings the people of Massena built. And the three-story white house that served as its convent seemed equally old. But the paint was new, the lawn and shrubs were freshly trimmed, and the whole place looked—cheery. In that instant, I knew I was going to love this place.

And I did.

We five new arrivals were shown into the convent's kitchen, where Sister Mary Julia was in charge. She was a large, ruddy-faced woman, rough-hewn and rough-spoken, but with a heart as big and warm as her giant cookstove. Hands on hips, she stood back and surveyed us. "You must be hungry after your long trip; how about some sticky buns?" She opened the oven door and withdrew a tray that filled the kitchen with a delectable aroma.

She led us into the refectory—a converted sunporch with red draperies framing the tall windows and a fireplace at the end. "Sit down now; these will tide you over till lunch."

"But it's almost lunchtime now," I blurted.

"Hush, child, and eat. You look puny."

After one bite I needed no further coaxing. Sister Mary Julia was the best cook I had ever known, and her specialty was baking. Bread, cookies, pies, buns, cakes—under her tutelage I would put on thirty pounds in my first year there.

We were just finishing, when Mother Annunciata came in. Physically she was exactly the opposite of Sister Mary Julia—a wee wisp of a woman who couldn't have weighed more than ninety pounds. But every ounce was filled with charm. "Well, look at my new girls—how are you, sweeties?" Before we could respond, she went on: "This is going to be a wonderful year! We're going to have so much fun, you won't believe it!"

She took us into the convent's chapel and assigned each of us to our chair and *prie-dieu*, a kneeler with a little shelf for holy books. In French, *prie-dieu* meant "for praying to God," and being so close to the Quebec border, we would soon be hearing quite a bit of French.

"Now we'll ask Jesus to bless your year here," she concluded, "and we'll ask His Blessed Mother to help you. Everyone who comes here must do their best, but we will do our best to make sure it's a good life for you."

There were sixteen sisters in the convent, tucked into every available corner. The older sisters had little private rooms on the second floor, but we young newcomers were dormed three to a room in the attic. We had a tiny sink,

a tiny closet, a tiny dresser in which we each had two
drawers, and a tiny window which looked out on the old
Methodist church across the street. The beds had iron
bedsteads, and I realized I was going to have to get used
to the sleeping sounds of others once again. But that was
hardly the main sound I was going to have to become
accustomed to—

Bong! Bong! Bong! I clapped my hands over my ears;
the church's bell, sounding the noon hour, felt like it was
going off inside of my head. But that was only the half
of it—

Bang! Bang! Bang! Now the Methodists' bell, two beats
behind and four and a half notes higher than ours, joined
in. The discordant tintinnabulation was so awful, I started
to laugh. Just then, an older sister looked in to see how
we were doing, and I had to shout to make myself heard:
"Does this go on every hour?"

She nodded.

"All through the night?"

"Oh, yes," she smiled, "but in a week you won't even
notice them."

"Thanks," I smiled back, wondering what I was going
to do for sleep in the meantime.

Putting the last of my things away, I hurried after the
others who had already gone downstairs. The stairway
was quite narrow and quite steep, and no sooner did I
start down, than an older sister came around the corner
and started up. Out of deference I started backing up the
stairs, but I tripped on my scapular and suddenly I was
rapidly descending, landing on each step with my seat.

When I arrived at the bottom, the older sister, seeing
that only my pride was hurt, observed with a smile, "Well,
we're certainly off to a bouncing start!"

I blushed—and then laughed. She laughed, too, and
introduced herself. This was Sister Mary Clementia, who

would become like a big sister to me.

The rest of the day was spent getting acclimated and preparing for the first day of school. I would be teaching first grade this year, instead of second, which meant there was no first-grade teacher to go to, to get a line on my prospective students. Also, I had to enroll at Pottsdam College eighteen miles away, to continue my work towards my degree. In all, it was a full day, and given the lack of sleep the previous two nights, I was more than ready, when it came time for bed.

I was just drifting off, when—*bong! Bong! Bong-bang-bong-bang.* . . I burst out laughing, as did Sister Mary Michelle and Sister Mary Peter. But I did not think it was so funny an hour later, or the hour after that, or the hour after that. As I pressed my pillow over my head, it was hard to believe it would ever become a lullaby.

In the morning we said Matins and Lauds in our chapel, after which Mother Annunciata came in and told us to put on our mantles; we were going over to the church for Mass. Our pastor was Monsignor Berube—middle-fifties, with jet-black hair and a distinguished bearing. I had never heard anyone celebrate Mass, as he did. He prayed every word—and created such an atmosphere of reverence, that when he elevated the host, you could almost see Jesus in it. I was stunned; no priest had ever made me feel so aware that I was receiving the actual Body and Blood of Christ in the Eucharist.

After Mass, Mother invited him and his two associate pastors over to the convent, to meet us "newies." Father O'Neill was a tall, skinny Irishman with red hair and steel-rimmed spectacles, and Father Billmeier was the opposite, probably weighing close to 300 pounds. As we chatted with them, Father O'Neill was an engaging contrast of shyness and quick wit, while Father Billmeier was jovial and funny—and both were extreme contrasts to the solemn

Monsignor Berube. When I thought of these three occupying the rectory together, I had to fight down a giggle.

The first day of school, I greeted my young charges, all 35 of them, in French, as well as English. More than a few came from homes where only a French patois was spoken, and while I would concentrate on helping them become comfortable with English, I wanted them to feel welcome. Happily they all seemed to come from solid homes, and as a class they were quick and happy. Mother Annunciata was right: this *was* going to be a wonderful year.

The following weekend, Monsignor led a retreat for us. Confession was part of it, and I chose to make mine with him. After it, he asked me: "What sort of books do you like to read?"

"Agatha Christie."

He was mildly startled. "Well, she's all right," he said in his low voice, "But that's not what I had in mind: what sort of spiritual books are you reading?"

"None," I admitted, hastening to add: "I just got here and haven't really picked any out yet."

"Then let me pick one for you: *Christ, the Life of the Soul* by Abbot Dom Marmion. If you don't have it in your library, I'll get you a copy."

We did have one, and I started reading it that evening. Dom Marmion was a Benedictine who had died in 1940, on the very day that I was born. Next to the Bible, his book became the most important book I had ever read, for it helped me to know the real Jesus. Periodically, I would check my understanding with Monsignor, who seemed to know my soul better than I did myself. He would make suggestions, things for me to think about as I read.

I was coming to see how important was the life of Christ within us, and how we needed to be always aware of Him dwelling there. We were to commune with Him whenever the need arose, and even when there was no pressing need—in fact, especially when there was no pressing need. We were to live, sensitive to His grace, and if we did—or spoke or thought—something that so grieved His Holy Spirit that He departed from us, then we needed to stop whatever we were doing and repent. If we asked Him, he would show us what it was that had grieved Him. Then, when we were convicted of what our sin had done to hurt Him and/or others, we could confess that sin and ask His forgiveness. And if we were determined to "go and sin no more," He would forgive us and wash us with His blood till we were "whiter than snow"—and grace would return.

Seeing that I was trying to live what I was learning, he asked me to convey my understanding to the little ones in my class, as I prepared them for their first Communion. I said I would try—and to my surprise they seemed to understand. I realized then, that it did not matter how young a child was; if you were imparting spiritual truth to them, on some level they were able to assimilate it, even if they could not articulate it.

When I first told them that as we grown-ups partook of the Eucharist, we were actually taking Jesus inside of us—and that this is what they would soon be doing also, they were dumbfounded. But gradually they were able to understand the nature of sin, and how it could deprive them of the life of God in their souls.

I believed it now, more deeply than I ever had before, and the kids believed it, too.

Their whole-hearted embracing of this Truth brought a gradual but profound change to our classroom: they began to respect the life of Jesus in each other. And the love and gentleness which they commenced to show one another was—awesome. I never had a single discipline problem with that class.

What was more, they went home and shared their understanding with their parents. *Out of the mouths of babes*—the parents began to view themselves and their relationship with each other in a different way. And now they started coming up to me and saying things like, "We can't thank you enough; I guess we always knew it, but we never really understood it or took it to heart."

I assured them I'd had nothing to do with it. I had merely shared a Truth that had only recently been awakened in me, as well.

The year passed more quickly than any I could remember. We had a lively bunch of sisters, young and old. They were wonderfully supportive of one another, and they all seemed to have well-developed senses of humor; I never laughed so much in my life. Plus, our parishioners could not have been more friendly; many of them had boats, so we were often invited to cruise the St. Lawrence and join them on picnics. When my parents called to see how I was doing (they could do that now), I told them the truth: I had never been happier in my life. Mother Annunciata had predicted a wonderful year, but she had way under-estimated it: it was a year of pure joy.

In all that hazy sunshine, it was easy to ignore the small dark cloud on the western horizon. Some odd things had begun happening. In the middle of a busy Saturday morning in April, for instance, Sister Mary Clementia and

I were in the convent's pantry, enjoying a coffee break. I was teaching piano now and art, and with a full day of lessons stretching ahead of me, I was grateful for a moment's respite with my good friend.

"I don't know, what's the matter with me," I yawned. "I can't seem to get started this morning. I must be getting older." I was all of nineteen.

Sister Mary Clementia replied in the creaking, menacing voice of a wicked wolf: "All the more reason, dearie, to have a nice warm cup of coffee," and she poured me one.

"I don't know if it'll help," I said, starting to reach for the little cream pitcher, then going instead to the fridge for some milk. In the past year I had gone from 120 to 150. Mother Annunciata insisted that was not too much for my big-boned, five-foot-nine frame, but I was determined not to reach 151. And I blamed the new weight for my increasing fatigue: who wouldn't be tired, lugging two fifteen-pound suitcases everywhere?

But this morning was worse than usual. "Sister," I said with voice that betrayed my concern, "I actually nodded off in the middle of Janic Bigelow's lesson."

Now she put on her Hercule Poirot voice: "I was wondering who had been dipping into the vat of midnight oil, and here is the culprit, under my very nose."

I shook my head, mildly mystified. "That's just it: my light was out before 10:00. I got eight hours of sleep last night."

"I wish I had," said Sister Mary Clementia, yawning. Seeing my expression she added, "I wouldn't worry about it; Janie's playing is enough to put anyone to sleep."

All at once, the cup I was holding fell out of my hand, sending coffee everywhere. Embarrassed, I grabbed some paper towels from the dispenser and started mopping up, before the light coffee could stain anything. My friend knelt to help me, noting that with my usual dexterity, I had managed to keep it off of our habits.

I laughed in gratitude, but inside I was anything but laughing. I was scared. Because I had not felt the cup leave my grasp; as far as my fingers knew, they were still holding its handle.

Bong—bong—coffee break was over; it was time for my next lesson. In the ordinariness of the familiar routine, the bizarre incident was soon forgotten.

With all the blue sky above, that cloud gathering on the horizon was of no concern; after all, it was no bigger than a man's hand.

17

Vaya con Dios

Ten days after my twentieth birthday, I awoke to see frost completely covering our little window. It was my second winter in Massena, and I knew how cold it could get in the snow belt. Our window was often rimed with frost, but never before had it completely occluded it. Yesterday it had reached 12 degrees below zero; it was probably even colder than that now.

I shivered and pulled the comforter around me. It didn't help; somehow the house's warmth never quite made it up to the attic. As if to confirm this, I noticed that I could see my breath. Well, there was one sure-fire way to get warm, and this morning—I glanced over at Sister Mary Michelle and Sister Mary Peter who were still tightly balled under their covers—I would have the luxury of having the shower to myself for awhile.

I reached a foot out and groped for my slippers. Finding one but not the other, I hurriedly retreated to the relative warmth of the bed. I calculated that if I could get my bathrobe on in ten seconds and find the other slipper in five, my combined pre-shower exposure might be less than a minute. My body didn't believe me, but staying in bed wasn't much of an option, so I was soon up and quietly scrambling.

I turned on the shower to full hot, and soon hot water and steam were rushing out of the shower head, transforming the little stall into a blessedly warm haven. Adjusting the temperature, I hung up bathrobe and nightgown and got under the thick spray. "Aaahhh," I sighed aloud, absorbing the warmth.

After awhile I noticed that the light was dimming— we must be having some kind of brown-out. I looked up at the bulb; it still seemed to be working, yet everything was getting dark. . . . Suddenly I felt a different kind of chill inside, that no amount of hot water could help. I was losing my vision!

In another moment, it was completely gone. Everything was black. Yet my eyes were wide open; I could feel myself blinking.

What was happening? Icy fingers of fear reached up into my entrails and closed in a deadly grip. I groped for the shower handle and turned the water off, then felt around for a towel. And then I had to keep one hand on the wall to steady myself, because in addition to losing my sight, I had lost my sense of balance. I grabbed onto the towel rack and just stood there, shaking with fear. *Dear God, what was happening to me?*

In a few minutes, as my body gradually cooled down, some of my vision began to return. I was able to make my way back to the room and get dressed. By the time I had my shoes on, most of my vision had come back. But things were still blurry, and I was still dizzy. And badly frightened.

In Lauds, I couldn't read the office, but by the end of breakfast I felt enough together to go to school. The moment I was done teaching, I went to Mother Annunciata. "Mother, I had some problems this morning: I couldn't see."

"You what?"

"I couldn't see."

She looked at me. "Well, dear, you can see now, can't you?"

"Yes, but—"

"I think you're just overtired. You told me that you were feeling fatigued—why don't you just go to bed now and take a little rest. I know you've been working awfully hard. Take the rest of the week off, and we'll see how you are then."

I did. And I did feel better. In fact, I felt so back to normal that I dismissed the whole episode as some kind of freak accident.

Until it happened again. The second time was not as severe as the first. Feeling terribly tired, I noticed that my vision was growing blurry. When I went to Mother Annunciata, she asked, "When was the last time you had your eyes checked?"

"I never have."

"It could be that you need glasses—but I think I'm going to have you see an ophthalmologist, so we can get a qualified medical examination."

In a darkened room, the doctor spent a long time examining different aspects of my eyes with one of those flashlights where the light came out through the center of a circular mirror. When he had finished, he said, "Have you been having any other problems besides blurred vision?"

I told him about going blind in the shower, but assured him that this had only happened once.

"Anything else?"

"No."

He looked at me. "Have you been feeling excessively tired lately?"

"Well, yes—but I've been trying to get some extra sleep."

"I'm not talking about normal fatigue; everyone

overdoes it from time to time. I'm talking about being more tired than you can ever remember being before."

I thought for a moment and then nodded. He did not seem surprised. "Look," he said, writing on a pad, "I want you to see a friend of mine. He's an optho-neurologist." Seeing my reaction, he shook his head and smiled. "Now don't go getting frightened; it's probably nothing. But we do have optic neuritis here, and that could mean diabetes—or MS." He was still smiling, but it did not offset the gravity of his tone, as he tore off the piece of paper and handed it to me.

When I got home I told Mother Annunciata, who made the next appointment for me. This doctor, in addition to examining my eyes, took blood and urine samples and tested my reflexes, even to tapping the knees of my alternately crossed legs.

When he was all done and had the results of the tests, he pulled a chair next to me and sat down. "What do you know about MS?"

I shrugged. "It stands for Multiple Sclerosis—whatever that is."

"Well, we may have a case of MS here. I can't make an absolute diagnosis at this point, because we don't have a test that says yes, it is, or no, it isn't. With MS, it's kind of a wait-and-see thing." (This was thirty-three years ago.)

Seeing I was at a loss as to how to handle that, he added: "I wouldn't let it upset my life. Obviously you need to rest and takes things at a slower pace." He paused. "The rest part is important; you need to make sure you get a good night's sleep—every night, not just once or twice a week." I smiled; to think he knew me that well, just from tapping my knee with a little rubber hammer.

"Exercise is important, too," he went on, "but never to the point of exhaustion. The main thing is to keep rested."

"Doctor," I forced myself to ask, "what does it look like for the future?"

"It's impossible to say; you may not have any more problems. Some people have one or two of these episodes and then never have another one." He sighed. "On the other hand, there could be more; if there are, we'll tackle them when and if they occur."

He got up. "The most important thing to remember is: you cannot let it rule your life. You have got to be the one in charge: you are ruling it, not the other way around."

As he showed me out, he smiled, "I'm going to call your Mother Superior now, and tell her exactly what I've just told you."

When I got home, Mother Annunciata informed me that she was moving me down from the attic and giving me one of the little rooms on the second floor. She was also relieving me of my religious education responsibilities, and my Saturday course at Pottsdam College, as well as the music and art lessons I was giving. "But I still want you to play and paint, so from now on you can regard Saturday as your own time, to do whatever you want."

I didn't know what to say.

"Sister Mary Raphael," she said, smiling, "you must not be discouraged by all of this. Trust God, and remember that whenever He closes a door, He opens a window."

Sometimes I chafed under the restrictions, and sometimes I just flat-out rebelled and stayed up late or worked too hard. But most of the time I really was obedient. And God honored that obedience: six months passed without an incident, then a year, then two years, then three. . . and gradually I became convinced that I was one of those cases which would never have another recurrence. As long as I didn't work obsessively or get seriously overtired, I would be fine.

Meanwhile, I grew to love Massena more and more. I knew enough not to expect heaven on earth, but I figured that this was about as close as we were likely to get. In August of '62, Mother Annunciata's five years would be up, and we wondered who would be taking her place. To my delight, it was Sister Mary James, who had been my principal at St. John Berchman's in Detroit, and who had taught me to play cards.

I spent a long time thanking God for this latest in the succession of wise and compassionate spiritual directors He had given me. Mother Loyola, Mother Carmelita, Mother Liguori, Mother Annunciata, and now Mother Mary James—I could appreciate how extraordinarily blessed I had been, for by now I had met enough sisters from other convents, including some from other orders, to realize that this was not always the case.

The winter of '63 was a particularly bad one for flu. It came like an epidemic to Massena, and did not pass over our convent. Several of our sisters came down with it, and in the middle of March, it was my turn. It hit quick and hard. One morning I knew I wasn't feeling well, but started to teach anyway. Suddenly struck with a blinding headache, I put my head down on my desk—and couldn't get it up again.

Sister Joy passed by just then, and seeing me, came in and lifted me up. She half-carried me over to the convent, putting me to bed and taking my temperature: 102. It was high, but not high enough to account for the loss of motor coordination: when I had to get up to use the bathroom, my feet felt like they were encased in cement. To walk,

I practically had to lift each leg with both hands—and I did not let myself think what that might mean.

Meanwhile, I slept and dozed and consumed hot chicken soup to bring the fever down—and was resolutely determined to believe the sister nurse who told me it was just the flu, and I would soon be fine.

The only thing which shook that belief was my right knee: it was demonstrating a propensity for collapsing without warning. I compensated by always walking near the wall, with an eye for something sturdy to grab and a place to sit down, in case I had to in a hurry. There were also times lying in bed, when I could feel my whole body going numb. But they never lasted more than a minute, and so I continued to believe that I had contracted an unusually severe case of flu, and these were all just symptoms.

Then one morning my knee gave out in the bathroom, and suddenly I was lying on the floor, unable to get up. I called and called, until someone heard me. They helped me back into bed, and the doctor was called.

"I've got this quirky knee that keeps buckling and caving in on me," I explained, when he arrived.

"Any other symptoms?"

I shook my head.

"What about numbness?"

With a sigh, I admitted that since the flu I'd had spells of numbness.

He examined the knee and my right leg and announced: "We've got some muscle atrophy here. I don't know why your quadriceps muscle and your ligaments aren't holding your knee in place, but we're going to find out. As soon as you get over the flu, we're checking you into the hospital at Ogdensburg."

A week later I was there, in the hepatitis ward, being subjected to all kinds of tests. "We're looking for a form of meningitis now," one doctor confided, "which means we'll have to do a spinal."

A spinal? "Doctor, I really feel a whole lot better; in fact, I feel fine. I've just got this stupid trick knee—"

He was just nodding and smiling, the way doctors did when they weren't giving any weight to what you were telling them.

"Well," he said agreeably, "we just want to check everything out."

I was in there for ten days, after which Mother Mary James informed me that Mother Loyola was concerned and wanted me to come back to Omaha for further tests at St. Joseph's Hospital, as soon as possible. In that case, said the doctor, I would have to fly; I was much too weak and debilitated for a 36-hour train ride.

So, at age 23 I experienced my first plane ride—in a little 12-passenger Mohawk Airlines commuter flight from Ogdensburg to Albany. No sooner were we off the ground than we encountered "severe turbulence" and started bouncing all over the sky. I grabbed the arm rests so tightly, I was sure I'd put permanent finger marks in them. Dear Jesus, I prayed, I think we're going to die! And even if we don't, it's definitely not worth it, just to save a day on the train!

Fortunately, the plane on the next leg from Albany to Omaha was larger—a Lockheed Electra with four turboprop engines. But they provided their own worry. I was in a window seat over the left wing and had a perfect view—of long streams of fire shooting out of the engines. Should I tell the stewardess?

I looked around, but no one else seemed concerned. So I prayed most of the way to Omaha that the flames would not work their way up the wing to the fuselage and consume us all. Finally I asked the grandmotherly type next to me, if those flames were normal. "Oh, sure, honey, that's just how an Electra does."

When we finally landed, I felt like I had been flying a whole lot longer than 36 hours.

I was met by two sisters who took me straight to St. Joseph's, where I was put in a room painted dark green with a window that looked out at a brick wall. I underwent two more days of tests there, after which I was discharged and went back to Massena (by train).

I never did learn what the tests revealed, but by now I was feeling somewhat better; at least, I was able to function. Fatigue came sporadically, and at its worst I would get dizzy and have to stop what I was doing and sit down, if I wasn't already seated. Also, I had to be extremely careful going up or down stairs, for I could never be sure when my knee might decide it couldn't bear my weight.

In August, as usual, we returned to the motherhouse for the Great Retreat, and this was my year to make my final vows. I was so proud! My mother and father were there, and all my brothers and sisters, as I processed down the aisle wearing my crown of white roses. There at the altar, before the Cross of my Saviour, I pledged to remain His bride forever and dedicated my whole life to doing His will.

I had one more year at Massena before my tour was up, and I savored every minute of it. The waves of fatigue came more frequently now, and sometimes when I was walking, I would think I was picking my feet up higher than I actually was. If there was the slightest wrinkle in a rug, I could trip over it, and more than once I even tripped over a carpet's pile. My knee became so unreliable that I developed a swing-gait: I would lock my right leg straight and swing the whole thing round, as if it was a wooden appendage. A ghastly sight, but it did get me from A to B without help, or having to use a wheelchair. I had not forgotten what my first doctor had told me, and I set my will that I would rule it, and not it me.

And it didn't. In many ways I had more joy and interaction with the sisters and the kids that last year than any year previously.

When it came time to go back to Omaha, it was the hardest leave-taking I had ever known. As I packed up my meagre belongings and said goodbye to the sisters and to the townspeople who had become my friends, I felt like my heart was going to break. I had no idea that I had put down such roots, and I marveled at the wisdom of whoever wrote the rule of life for the Servite order; one more year in Massena, and I might never have been able to get my roots up!

Dear Sister Mary Clementia knew what I was going through, because she would soon be leaving herself. She put her arms around me and gave me a great hug, and I fought back tears.

"I just hate this!" I exclaimed. "Why does God allow us become so attached to a place? Doesn't He know how much it's going to hurt when we have to leave?"

She smiled. "He knows. But the reason you've become so attached to this place, is because here is where you really drew close to Him." She paused. "Your spirit is afraid of losing that closeness; that's why it's grieving."

She looked out at the maples, going down the road. "Sure, you are going to miss Massena. But you will be taking that closeness with you. You're only leaving a place; you're not leaving Him. He's going with you."

I nodded and smiled—and felt peace coming into my heart; she was speaking for Him.

"He has a special plan for you, Sister, and you've got to cooperate with it. Who knows, He may even bring you back here one day. But in the meantime, the main thing is for you to stay open to Him, and let Him take you where He wants you to go. You go with Him, and He will go with you—*Vaya con Dios.*"

I would soon have occasion to recall her words. A small change had taken place at the motherhouse that would eventually lead to a very great change in my life: Mother Beatrice and Mother Loyola had exchanged roles.

18
MS

Having put my two habits away in the little closet, I laid the new, simplified wimples in the drawer. I missed the old, handmade ones. I had never minded the enormous amount of work that had gone into the making of each one, or the fact that the wimples had to be reshaped by hand after each washing. They were works of art, and they had an aura of holy mystery about them that went with Latin chant and all the other ancient traditions of the religious life. Wearing them and chanting the Magnificat, I had felt one with all the other brides of Christ through the ages who had chanted these same words. It was as if we were one family still, and they were processing beside us and joining their voices to ours. . . .

Now, in the wake of Vatican II, modernization was doing away with many of the old traditions. At least, we still had our beautiful habits—but for how much longer?

With a sigh, I unpacked my life's belongings—the little statue of Mary which my second-grade class in Detroit had given me for Christmas. I placed it on the desk, next to my bed—it was the only thing which made my little room any different from all the others down the new convent's long corridors; even the shades were lowered to precisely the same point. I was grateful for it, because now instead of having to check the number on the door, I could just glance in and see the Blessed Mother and know it was my room.

That was the hardest part about moving back to the motherhouse: it was like being institutionalized. At Massena, in the interest of our becoming fully-rounded and well-balanced, minor expressions of individuality and creativity were smiled upon (within reason). So we had put a few little personal touches in our rooms which brightened them considerably.

But here, conformity was the rule. For the sake of setting the right example for the novices, we followed all observances of our rule of life to the letter. That had been equally true, of course, when I'd been a novice six years before, and I reminded myself how much I had come to love this place and how homesick for it I had been when I had to leave.

Yes, but back then there were only 26 sisters and 26 novices. There'd been a warmth and a shared intimacy to it all, in spite of the disciplines. Now, there were, all told, 130 of us—130 perfectly-made beds covered with white, crinkle-crepe seersucker bedspreads. . . .

You should be glad that God has prospered the Servite Order, I rebuked myself, especially at a time when other orders are in decline. Some are even giving up wearing habits entirely!

Well—I am glad, I suppose; and the new convent is certainly impressive. But I can't help missing the way things were.

When I mentioned how I felt to Mother Loyola, who was no longer Mother Provincial but was still our Mother Superior, she understood.

"Try looking at it another way," she said. "Only the best examples of professed sisters are brought back here— the ones who can be counted on to inspire the novices to persevere in their vocations."

I chuckled; Mother Loyola well knew the problem I'd had with pride—and obviously suspected that I was still susceptible. As usual, she was right.

I was assigned to teach at Pius the Tenth School, which meant that like the other teaching sisters, I would have to commute daily by car, as the parishes did not have their own convents. I would even be away Saturdays, taking courses at Duchesne, to complete my degree. How I envied the non-teaching sisters who got to stay home and chant the offices and have lunch together and—

Girl, you are really perverse, I scolded myself. When you were a novice, you envied the sisters who got to go out into the world; now you envy the ones who get to stay home!

I had to smile: jealousy was never rational, and at times it was just plain crazy. But I knew the antidote for it, and I started thanking God for all the things I had to be grateful for.

When I came back to my room to go to bed that evening, the statue was gone. Looking for it, I opened the desk drawer, and there it was, along with my Bible and my copy of *Christ, The Life of the Soul.*

Irked, I put it back out where it belonged.

The next evening, when I returned, it was back in the drawer again.

Now I was *really* irked! I took the statue out and practically slammed it down on the desk—and then apologized to the Blessed Mother. "I'm sorry; I don't know who is doing this, but I am going to put a stop to it!"

The following evening, after we had processed out of the chapel singing the *Salve Regina,* we had just been given *Deo Gratias,* permission to speak, when one of the sisters came up to me and said, "Mother Provincial would like to see you."

"Now?"

"Now."

I went over to were Mother Beatrice was sitting and knelt down before her.

"That statue will remain in your drawer," she commanded, loud enough for those around to hear. "Do you understand me?"

"Yes, Mother."

She gave a curt nod, and I got up and went back to my place.

I said nothing, but inwardly I was seething: she's the most unreasonable person I have ever met! Why should she care? What a stupid rule! I'm not a machine! I'm a person, with likes and dislikes! I'm sorry they ever brought me back here! I wish I was in Massena; there, I was treated like a human being, a person. Here, I am a non-person. When are they going to realize that we are not a collective mass; we are individual people?

On and on I went—like a mouse on an exercise wheel, running furiously around and around, until my pride had to stop and catch its breath. Then I would get back on and run some more.

Finally, with my soul temporarily exhausted, I was able to hear a few still, small words from my spirit: had I forgotten that a year before, I had vowed to do God's will? No matter what it cost? For the rest of my life? So my will had been crossed, and my pride humiliated—so what? That had happened often enough before, and it would happen again. And remember something, admonished my spirit: it was He who brought you back here, not "them."

I left the statue in the drawer.

Two weeks passed—and then one evening I returned to my room to find the statue on my desk. Quickly I put it back in the drawer; who had been in my room?

The following evening it was out again; I put it away again. What was going on?

After the *Salve* the next evening, Mother Beatrice again called me over. I knelt in front of her, and she said, "I have noted your compliance with my request."

"Yes, Mother."

"Well, I have decided that it was not such a bad thing for you to have that statue. So I put it back on your desk. You may leave it there."

"Thank you, Mother."

I got up, inwardly ashamed of all the feelings I'd had before—and the few sessions I'd spent on the exercise wheel since.

I did have one other thought after that: that it was a little odd for the Mother Provincial of our order to be patrolling corridors looking for infractions. But I quickly put that out of mind; that was just Satan, trying to lure me into judgment of my superior.

I had only one other communication with Mother Beatrice that summer: I asked her if I might learn to drive. It was a brief meeting: I was informed that the convent already had enough drivers, and it was not something I needed to know.

One Saturday morning in early October, my right leg collapsed as I got out of bed. It happened again on the way to the bathroom, and again on the way back. It was so bad that even the scissor-gait couldn't cope with it. And as I sat on my bed in despair, I could see why: my right kneecap had slid around to the inside of my leg.

I was scared.

But this thing was *not* going to rule me; I was still in charge. Somehow I got dressed and went down to chapel. But where once I had flown down, barely touching the steps, now I had to take it a step at a time, constantly relocating my center of gravity and keeping it above my feet.

By sheer grace, I arrived at the chapel doors, just as we were forming up two by two, to process down the aisle. As always, the pace would be slow and solemn—it would take an eternity! And what was I going to do at the front of the church, when we genuflected and separated, filing into the choir stalls on either side?

Our turn came, and we started forward. We were supposed to process with our hands folded under our scapulars, but there was no way I was going to make it without cheating—and I slipped my left hand out to make contact with the end of each pew, as we passed. When it came time to genuflect, I could not get up, and the sister next to me had to help me.

Badly frightened, right after church I went to Mother Loyola, our Mother Superior.

"What's the matter, Sister?" she said, concerned. "You were swaying like a palm tree, as you went up the aisle."

When I told her, she was shocked. "I'm going to see that you get to a doctor, a good one, as soon as possible."

Later that morning, I was called to the Mother Provincial's office. "You're having problems again?" Mother Beatrice asked from behind her desk.

"Yes, Mother."

"Well, you look strong and healthy to me. I don't see how there could possibly be anything wrong with you."

I was about to respond, then thought better of it and stood silent.

"I think you're doing it just to get attention."

"Mother," I blurted out, "why should I try to get attention? I sing, I'm an artist; I get plenty of attention from the things I do."

"Well," she declared, "I am going to say something: You may go to a medical doctor, but you are going to see a psychiatrist first. Because I am convinced you don't have anything seriously wrong with you; it's all in your mind."

My mouth opened; I shut it.

"You're sick, then you're well, then you're sick again, then well again—it doesn't make any sense!" She looked at me, expecting another outburst. When there was none, she repeated, "You are going to see a psychiatrist—someone we've occasionally had to use before."

"Fine," I said, meaning it. "If this thing *is* mental, I want it taken care of immediately. I don't want to go through the rest of my life a half-person."

Two days later, I was in the psychiatrist's office, and he was asking me about my life—how I spent my time and what I liked to do. Mostly his questions were to stimulate a response and keep me talking. Occasionally he would make a note on a yellow legal pad, but mostly he just listened. Mostly I just talked about how much I liked what I was doing.

The ensuing sessions were much like the first, and at the end of the fifth he put his pen down and said, "If all my patients were like you, I'd have no more practice." He smiled. "Mentally, there's nothing wrong with you, but physically—well, I'm also a medical doctor, a neurologist, and if it's all right with you, I'd like to give you a complete physical, and a neurological exam."

"I would have to ask Mother Provincial; she—"

"She'll give her permission," he said with certainty. "She's already told me that she'll abide by my recommendation. What do you say?"

"Fine."

He went to make the call, and in a few minutes returned with a nurse. "Let's do it right now."

When he got to my right leg, his eyes widened. "My God, what *is* this? Your leg is deformed! Your quadriceps is almost gone, and—" he started to probe the leg. "Can you feel this?"

"No."

"And this?"

I shook my head.

"There's partial paralysis here," he told the nurse who was taking notes, "and I don't know what's causing it." He thought for a moment. "Have you ever had any other problems?"

I told him of the optical neuritis, the spells of numbness afterwards, and the episodes of intense fatigue, accompanied by dizziness and loss of balance.

He frowned. "Has anyone—ever diagnosed what might be causing this?"

"The doctor in Massena thought it might be MS."

He nodded. "That's what's going through my mind, too. But first, we've got to get this leg taken care of." He stood up. "I know an excellent orthopedic surgeon who is up on the latest procedures. I want you to see him right away."

Anticipating what I was about to say, he raised his hand. "Don't worry; I'll talk to your Mother Provincial."

The surgeon, as shocked at the condition of my leg as the previous doctor had been, scheduled me into the hospital for an immediate operation. He carefully explained to me each step of the operation. First, he would scrape out the knee-cap and reposition it where it belonged. Then he would put a long steel pin through the femur above the knee, and another through the tibia below it. These would extrude through both sides of the full-length cast up to my hip. They would serve two purposes: they would keep the knee from rotating within the cast, and they would be joined by springs on either side of the knee, to keep the joint compressed.

There was only one thing he didn't tell me: on the

day of the operation, I discovered that this was all going to be performed with only a local anesthetic; he explained (belatedly) that he needed me conscious, to help keep the leg properly aligned.

Until the moment the drill penetrated my femur, I had thought I could endure pain; in fact, I had been a bit proud of my high threshold of pain. All that vanished in an instant, with the heart-stopping shock of that bit entering into the marrow of my bone, where no local anesthetic could reach. My last rational thought was: this is what Jesus must have felt, when they nailed Him to the Cross. I tried to unite my suffering with His, and to offer it up for all the lost souls who had no one to pray for them. But by the time the drill came out the other side, in my heart I was just screaming for Him to get me through this.

And then came the second pin. . . .

When it was over, I would spend three weeks in the hospital, the first in traction, the second two in therapy. But even as my right leg was suspended in air by a system of ropes and pulleys, the therapists started working on the left leg, for it, too, had begun to atrophy.

As I lay there contemplating my condition, I decided it was about time I found out what I could about MS. So when my neuro/psych doctor came to see how I was doing, I asked him.

"First of all, he said, "We're not 100% sure that you have MS. There's no positive test for it."

Then he laid it out in layman's terms: MS was a disease of the central nervous system, in which the myelin sheathing that encased all the nerves became ulcerated. It developed what they called lesions, and they had no idea what caused them, where they came from, or why. There were many possibilities, like adult cases of measles, or—

I interrupted, to tell him of getting measles when I was 19, as a teacher in Detroit. As the lesions healed, he went on, scar tissue formed over them. And if there were numerous lesions, eventually the scar tissue would begin to block the nerve passages, impairing the nerves' signals or preventing them completing their circuits. The medical term for this scarring-over process was *sclerosis;* when there were many lesions simultaneously, you had Multiple Sclerosis.

"What did you mean by the signals not being able to complete their circuits?"

When a person perceived or felt something, that was actually a nerve impulse, flowing through the nerves to the central nervous system. If you stepped on something sharp, for instance, the signal would go up the nerves in your leg, into your spinal chord and up through the stem of your brain, into the area which processed such information. Then the brain would send back the appropriate response. Sharp object? Withdraw foot. The brain sent a signal to the appropriate muscle groups to contract and get the foot out of there. Similarly, when a thought formed in your mind, like: I think I'll go upstairs. Through the nervous system the brain sent contract or relax messages to the different muscle groups which would accomplish this.

"How does MS affect it?"

If the nerve pathways were covered with scar tissue, the messages got distorted. Think of telephone wires in a cable, each with its color-coded coating. Normally, it was a complex yet smoothly-functioning system. But if those coatings got abraded or worn away, and exposed wires were allowed to touch each other—there would be static on the line, or the calls might not get through at all. They might even go to the wrong place, without the caller knowing it.

"You mean, I could step over a door sill and think my foot had cleared it—and then trip over it, because I had not actually raised my foot as much as I had felt I had?"

"Exactly. Or you might touch hot water and experience it as cold."

"That's beginning to happen to me, too," I said sadly. "At least, I can't tell whether things are hot or cold anymore. Is it—going to get worse?"

There was no way of telling. A quarter of the people who experienced these symptoms also experienced complete remission—and were never bothered again. For the rest, there was a gradual, progressive deterioration, and more often than not, it ended in death.

"Not a very cheerful prospect, Doctor," I mused.

Over in the visitor's chair, he nodded thoughtfully. "It's my belief that if a patient can handle it, the truth, right in the beginning, is a lot kinder in the long run than in giving vague generalities or worse, false encouragement, just to keep from frightening them or hurting their or their family's feelings." He smiled at me. "I've gotten to know you pretty well, Sister Raphael, psychologically as well as neurologically. I feel you can handle hearing it the way it is."

"Thanks, I think."

He got up and came over to the bed. "Remember this: we don't know for sure that it *is* MS. The thing for you to do is to go on living your life as normally as possible. We'll just take things as they come—*if* they come. I think you should assume they won't. If they ever do, do not hesitate to get in touch with me. But right now," he patted my cast, "the main thing is to rehab this leg."

Several sisters came to see me during that first week, but the visit I enjoyed most was from Mother Loyola. What fun it was to chat about old times, and to tell her how much I'd loved Massena and all that I had learned from Mother Annunciata and Mother James.

"I can't thank you enough for sending me there, Mother."

"We both know that it was God who sent you—and now He's telling me to tell you something I would normally not: I did not agree with Mother Beatrice's handling of this. But I can now see the hand of God in it: if she had not sent you to that psychiatrist, you would never have received the treatment you needed," and she nodded at my suspended leg.

We sat in silence, in the darkness on either side of the pool of yellow light cast by the lamp on the bedside table.

"I'm telling you this," she resumed, "because she is coming to see you tomorrow, and I want you to be understanding with her. She was acting in what she thought was your own best interest."

"I will try, Mother."

When Mother Beatrice arrived the next afternoon, she came right to the point: "As soon as you get home and back on your feet, we're going to put you right to work. You will receive no special consideration, is that understood?"

"Yes, Mother; I didn't expect any."

She glanced at my suspended leg. "How is it?"

"Well, the pain's subsided, if that's what you mean. But the surgery was unbelievable."

"You didn't have surgery," she said quietly but with a steely edge to her voice.

"Yes, Mother, I did."

"You did not have surgery!" she insisted, her voice rising.

I glanced at the pins sticking out of the cast and the wires connecting them—and remembered what Mother Loyola had asked. "All right, all right," I said placatingly, "that's fine."

"It was not surgery, and you are never to refer to it, as such."

"Yes, Mother."

She got up to leave. "I want you to know, I do not approve of what's been done here—not any of it. The only reason I allowed it is because I told the psychiatrist that I would go along with his recommendation. But I had no idea it would lead to this!"

At the door she paused and turned back. "I am convinced there is absolutely nothing wrong with you. You've done all this to focus attention on yourself." And with that, she left.

I stared at the door long after her footsteps receded down the hall. Then I looked down at the knuckles of my left hand, gripping the bed railing; they were white. Consciously I released my grip—and started to cry. Soon I was shaking with rage—and fear, because this woman had absolute control over my life.

Then, remembering who was the author of fear, I rebuked him and turned in prayer to the Lord. "I know that whatever she says, it is only with Your permission. And so, with all my heart I am asking You to help me be a gracious and obedient servant." I shuddered. "But Dear Jesus, You're really going to have to help, and I'm going to need a lot of grace."

19

Pieces

God was good. I had numerous other visitors during the next two weeks, including all the sisters who knew me, and two instructors from Duchesne who came to tutor me in Chemistry and Children's Literature, so that I wouldn't lose the credits I had been working on in summer school.

I could not believe that they were willing to do this for me! But Mother Shirley McDonald, of *Madame de Sacré Cœur*, who was head of the Science Department, said: "If you're willing to learn, we're willing to teach you. You're going to get that degree in Biology on time!" I was willing; the desire within me to learn was undiminished. And the studies gave me something to keep my mind off what was happening to my body.

After three weeks in the hospital, I was more than ready to return to the motherhouse, even if it had to be by wheelchair. As I was wheeled up to the front door with my casted leg sticking out straight in front of me, I felt like some medieval siege engine, arriving to batter down the castle door.

They had cut off the end of the cast, so that I could wear a shoe, and thus I was marginally mobile—just enough to enable me to teach when school opened the following week. It was, nonetheless, a humbling experience, especially when it came to getting in an out of a car. But by far the worst was having to ride the elevator. In my immortal, invincible youth (ten years before), I had raced such elevators as this, disparaging them as O&I conveyances—strictly for the Old and Infirm. Now I was one.

But remembering the words of my first doctor, I refused to get discouraged and worked with total commitment at my therapy. When the cast was removed, the doctors were delighted. My illness, whatever it was (I still refused to acknowledge that it might be MS), appeared to be in remission! My legs were still puny, particularly the right one, but they were still better than before. The doctors took measurements and found that because of my knee's former dislocation and also scoliosis, my right leg was now a full inch shorter than my left, and I would have to wear orthopedic shoes with a one-inch lift in the right one.

I redoubled my rehab efforts. The therapy exercises, the walking, getting extra sleep—I was not just faithful to the regime, I was religiously faithful. And after three months, my legs came almost all the way back—with my kneecap staying in place! I still couldn't run up the stairs, but I could walk up them with no difficulty. Indeed, the only difference now was the orthopedic shoes—a small price to pay for almost complete recovery.

And of course, now that my health was restored, in my mind it was once again as if I had never been sick! I threw myself totally into everything—teaching and giving music lessons, plus all the community work in the convent I had once been responsible for, plus any other extracurricular activities that came along. I was maxed to the hilt, as the kids say now, and loving every minute of it!

I sailed through the Christmas season with all its extra

preparations and special events, the highlight of which was a special visit from my whole family. Plus, two of my oldest friends from novitiate days were back in the motherhouse now—Sister Mary Emmanuel and Sister Mary Joachim. Peace on earth, goodwill to men—it was the happiest Christmas I had ever known.

And then, in with the bone-numbing chill of February, I began to get tired. At first, I told myself I had just been overdoing it—and that was certainly true! I cut back on my extracurriculars, and started getting to bed earlier—but it didn't seem to help. I slept in almost all day Sunday—and could hardly drag myself to school Monday morning.

I tripped going up the steps to school and sprawled forward, books and papers going everywhere. Darn orthopedic shoes! But deep down, I knew it wasn't their fault. The symptoms were returning.

My legs which had done so well under therapy, once again began to deteriorate, indicating the presence of new lesions. As the muscles in my right leg atrophied, the ligaments holding my right kneecap in place tried to compensate—and began to stretch. My kneecap began to slip around to the inside of my leg.

Now, the relentless fatigue intensified, and with it, the dizziness and loss of balance. The tiredness was so deep that I often did not hear the bell for morning prayer—and that bell was as loud as the alarm-bell in a fire station! Morning after morning I would find myself going down to Chapel late, so bone-weary that I could scarcely move.

The doctor had told me repeatedly that I must contact him, if these symptoms ever recurred. So now I faced a dilemma: I was under obedience. In any other house, I would simply have gone to the Mother Superior and let her make the arrangements. But this was not any other house; this was the motherhouse, and here the Mother Provincial, for reasons know only to herself, had taken a personal interest in my case from the beginning. Knowing that sooner or later I was bound to have to face her, and not wanting to put Mother Loyola through the possible humiliation of being over-ruled again, I found myself once again standing in front of Mother Beatrice's office door.

I was scared again, but I'd had three years' experience living with and overcoming this fear. Jesus, help me, I prayed, and taking a deep breath, I raised my hand to knock.

This time Mother Beatrice did not even have me sit down. "Yes?" she asked, as I stood before her desk.

"Mother, my symptoms have returned—the deterioration in my legs, especially in the right one, and the right kneecap has slipped again. Also, the fatigue is back and the dizziness and loss of balance."

She tapped her fingers together. "And?"

I took a deep breath. "And the doctor had said to notify him, the moment the symptoms returned—if they returned." I paused. "He was hoping—we were both hoping—they wouldn't."

She glared at me. "Do you think I am going to allow all that disruption again? Absolutely not! You don't need to see a doctor; you look perfectly healthy to me."

"But Mother, the doctor said to tell him if this happened; there might have to be more surgery—"

"You are not going to see the doctor, and that's final, so put it out of your mind."

"Mother, I—"

"Also, you will carry on with your normal duties; if you think this is going to be a way to get out of community work, you are sadly mistaken."

"Mother, *please*—"

"That's all, Sister."

"Yes, Mother."

After that, I asked God for strength and tried to do

the best I could. The time I had the most difficulty was in the early morning. I would be so tired, I would sleep right through the bell for morning prayer—and that clanging was loud enough to send Engine Station #4 racing to a fire! In desperation I asked Sister Mary Emmanuel and Sister Mary Joachim for a huge favor: would one or the other come in and make sure I was up? So each morning, as soon as the bell went off, one or the other would pull on her robe and come in and wake me.

In the evening the fatigue was so great that I repeatedly had to ask permission to go to bed before Compline— by 8:00 PM, actually; later than that, my eyelids simply fell shut.

"C'mon, Sister, wake up! It's ten minutes to chapel!" It was Sister Mary Joachim, shaking my shoulder. "I had you up once," she said, helping me sit up, "but you must have fallen back asleep!"

"Sorry," I mumbled, "and thanks for coming back."

"It's okay. Look, I'm going to make my bed, and then I'll come back and help you down."

I nodded and headed for the bathroom.

In five minutes I was back in my room, pulling on my habit; a minute later, Sister had returned and was pulling my bed together. Then she helped me down the hall, running ahead to summon the elevator. When we were in it with the doors shut so no one could hear us, she almost shouted: "Rafe! You have *got* to see a doctor! This is insane!"

I promised her I would ask again.

Others had apparently already brought my condition to Mother Provincial's attention; she granted me permission without objection. But not to go to the neuro-psychiatrist who had betrayed her trust, nor to the specialist who had taken over my case. Nor to the orthopedic surgeon who had said he would probably have to perform further surgery, should the condition return. I was allowed to go only to our regular GP, the old doctor who had been treating the sisters long before I first came, and who donated his services.

That afternoon as he examined my legs, like the doctors four years before he was appalled at the condition to which they had been allowed to deteriorate. Then he asked me for my entire case history, in detail. So I told him—everything.

When I finished, he made an observation that was hardly medical and took me by surprise: "Sister, sometimes God has strange ways of making us see things that we don't want to look at. Has it ever occurred to you that perhaps He is speaking to you through all of this? That it may be time, His time, for you to leave your order? That He may be using your Mother Provincial to make it impossible for you to stay?"

I was speechless—then angry: how dare he presume to say such a thing!

But he did not stop there. "The work load that you have described as your normal routine would drive a person in perfect health to their knees." He pointed to my leg. "And speaking of knees, Sister, your health is far from perfect. We are going to have to lift as much of that load from you as possible; the stress of it, on top of your—well, I won't call it MS, but that's what I think it's going to turn out to be—is literally crippling you."

I smiled ruefully; I had not mentioned a word to him about what was causing the most stress of all.

He misread my smile and became angry. "Do you think God *intends* you to become a permanent cripple? I don't! But if your circumstances don't change, that's what's going to happen! It may happen anyway, but if you keep going as you are, it's guaranteed!" He slammed the top of his desk.

"But I've made my final vows!" I cried.

He waited a moment before replying, then in a more gentle voice, said, "Let's not talk about vows now; let's talk about you. I'm just afraid that you're headed for a complete breakdown—nerves, emotions, everything. And if that happens, you may never recover."

I burst into sobs.

He located a box of tissues and handed it to me, then waited patiently till my crying subsided. At length, he said very tenderly, "Pray about what I've said, and if you have a priest you can confide in, go and have a serious talk with him." He smiled. "And it wouldn't hurt to talk to your mother, either."

"My Mother Superior?"

"No, your mother mother. The one who bore you—and who probably knows you best of all."

As soon as I got back to the convent, I called Father Thomas Halley, SJ, at Creighton University. He had been my theology professor at the convent during my canonical year, and had also been one of my confessors while I was at the motherhouse. Now that I had returned, he was once again in that role.

When I started to tell him my situation, he suggested I wait until we could meet at the motherhouse; in the meantime we should both pray over it.

In the guest parlor the next day, I told him about my illness, the doctors' prognosis, the treatment I'd received, Mother Beatrice's response to it, and the sudden return of the symptoms. I concluded with my visit to the doctor the previous afternoon, and what he had said.

For a long time Father Halley sat without speaking. Then he said, "Let's pray on this now."

I had been doing nothing else since I'd left the doctor's office, but more prayer never hurt. Father in Heaven, I ask only to know Your will—and to be absolutely certain it *is* Your will. But at the moment, I pray that You will give Father Halley a double measure of Your gift of wisdom, because he's going to have to do the thinking for both of us.

Outside, the late afternoon shadows had already crossed the lawn and were creeping up to the motherhouse, when Father Halley broke the prolonged silence: "You've made your final vows—But let's look at what those vows signify: on your side, they were a final commitment to the Lord, and on His side, proof that He wanted you here for the rest of your life."

I nodded.

"But let's go back and look at your original vows: how old were you, when you came here?"

"Fifteen."

He rubbed his chin. "And how old were you, when you took your first vows?"

"Eighteen."

He thought some more. "And you received adequate instruction on the meaning of those vows?"

I nodded again.

"On the vow of chastity—what exactly did you know about the, um, facts of life?"

I shrugged. "I really didn't know anything, beyond what I had learned in Biology."

He shook his head. "I really doubt that the vows you made were even valid. Eighteen is too young for a person to make such a commitment. That's why we've closed most of our minor seminaries, and why we do not encourage our young people to marry at that age. They simply do not have the wisdom to make a responsible decision that will affect the rest of their lives."

I disagreed. Even if the vows I made were not valid in the Church's eyes, in God's eyes they had been made in all honesty and with all my heart.

But as he spoke, a recent vivid memory returned unbidden. Earlier that summer, when I was still in a cast recovering from surgery and unable to do much, at the doctor's suggestion I had asked for and been granted a leave to see my sister Ruthanne who had just given birth to a little boy named Gregory. She was anxious for me to see him, and I had never seen such a beautiful baby! Less than a month old, he had a serenity about him that he seemed to have brought straight from Heaven.

I had always loved kids, especially the little ones, but had never regretted that I would not have any of my own. For me, what Jesus told Peter fit perfectly: "There is no one who has left house, brothers, sisters, mother, father, children or land for my sake and for the sake of the gospel, who will not receive a hundred times as much—houses brothers, sisters, mothers, children and land. . ." (Mark 10:29,30) And it was true: mothers, sisters, and classrooms full of children—I had received them all. And they had been enough.

But now, as Ruthanne handed me her infant son to hold, and I took him and held him to me, gazing down at his face and thinking, this is how Mary must have looked upon the Babe,—all at once I was overwhelmed with longing. In fact, I felt such an ache in my heart—such grief that I would never have a child of my own—that I had to hand him back. "Here," I said, my voice breaking, "I just can't hold him."

I had willed that shattering remembrance out of my mind—until now. Was it the Lord who had brought it back?

As Father Halley built his case, I could see where he was heading,—and I was not at all convinced I wanted to go with him. The procedure for obtaining a marriage annulment involved demonstrating that the marriage vows were invalid, that they had been entered into without full cognizance or disclosure of all pertinent information on the part of one or both parties. I assumed that applying for an annulment of religious vows involved much the same process.

Sensing my growing resistance, Father Halley took a different approach: "How would you feel, if I told you that I felt God wanted you someplace else?"

"I would be devastated."

"Would you be devastated at the thought of not being a sister? Or because you know no other life, and would have no place to go?"

"I—I don't know. I'd be devastated because this is my home, and these are my sisters, my family."

"Then the other *is* a factor here."

"No," I insisted, "it isn't! I'm not leaving!"

"Sister Raphael," he sighed, "I'm not trying to persuade you to leave. Believe me, all I'm trying to do is discern God's will."

He got up and smiled. "Look, I think we should give it a rest. Pray on it, and I will, too, and come back to see me in two month's time. I have a feeling you'll know one way or the other, by then."

The next two months were unlike any I had ever known. Remembering where Mother Carmelita used to go, when she needed to regain her spiritual equilibrium, more than once I walked alone up the hill to the cemetery in the late afternoon, after Tea. There, I would sit on the bench where Margaret and I had once sat as postulants, so long ago. And as I watched the sun settle on the horizon, I tried to work things out with God.

Until my appointment with the doctor and my talk with Father Halley, the possibility of leaving the order had never entered my mind. Once a nun, always a nun. . .

God had brought me here; I knew that, beyond the shadow of a doubt. And here I had become a Bride of Christ—in sickness and in health, till death did us eternally unite. And I was prepared for that, too: if what I had did turn out to be MS, and did prove fatal, well, I would simply occupy that plot over there a little sooner than anticipated. No matter what Mother Beatrice did, no matter how grave my condition became, here I would remain. Bernadette of Lourdes had stayed to the end; so would I.

But what if it *wasn't* God's plan for me to stay? What if, as Father Halley had suggested, He was using my illness to cause me to leave?

The only thing to do was go to the foundation: what was the gist of my final vows? To love God and serve Him with all my heart and mind and soul and being. That was also the gist of my first vows, and of my intent on the day of my Investiture as a novice—in fact, it was what had brought me here in the first place.

If, then, it *was* God's will for me to leave this place, then to *not* go would be disobedience. And it would be a reflection of my core sin of pride: Saint Bernadette and Saint Mary Raphael. . . .

Suddenly the thought came: you're just playing mind games. This is all nothing more than an elaborate rationalization to justify leaving.

Dear Jesus, is that true? Is that from you?

It was crucially important now that I discern His will—more important than it had ever been in my life. And I had never felt less sure of my ability to do so.

It would have been so much easier to just let Father Halley or Mother Loyola—or even Mother Beatrice—make the decision for me.

But on something of this magnitude, which was going to set the direction of the rest of my life, I sensed that no one could do it for me.

One day I would have to stand before the throne of God and answer for the decision I was about to make— and no one else would be standing there for me.

My prayer became simply: make Your will known to me. And make it so clear that I will never doubt it for the rest of my life, wherever and however You might have me live it.

Once again I felt like I was viewing the upside-down pieces of the puzzle of my life. Only now He was permitting me to turn over a few of the pieces which had already been fitted together, to see how they had been part of His plan. Why? Because it was so important that I not use force, in putting the next pieces together.

I saw, for instance, that my coming here at such an early age had not been merely within the broad parameters of His permissive will; it was right down the center-line of His holy perfect will. He had brought me here at such an early age, for my own protection. To protect the call on my life, which had been sealed right after my baptism, when my great aunt had consecrated me to the Blessed Mother. And I had come to know myself well enough to know that had I tarried one more year (let alone until I was 18), I would no longer have been so innocent of the facts of life. I never would have come; it was doubtful I would even have heard Him calling.

I smiled at the next piece: if God had wanted to put me in a spiritual holding pattern, so to speak, He could not have picked a better one!

That was being too negative: probably nowhere else

could I have received the depth of spiritual training and preparation. Certainly nowhere else could I have had such a succession of outstanding spiritual directors.

Had it originally been His will for me to remain?

Perhaps—but that was a holy mystery that would only be revealed to me when I stood before Him, face to face.

Had it been the devil's intent to destroy me?

Almost certainly. But God had allowed it.

For what purpose?

Ahh—that was the question.

The sun was down. In the gathering shadows I shivered and got up; it would soon be time for Vespers.

20

The Hardest Part

Sitting in the visitors' parlor, awaiting my mother's arrival, I remembered so clearly that Sunday afternoon thirteen years before, when our whole family had arrived. We had all come into the visitors' parlor in the old convent, where Mother Loyola served my family iced lemonade and cookies. Then it had been Mom and Dad and Ron and Ruthanne and RJ and Ricky. . . .

Now it would be just Mom. My doctor had recommended my having a talk with her, and Father Halley had concurred that it would be a helpful part of the sorting-out process. So I asked for permission and called her. I didn't tell her what was on my mind or give any indication that it was urgent or serious. But since I'd never made such a request before, I didn't have to. They had recently moved to Cedar Falls, Iowa, which was three times as far away, so it would take her all afternoon to get here. She said she would drive over on Sunday, right after church.

After making the call, I'd gone to the chapel to pray— again. I still did not know God's will, and the more I prayed, the more frustrated I became at not getting a clear answer. I had forgotten the advice I used to give young novices: Sometimes you just have to ask God to make His will known, and then trust that He will—and relax until He does.

Excellent advice—easy to give and almost impossible to receive.

My prayers had become increasingly strident and demanding. But at Mass that Sunday, shortly after I had begun railing at God yet again, all at once a great calm settled over me. And in my heart I seemed to hear: *Do as you are directed. Just be obedient and do as you are directed.*

That calm was still with me, as I waited for my mother. What would she think? One thing, however, was certain to please her: my illness, for reasons of its own, was in remission again. I had worked diligently at the therapy all winter, and now by late spring my legs, even the right one, had recovered most of their strength. And though I still had to use orthopedic shoes, I could walk with a normal gait—and with no fear of falling.

When my mother arrived, I served her some tea, and then sat down and told her what had happened and what was on my heart, and that I was really confused about what I was supposed to do. I did not tell her that it was Dad, not her, whom I was mainly concerned about, should I decide to leave. He was so proud to have a daughter who was a nun!

When I concluded, she said, "Rita, I'm just your mom. And I wasn't born Catholic; I'm just a convert." She paused. "But I've tried to be a good mom, and I've tried to do what God wants. And now, since you asked me to come here, and have told me what you have, I feel I'm supposed to tell you something: I never felt you were supposed to be here."

"And Dad?"

"Don't worry about your father. To tell you the truth, we both felt you were too young when you first came here, but we never said anything to you, because we didn't want to influence your decision—or interfere with what God had planned for you. So now I want you to come home."

I started to object and then remembered: *Just be obedient and do as you are directed.* Was this what it meant? It must be—it was the only direction I had received.

"Mom," I smiled, "I thought you were going be ashamed and—"

She came over and hugged me. "I would never be ashamed of you! I love you!"

We both laughed and cried. As she left, I told her I would let her know my plans—as soon as I knew them myself.

When I told Father Halley of the visit, he said, "I gather from this that you have prayerfully made your decision."

"As nearly as I can tell, yes."

"Then as your confessor I have to tell you: if you feel that what you are about to do is God's will for you now, then in conscience you are bound to do it."

He added a word of counsel: "Never think of your years in the order as wasted. I have no idea what God has in store for you, but someday you will see that everything you've learned here and done here has been preparation."

Did he have an inkling of what the future might hold? I looked at him expectantly.

He just smiled and shook his head. "I have no idea what your mission will be, but I know He's not finished with you."

He sighed. "In the meantime, I will write the necessary letter to Rome, petitioning for you to be released from your vows on the grounds of your extreme youth, and will help you with the one you must write, as well. There'll be no problem; your vows will be rescinded. I'll also take care of everything on the canonical end." He paused and looked at me. "But *you* are going to have to inform your Mother Provincial."

My heart sank. Later I admonished myself: who did you think was going to do it for you, Father Halley? He's doing more than enough already! If this is of God, then He will give you the grace to face her—and tell her the truth, no matter what.

And so, once again I stood outside her office door and knocked.

"What is it, Sister?" she said, when I had entered.

"I need to talk you."

"I gathered that; otherwise, why would you be here? You may sit down."

I did. "I don't know how to begin this—"

"Let me guess: you want to leave the order."

I looked at her, startled. "Yes," I admitted. "I feel that may be what I am supposed to do."

"You mean, you've decided this is what you *want* to do."

"No," I said firmly. "I feel it may be what I'm *supposed* to do."

She got up and walked to the window. "I'm not going to ask you why. What I'm wondering is: why, if you had this in mind all along, did you bother to take your final vows three years ago?"

"Mother, I—"

"Don't interrupt me!" she commanded, turning to face me. "You had no intention of staying, even then! This whole thing has been a charade from start to finish!"

"Mother, *that is not true!* I made those vows with all my heart. And I intended to keep them for the rest of my life!"

She returned to the desk and sat down. "I knew all along you didn't belong here, from the very beginning. When you first petitioned this order, I knew it. I don't know why it was ever allowed to get this far."

She clasped her hands in front of her. "So—you would

like me to petition Rome for your vows to be invalidated."

"Actually, Father Halley has already said he would do that."

She glared at me. "Well, I see we've been planning this for some time!"

She was not going to intimidate me. Just tell the truth: "No. I *have* been praying about it for the past two months, but believe me, it was not premeditated."

She waved her hand, dismissing what I'd just said. "Have it your own way, Sister. I have no objection whatever to your leaving the community. But I want to say one thing to you: If you are leaving your vocation, and if it is truly a vocation from God, then do you realize that you are in peril for your soul?"

"Pardon me?"

"You are in danger of losing your immortal soul."

I stared at her.

"If this *is* where God wished you to be, and you are not here, in His will, then you are in the gravest peril."

I felt a crushing weight inside of me.

When I didn't reply, she added, "I'll say only this: may the Lord have mercy on you."

I looked at her like she had just sentenced me to eternal fire.

She changed the subject. "Do you plan on getting married, Sister?"

"I—I don't know; I've never thought about it."

"Well, do you like children?"

"Of course! I love them; you know that."

"Then you *do* plan on getting married." A slow smile came to her face. "You're leaving to get married."

"I am *not* leaving to get married! I don't even know anyone!" Then, for the first time, I actually considered the possibility. "If the Lord does lead me to get married, then I will pray that He find me a good man who will love and honor me, and I will love and honor him."

"A pretty speech, Sister—but you do know someone, don't you."

"I know absolutely no one!" I cried, feeling like my insides were erupting. "Before God, I tell you: *I know no one!*" I felt like I was about to be physically ill.

She held up her hand. "All right, all right. But now I am going to tell you something: you are to speak of this to no one. No one is to know you are leaving, do you understand me? *No one.* When you leave, it will be done in secret."

She stood up and made it a formal order: "You are hereby forbidden to speak to anyone."

"Pardon me?"

"You heard me: you are forbidden to speak further with anyone in this convent."

Surely she couldn't mean that literally! "I don't understand."

She pointed a finger at me. "I mean exactly what I said: until you are released from your vows, or until you leave this house, you are not to communicate to anyone."

"You mean, I can't talk to *anyone*?"

"You have heard me correctly."

"I can't even say goodbye?"

"Absolutely not."

After leaving her office I went straight to the chapel. Dear Jesus, this is my family! I've spent nearly half my life with them—how can I leave without saying goodbye? You really don't expect this of me, do You?

But I heard nothing in my heart, felt nothing but emptiness. I felt so dry inside, it was like I was dead.

On my way up to my room, I met Sister Mary Joachim coming out of hers. Seeing that I had been crying, she said, "Come in here a minute; let's talk."

"I'm not allowed to talk to you."

"What do you mean? Of course you can talk to me; I'm your sister!"

I shook my head.

"Listen, Rafe," she said, guiding me into her room, "remember all the times I wept on your shoulder? Well, now you're allowed to weep on mine."

So—I told her everything, and she just sat there, tears streaming down her face, as they were on mine.

"Oh, Rafe, I hate this! I hate seeing you go!" She cried and gave me a hug. "I'll be praying for you all the way!"

That evening, because I couldn't tell Sister Mary Joachim without telling my other closest friend, I told Sister Mary Emmanuel, as well.

Three days later, I was summoned to Mother Beatrice's office. She was furious. "I told you, you were not allowed to tell anyone! Now the whole convent knows you are leaving!"

I said nothing.

"What am I going to have to do? Put you someplace where you can't contaminate the others?"

She thought for a moment, then announced: "I do know what I'm going to do with you: something that has not been done for a long time. We are not going to wait for the dispensation from your vows. You are going to be out of here a lot faster than you ever planned!"

I was dismissed.

What did she have in mind? What difference did it make, my spirit chided me; whatever it is, God is allowing it. The important thing is your response to it.

In the meantime, I concentrated on simply carrying on. I continued teaching, and as the school year drew to a close, I made plans to attend summer school—at Maryville College in St. Louis. The Sisters of the Sacred Heart had closed Duchesne the previous year, and transferred their faculty to their other college, Maryville.

The first Saturday after the close of school, Mother Beatrice called me back to her office. "You'll go down to Maryville as scheduled, but you won't go as a sister; you'll go as a layperson."

"What?"

"You heard me: as far as I'm concerned, you are no longer a member of this community. Your tuition and expenses have already been paid, but you will be expected to reimburse the order as soon as you are able. Your dispensation should arrive while you're at Maryville. When it does, we'll send you a copy, and you're on your own."

I sat there staring at her.

"I will give you a clothing allowance of a hundred dollars, and someone can take you shopping next week. I will also give you a hundred dollars cash when you leave. But from then on, you will have to support yourself. So you'd better start looking for a position for next year."

The following week was a flurry of activity. When I told the school nurse I was leaving, she offered to take me in her car and help me pick out some clothes. A hundred dollars seemed pretty generous—until I discovered how much less it bought in 1968 than in 1955, the last time I'd gone shopping. We picked out a brown suit and two dresses, plus a pair of black shoes that would go with everything.

As for a job, I had sent my resume in to an educational placement bureau. I received a call about an opening in a place called Mars, a little town of barely a thousand people, about half an hour north of Pittsburgh. And that same afternoon, I got another call, from Lois Wolfson, whose children I had taught at Pius the Tenth School. Her husband had been transferred to Pittsburgh, and she had just gotten a call from a mutual friend that I was considering a job in their neck of the woods—would I want to stay with them until things got settled?

Two offers from the same place? On the same day? It appeared that God might want me to locate in Pittsburgh.

Now all that was needed was for me to go east for the interview. This time I went to Mother Loyola, the convent's Mother Superior. "There may be a job for me in a little town in Pennsylvania, called Mars. They're looking for a junior-high science teacher, but I'll need to go for an interview."

She smiled. "I'll arrange the ticket. Will they see you on a weekend? We'll fly you out right away, and you can be back by Monday for school."

"That would be great, Mother."

Slowly she shook her head. "I am so sad about this; you have no idea. . . ."

She could not go on, and as she looked at me, her eyes began to fill. "You, of all the sisters—and I am going to tell you this now—of all the sisters I have ever watched come through here, I had the highest hopes for you. I thought you were going to be a future leader of the order." Her voice broke. "I know you have to do what you feel the Spirit is leading you to do. So—" she managed a smile, "I will tell you again what I told you once a long time ago: unto whom much is given, much is also required."

She nodded toward the window. "When you leave here, you'll be taking with you not only the traditions of your family in Cedar Falls, but those of your spiritual family, as well. All the ways of this life, all the prayers—they'll be yours forever. They're part of you now. So take them and use them for the honor and glory of God."

My eyes, too, were beginning to fill. This, right here, was the hardest part of the whole long ordeal. For some reason I thought of that first day when she had given me a hug, and I'd been surprised at how soft her cheek was. She had been like a like a mother to me in those early years. I had not seen that much of her recently, but I loved her no less.

Apparently her thoughts were going in the same direction. "Now I have something else to tell you, as a mother—a small 'm' mother: I've always felt as if God had intended me to be that to you. When your own mother left you here at such a young age, I had the sense that God was entrusting you into my care, that He wanted me to fill the void that was left when your mother said goodbye. Not," she hastened to add, "to usurp the place of the Blessed Mother, but to be an actual, physical mother and watch over you, as I had promised your mother I would. I've always loved you and believed in you."

I was brushing away tears now; so was she.

"I want to give you a special blessing," she said, coming over to me.

I got out of the chair and started to kneel before her. "No," she said, "we don't need to do that."

I returned to the chair, and she put her hands on my head. Then softly she prayed: "May the blessing of God go with you. May the Spirit of God overshadow you. And may all your life be blessed."

We hugged. And wept. And she said, "Now, come on; we can't act like this. And you certainly can't go out of here, looking like that; you'll have everybody in the convent wondering what happened in here."

Picking up the intercom phone, she called down to the kitchen and requested some iced lemonade and cookies. I smiled; it was the same thing she had served when I first met her.

When we had enjoyed our cold drinks, and I had regained my composure, she said, "I did intervene on your behalf and mediate wherever I possibly could."

I nodded. "I sensed you were doing that."

"Well, somehow, in your heart you are going to have

to forgive her. She acted in what she felt was your own best interest, how she felt the Spirit was directing her."

I said nothing. I knew she was right: I did have to forgive Mother Beatrice, and I knew I would one day. But I wasn't there yet.

When I did not respond, Mother Loyola said, "Well, I pray that you can forgive her—and you must pray for that also, so there can be healing. It may not come right away; it may be a long time in coming. But it has to come."

I nodded, and the bell rang for Vespers. It was time to go.

As we put on cheerful faces, Mother Loyola laughed, "Listen, Sister, I want you to remember that this is also your home; any time you want to come back, I don't care if you're married and have ten children, you come! And bring your husband and children with you!"

At the door, she repeated in a more serious tone: "You are always welcome here; this is your home."

21

Goodbye, Mary Raphael

The flight to Pittsburgh was the best kind: uneventful; in fact, I hardly even thought about it. I was met at the airport by Lois and her husband and children, and the next day she took me to my interview with Dr. Manerino of the Mars area school system.

The first thing he asked was how my work towards my degree was progressing. I told him I was now within three credits of completing it. All that remained was the seminar for majors, and taking the 24 hours of written comprehensive exams. Did I plan to pursue a graduate degree? Yes, I had already taken courses towards a Master's in Special Education. As part of my degree work, I had done some student teaching in the upper grades and found I had a real concern for kids who had a hard time learning anything. We were having to shift them to public schools, because our parochial schools had no programs for them.

Also, in the past year I had gotten involved in helping children with emotional and learning deficit problems and had attended a number of seminars and workshops designed to train teachers to deal with this type of child. Perhaps because of my own illness, I seemed to have an affinity for such children: I understood them, and they knew it. That rapport enabled me to help them work through their problems and become whole again.

"You know," said Dr. Manerino smiling, "I may have an even better job for you. I have a friend in the Butler Special Education Office, and I know there's an opening there, if you're interested."

It sounded ideal, and though it was Saturday, he was able to arrange an interview, and Lois drove me there. It *was* ideal! I would be assigned right back in Mars, to work under Dr. Manerino, teaching educable retarded children from intermediate age up to high school. I signed the contract and flew back to the motherhouse, all in one weekend.

On the second leg of the flight home, as we climbed to cruising altitude I gazed up at the massive cumulonimbus build-up of a storm towering above us a few miles away. Dark and roiling, with flashes of lightning in it, it was a frightening sight—or would have been, if one did not have confidence in the pilot's ability to plot our course.

Concerning the future, I was still deeply apprehensive—but as I thought back over the remarkable string of coincidences in the past 48 hours, I had confidence that the Pilot was still at the controls.

No sooner had I entered the motherhouse, than I was informed that Mother Provincial wanted to see me. Now.

"You're leaving on Saturday. Everyone knows you're leaving, so there's no need for further discussion with anyone. You are therefore to maintain a prayerful silence all week. You are to consider yourself on retreat, and speak to no one."

There was more. "On Saturday morning, a car will be waiting at the back kitchen door at 5:30. It will take you to the bus station. The bus for Waterloo-Cedar Falls leaves at 11:00."

"But Mother, it only takes half an hour to get to the

station—why am I leaving at 5:30?"

"Because that's the way I have arranged it, and that's the way it will stay. What you do when you get to the bus station is your business. You will no longer be my responsibility."

She was not finished. "Now, about personal effects: the *only* things you may take with you are the clothes which you recently purchased. Everything else is to remain here."

"What about my banjo and my guitar? They were both given to me."

"You may take one; you decide which."

It was a hard choice: my first-graders had given me the banjo, but my parents had given me the guitar. "I'll take the guitar, I guess."

"Fine. Everything else is to be left on your bed."

She returned her attention to the work before her on the desk, and I got up to leave. "Oh, one more thing," she said, looking up. "Saturday morning, after you have left, a notice will be posted on the board. It will say that you are no longer with us, and to pray for your soul."

It was still dark out on Saturday morning, as I made my bed by the light of the little desk lamp. I pulled the bedspread tight, then laid out the suit I would wear that morning and packed the two dresses in the old suitcase I had been given. I started to put the suit on—then took it off. There was something I had to do first. I went to the little closet and put my habit on for the last time. As I put on the veil, I instinctively recited the prayer that we always prayed while we did that.

When I was dressed, I went over to the mirror above the sink and gazed at my image in it. "I have to leave you now," I whispered at length. "Goodbye, Sister Mary Raphael; I pray the archangel Raphael will go with me."

Then I took the habit off and laid it on the white spread. And tried not to look at it again, as I got dressed and started putting the other things on the bed—the banjo, my copy of *Christ, The Life of the Soul,* the leather brief-case I'd been given in Massena. . . it was like laying out my life.

Harder to part with was the leather-bound copy of the Divine Office which my parents had given me on the occasion of my becoming a professed sister. It had "Sister Mary Raphael, OSM" in gold letters on the cover, and I had carried that little volume with me almost everywhere. Holding it now, I recalled the countless times I had let the rhythm of the Psalms flow through me, cleansing the inside of my cup, uniting me with all the sisters of untold generations who had sung these same words in the same way. I put it on the bed, next to the veil.

Harder still was parting with the little statue of Mary. I cradled it in my hands and looked at it until I couldn't see it any more, because of the tears. I put it on the other side of the veil.

Then came the part I dreaded most of all. I looked down at the gold band on the third finger of my left hand. I couldn't do it. I just couldn't take it off. Finally, I did, and placed it on the veil.

At that moment, everything in me wanted to put it back on and the habit and the veil, and go down to the chapel and wait for my sisters to come to morning service.

"Oh, God!" I whispered, muffling the sobs, "God, please help me." But the deep, agonizing ache I felt did not diminish. I took a last look at the pieces of my life, the habit, the veil, the ring. Goodbye, Sister Mary Raphael.

As quietly as I could, I made my way down the hall and down the stairs. It was still a few minutes to 5:30, and so I went into the chapel for the last time. The vigil candle was still burning, but the pre-dawn light was just enough to make colors distinguishable. I stood at the back, taking it all in, a full-page photo for my memory-book. There was St. Julianna, to whom I'd prayed every morning, and dear St. Philip—"Please come with me, you two," I said softly. "I will never forget you; please—don't forget me."

I felt dead. I had failed—God, first of all. And my community. And myself. And my family—all the people who had told me what a beautiful nun I was going to be.

And I felt alone—for the first time in my life I felt absolutely alone. I did not feel the presence of God in any of this, not even a glimmer. I was just alone and dead.

I looked at the Pieta, at the Blessed Mother overcome with sorrow as she cradled the dead body of her Son. All of a sudden, I felt like it was me she was holding. Weeping, I said to her, "If this turns out to be not God's will, I won't go to heaven. I came here, because I wanted to go to heaven. I wanted to be a saint and go to heaven. And now I'm leaving. I don't understand. I just don't understand any of this."

It was time. "Please," I said to her, "be a mother to me," and I turned and left.

The car, a station wagon, was waiting for me, when I went out the kitchen door. The sun was just up now; a shaft of first light fell on the little plot of flowers which I had planted around the back entrance, mostly moss roses. I loved flowers, and in the summers when I was at the motherhouse, I had always volunteered to do the weeding and plant the new blooms—I'd planted them everywhere.

I had planted these—and now, as I looked down at the little moss roses bathed in golden light, all bright yellows and reds and pinks and corals, they seemed to be looking up at me—and saying: It's all right; you're going to be okay. And with that, came a sense of peace. The terrible, wrenching ache was still there. But there was peace there, also.

22
Maryville

Resting my head against the cool bus window, I gazed out at the Iowa countryside rolling past. The last time I'd done this, I realized, was on that train eight years before, on my way to Massena. I'd been full of hope then, full of eager anticipation, facing the unknown with the calm assurance that I was in the center of God's will.

I had no such assurance now. I had no sense whatever that God was with me—or I with Him. And that had never happened before. My vows had been both an anchor, helping me to withstand the pull of powerful currents and tides, and a foundation, bedrock on which to build a spiritual life. Now I was adrift. I felt totally numb—with no indication that the novocaine was wearing off. Not that I wanted it to; I'd had enough spiritual pain to last a lifetime.

I had tried to pray, but I had no sense that my prayers were being heard. To me, they sounded like just words, nothing more. Even so, I kept at it—because there was nothing else to do *but* pray.

I was strongly reminded of Theresa of Avila's definition of hell: to be separated from God. I was in hell. And I had put myself there.

I was going home now—and the thought made me

wince: until this morning, home had been the mother-house. Now, I supposed, it was where my mother and father lived. I was going to spend a week with them, before going to Maryville to complete my work on my bachelor's degree. We had always been a strong, closely-knit family, a safe harbor, if you were caught in a storm at sea. I knew that emotionally I was hanging by a thread until I could reach that harbor. So the passing rural vignettes held little fascination for me now, nor was I stirred to imagine where the old pick-up with the two kids and three dogs in back was going, or why. The only mental scene that held any interest for me was the faces of my mother and father greeting me at the Waterloo bus station.

Imagination and reality merged a little after 4:30 PM. They *were* glad to see me—gladder than I had dared hope. There was no silent recrimination, no suggestion of disappointment: their daughter Rita, their eldest, who had been away on a long journey, had at last returned home. They welcomed her with unfeigned joy. I relaxed—and the tears started to come.

I spent most of that week crying. I felt like I was grieving for the loss of someone who'd been very dear to me—and I realized the truth of that: I was grieving for the death of Sister Mary Raphael.

In ten years of teaching, I had learned enough about grief not to cut a child's grieving process short; it had to be allowed to run its course. And now that was true for the teacher, as well. I did hope that would happen before I had to leave for Maryville.

Meanwhile, I was learning the truth of Thomas Wolf's caution: you can't go home again. On a subconscious level, my parents were responding to me as if I were still the age I'd been when I left home. And as much as I would have liked to buy into their fantasy and turn the clock back to 1955, I couldn't. It was 1968, and I was not even remotely like that person.

My first impression of my new home was how noisy everything was. All my years in our community had trained me to avoid making unnecessary noise, or speech. As a result, I was acutely aware of my mother talking incessantly, filling the air with aimless chatter as if silence were an enemy to be overcome, instead of a comforting friend. And when I wouldn't respond and she wearied of her one-sided dialogue, she would turn on the television or the kitchen radio.

Finally she got angry: "Why won't you talk to me?" she demanded.

"Mom, I'm just not used to it. I've had all those years of being quiet and prayerful."

"So you're telling me I talk too much, and make too much noise."

"Mom," I pleaded, "it's not that; I'm just not used to talking all day long."

"Well, you talk in the classroom."

I shook my head. "Somehow that's different." Then I smiled. "Look, you talk about the neighbors and shopping—I just don't have anything to talk *about.*"

I didn't tell her what fun we used to have, sharing stories and making little jokes about our community life. . . from which I now felt so terribly separated. I was in the world now—and realized I didn't know how to just *be.* Jesus had called His disciples to be in the world but not *of* it. I had changed too much to ever be of it, but I hadn't the first clue of how to be *in* it.

My father didn't want me in the world; he wanted me home. "I assumed that when you came out, you would be living with us."

"But Dad—"

"If you're worried about losing your Blue Cross coverage, don't; we can take care of you. We don't have a lot, but we're not poor. I want you to stay here."

"Dad, I can't. It wouldn't be good for either of us. You and Mom would want to protect me and take care of me, like I was your little girl."

"Well, what's wrong with that?"

"I'm not fifteen any more; I'm twenty-eight. I've got to make a life for myself now."

He nodded, but he was clearly hurt. "Do you know how to take care of yourself? You don't know how to drive; I'll bet you don't even know how to keep a bank account or write a check."

I laughed. "You're right, I don't know any of those things." I took his arm. "So you're going to have to teach me."

I smiled at him, and he grumped, "Do you have a Social Security number?" I nodded. "Well, that's something," he said, and the twinkle returned to his eye.

He went with me to set up a checking account, insisting on giving me a loan of $500 to get started with, even though my summer courses and expenses were prepaid. Then he went out and got my bus tickets.

Mom, meanwhile, was delighted to be able to fuss over me. "You certainly can't go through the summer with two dresses and a suit!" And since we were about the same size, she started going through her closet and her drawers. "I don't need this," she would say, adding a silk blouse to the growing pile of clothing on the bed. And "You'd look good in this," she nodded, following it with a dressy skirt.

"Mom, you can't give me all this."

"Don't be silly, I never wear any of those things."

I was about to insist on her stopping, when I realized how much she was enjoying this, and how much it meant to her, to finally be able to do something for me. So when it came time to leave, I had a full suitcase and a hanging-bag. I also had a shopping-bag full of new keepsakes, including a new statue of Mary, thanks to my brothers and sisters. All the McLaughlin kids except Rick and Regina were married now, yet all of them but Russ were near enough to make the trek over to see me, and they did. Again, there was no unspoken disapproval, only love, as we reminisced about night baseball and getting lost in the storm drains, and the morning our dog Ginger came down the main aisle of church and settled under the pulpit to hear Father Wingart's sermon.

As I was still numb, they did most of the reminiscing. We'd been a tight bunch when we were growing up, and now they made allowances for me, keeping it light, letting me take it at my own pace and enter in as much or as little as I felt able. I loved them for that—and felt closer to them than ever before. Swiss Family McLaughlin. . . .

And when there were no brothers or sisters around, my mother took me to lunch or to meet her friends, making sure that as much of my time was occupied as possible. Which was a good thing, because when I was alone, I began to feel massive guilt that I had truly violated my vows. I did my best to suppress the guilt, reminding myself how confident I had been that it was God's will for me to leave. (Nor was there any point in asking Him to confirm it now; at the moment, He and I were not on speaking terms.)

But the truth was, I was no longer at all confident that I was in His will. What I was, was scared—almost to the point of shaking. And each time I thought about it, the guilt would return, and I would weep, devastated. And pray: Dear God, I am sorry. I am so sorry. Nothing else would come, except that: I am just so sorry.

Aboard the bus for St. Louis, I was determined to be upbeat. Well, I said to myself, you're finally going to get your degree! It's about time; you've only been working on it for twelve years! Which was true: ever since becoming a sister, I had held full-time jobs; what studying I was able to do had to happen in the summer and on weekends. But this summer would mark the end of it—at least of that phase; I did plan to go on a get my master's.

There was something else to be grateful for: the grieving process had apparently progressed to a new stage; I was no longer undone, any time my thoughts happened to go the sisterhood.

But I was no less empty, no less separated from God. I had read enough lives of saints to know that such prolonged dry periods were not unusual, and so I kept praying—despite it being a strictly one-way conversation. He had not abandoned me, I reminded myself; He promised us in Scripture that He would never leave nor forsake us (Heb. 13:5). He was there.

But in my heart, I feared that I had abandoned Him. And that nothing would ever bring us together again. Saint Theresa was right: it *was* hell.

I arrived at Maryville acutely aware of the fact that I was practically the only summer student not wearing a habit. I was summoned to the head of the Science Department—and received a delightful surprise: it was Mother Shirley McDonald, the former head of Science at Duchesne, who had come to the hospital to tutor me! During her visits we had grown close, and more than once she had offered to speak to Mother Beatrice on my behalf, but I had always said no.

Now she gave me a big hug and stood back to survey me. "It's good to see you mobile! How long have you been in remission?"

"More than a year."

She shook her head. "Considering the condition you were in the last time I saw you, I'd say that was miraculous." Noting my dress, she asked, "How long have you—been a layman?"

"I left the order a week ago."

She sighed. "I suspected that God had other plans for you." Inviting me to sit down, she asked, "Do you want to talk about last week?"

I shook my head; no, I was over that. But then my tears betrayed me.

"You talk," Mother McDonald smiled, "I'll listen."

Everything spilled out—my grief, my guilt, my anger. . . . Finally, when after nearly two hours there was no more to say, she observed, "One of those times I visited you in the hospital, it came to me that maybe this was God's way of letting you know that He wanted other things from you." She smiled. "This may sound very strange, but I believe He has something wonderful planned for you."

I looked at her, open-mouthed. "Father Halley, my confessor at the convent, said almost the same thing."

She nodded. "He has something wonderful planned for you, but you have to be open, and you have to be healed first. You're angry, and laden with much guilt—and the Holy Spirit cannot work within you, while you're in this condition."

As she spoke, I sensed that God was speaking to me through her—what a relief! And I realized that I'd been afraid He would never speak to me again.

The healing she was speaking of, had already begun.

"Let's talk about your physical condition," she said now. "You are going to need real exercise. I'm going to get you a bike, and I want you to ride it to all your classes. Also, I want you to swim. Every day."

"Swim? Where?"

"In the sisters' pool. They won't mind; I'll explain it

to them." She smiled. "We're going to adopt you into our community for the summer. As long as you are at Maryville, you are to consider yourself an adopted sister; you are welcome at all our liturgies, prayer services, everything that we do."

I started to cry again—tears of joy. But she wasn't finished. "I'm remembering now that you have a beautiful singing voice—did you bring that guitar with you?" I nodded. "Well, you probably don't feel much like singing now, but when you feel you can handle it, we could use some music at liturgy in the morning. But only if you want to; I don't want to impose anything on you."

I left her office and went straight to the chapel. I could feel God in my soul; it was like He was holding me and calming me. His Spirit was like a balm of cool water, flowing over my heart, relieving the searing ache that had been there so long.

I didn't pray. I just sat there, enjoying His presence, sensing His love and His care. He was with me—*I will never leave, nor forsake you.*

That summer at Maryville was a pure gift from a loving God. He knew I needed a period of transition—and what He arranged for me was more than I could have dared hope for. Maryville was like a spiritual half-way house: I was not a sister anymore—and yet I was still treated like one and still had the fellowship of other sisters.

My roommate was a sister, a Servite, in fact: Sister Pauline who had been two years behind me in the novitiate. I was glad, because she was fun and had a good sense of humor. But I was a little nervous about how she might feel, when she learned I would be her roommate. I needn't have been: the moment she came in, she dropped her bag and gave me a great hug. Then she started to tell me everything that had happened when I left.

"I knew you weren't dead! But the way that notice was worded, 'Pray for her soul,' a lot of others assumed you must be. It made me so mad, I wanted to tear it down!" And she got mad all over again, thinking about it. "How could they say good-bye to you like that! After all the community we'd had together!" She clenched her fists. "I can't believe they treated you like that!"

"Calm down, Sister," I said, laughing. "Whatever happened, God allowed it. It's over with now, and it's in His hands."

She did calm down and continued in a more normal tone. "The other sisters were so surprised—and no one more than me: you were the last person in the world I would ever have expected to leave." Seeing my surprise, she explained: "You don't know how I looked up to you in the novitiate! I was shocked!"

Now I was *really* surprised. I'd never thought of anyone looking up to me; I was always too busy looking up to somebody else.

"It was just that you'd made such a contribution to the community," she concluded. And then she asked, "Can you tell me why you did leave?"

I shook my head. "No, that's a closed chapter, and it's best to leave it that way." I had told Mother McDonald; that was enough. It was also different: she had asked, she was in charge, and she was not of our order. Besides, thanks to her willingness to be my confidant, I had regained my peace and the presence of God. Which I was not about to jeopardize for anything.

That summer was truly a God-given oasis: I rode the bike Mother McDonald had gotten for me. Not just to classes but everywhere. And what fun it was to go whizzing through the campus with the wind on my face! The swimming was fun, too—I felt graceful in the water, and as the weeks went by I began to feel more graceful on land, too. Also, my muscle tone was returning, and with it, my strength and stamina; I could climb three flights of stairs now, without breathing hard. Was this what Samson felt like in that Philistine prison, as his hair began to grow?

The mind can be a powerful ally to the healing process. I no longer regarded the exercise I was doing as therapy; it was just fun—and exactly the sort of extra-curricular activities I would have chosen for myself, even if the doctor in Omaha hadn't recommended them at my last physical. "You're definitely in remission," he'd said, "for more than a year now, and hopefully for good. But you need vigorous aerobic exercise on a regular basis, and the more, the better. One thing, though: it must be no-impact aerobics, like swimming or cycling. You'll have to avoid running or jogging at all costs: your knees, especially the reconstructed one, will never take the impact."

He had also advised me not to mention MS in my job interviews. The public's perception of Multiple Sclerosis was that it was a progressive, degenerative disease of the nervous system that was irreversible and usually fatal. And the public's perception was by and large correct. "But," he said, holding out the golden carrot, "we still cannot say with absolute certainty that you have MS. We're 85% sure that you do—but that leaves a three-in-twenty chance that it may be some other type of chronic disease, and you will never have another episode. The main thing is, you're fine now, and to anyone interviewing you, you look perfectly healthy. As for the orthopedic shoes, a lot of people wear them just because they're more comfortable."

A three-in-twenty chance—that was enough for me. And as month after month went by, I became convinced that I was one of those three. I could swim a lap under water, ride sixteen miles in an hour. Whatever it had been, it was part of my past, like a bad dream, already half-forgotten.

Besides, I was too busy looking forward, to look back. August was still transition-month for me, and this August, 1968, I would be starting a new life in a new part of the country. *Vaya con Dios*—go with God. I was—and He was going with me.

23

Mars

In a trailer park on the outskirts of a little town half an hour north of Pittsburgh known as Mars, sat a small but gleaming silver trailer. It had a tiny kitchenette, a tiny bathroom, a tiny living area and a tiny sleeping area that was all bed. It was my home, and I loved it.

It was also the first investment I had ever made. My parents would have preferred me in an apartment. But there were so few that the rents were astronomical. Meanwhile, I had come across this unique opportunity to lease a trailer with an option to buy. Once I owned it, I reasoned, I could always sell it; in the meantime, instead of throwing rent money away, I was building equity.

I thought my father would be proud, but he remained extremely skeptical. "Rita," he said over the phone, "I'm just really concerned about you and money; you don't know the first thing about it, and I'm just afraid you're going to get fleeced, every time you turn around."

He was right, of course; I'd never had to buy or rent anything major in my life. But I had too much McLaughlin pride to admit it. "Please, Dad, stop worrying about me! I'll be fine!"

I decided not to tell him about the Rambler.

When I'd arrived in Mars, my friend Lois had said,

"You'll stay with us, till you find a place of your own. But the first thing you're going to need is a car."

"Lois, I don't even know how to drive!"

"Well, kiddo, there's no bus transportation to your school, and it's way out in the country. You can't very well walk it."

"So —"

"So you're going to have to get a car."

"Shouldn't I learn how to drive first?"

She thought about that for a moment, then wrinkled her brow. "No! First, we'll get the car; then you'll learn to drive it. You'll *have* to!" Lois and I got along so well, because she was as impulsive as I was.

"How much money have you got?"

"My dad loaned me five hundred dollars, and my sister gave me a little more, but it's supposed to go for a deposit on an apartment and—everything."

"Five hundred," she mused. "That's not very much." Then she brightened. "You know what? I just remembered: our neighbor has a car in his garage he's been trying to sell for four years! I think it's a Rambler."

"I've never heard of a Rambler," I confessed.

"Well," Lois shrugged, "it won't hurt to go look at it."

So we did. It was a Rambler, all right; red with a white top.

The neighbor stood there, waiting for me to ask questions, but I didn't know what to ask. "Um, does it run?"

"Of course," he said, starting it up.

"How much do you want for it?"

"What are you looking to pay?"

"I don't have very much—"

"All right, $300."

"I can't give you that much."

"$250, then."

"That's still too—" Lois kicked me. "I'll take it," I lamely concluded.

When Lois's husband Bob got home, he said, "What about insurance?"

"What about it?" I countered.

"Well, you can't drive in this state without it."

So the next morning Lois took me to get it, which took most of the money I had left.

Now I had a car I didn't know how to drive. "Not to worry," said Lois blithely, "I'll teach you." She took me to get a learner's permit, and we found some secluded country roads north of Pittsburgh, and I started to learn. Driving was fun, I thought, as I whipped around the countryside.

In a week, I had a driver's license; in two weeks, I was on my first long-distance solo flight, fifteen miles up Route 8 to the special ed office in Butler. I had just passed the point of no return, when steam started to escape from under the hood. I looked at the temperature gauge; the needle was all the way up in the red.

I managed to get it over to the shoulder, but I hadn't the foggiest idea how to open the hood—let alone what one was supposed to do then.

A trucker stopped to help, raised the hood, and burned his hand getting the cap off the radiator. "Bone dry," he said, squinting down into radiator. "When was the last time you had your coolant checked?"

"Huh?"

"Your anti-freeze—when was the last time it was checked?"

"I—I don't know; I just got the car a couple of weeks ago."

"And you bought it privately, right?"

I nodded.

"Oh, boy," he muttered, shaking his head. I knew I

was in trouble. "It's not a good car?" I asked.

"Lady, it wasn't a good car to begin with. And it's nothing but junk now; engine block's seized."

I started to cry.

"Look," he said more softly, "I've got a friend up the road who runs a garage. He's got a tow truck; I'll send him back for you."

Half an hour later, a man in a tow truck arrived. He got out and winched up the Rambler. "Where do you want me to take it?"

"I don't know." I started to cry again.

"Well, I've got a friend in Butler who sells Volkswagens—you like VW's?"

"I guess so."

The Volkswagen dealer looked over the Rambler, then said, "I'll give you $35 for it."

"But I paid $250 for it two weeks ago."

He shrugged. "It's not worth fixing, and frankly I'm doing you a favor; I doubt I can get $25 for it, for junk."

I was in despair—but I was not about to cry again.

He looked at me. "You don't have a ride home, do you." I shook my head. Don't you start crying, you big jerk! "You're going to need another car, I guess."

"I guess."

"How much money have you got?"

"None," I answered truthfully.

"But you're working, right?"

"Yes, I've just started teaching school."

"What's your take-home?"

"My what?"

"How much is your paycheck for?"

"$390 a month—but most of that's going for rent and food." (I had the trailer by this time.)

"Tell you what," he said, like he was doing me a favor he really didn't want to do, but he was so full of compassion, he just couldn't help himself. "You see that little beauty over there? That's a demonstrator. It's been driven some, so—even though it's a '68 and a fastback which means it'll soon be a collector's item, I can let you have it for—$2,200!" He looked at me a little cautious, like he expected me to throw myself on him and hug him out of sheer gratitude.

I didn't feel like hugging anyone just then. "I just told you, I don't have any money."

"Oh, you don't have to pay me *now*. You'll just pay a hundred a month—and the $35 for your car can be the down-payment! Have we got a deal?" He beamed.

"I don't have a whole lot of choice."

The car had a D title on it which meant, I learned later, that far from being a demonstrator, I was the car's fourth owner. And later still, I learned from someone who knew one of the car's former owners, that it had been wrecked—so badly that the frame was bent. Which explained why they could never get the wheels aligned.

And like the Rambler, this car, too, was a dog. I soon discovered why Volkswagen may have stopped making this particular model: its distributor had to be taken out and hand-dried on damp mornings, just to get the car to start. I also soon learned that the Allegheny foothills of western Pennsylvania were notoriously damp in the early morning.

One other thing I learned: never buy a car without checking the tread on its tires—mine had none. Needless to say, I never told my father any of this.

But Mars itself I loved from the moment I got there, much the way I had loved Massena. And the best thing about my new life was the special ed kids. There were nine of them, from nine to fourteen years old, and unlike my previous teaching situations, they would stay with me for the duration of their time in junior high.

My first impression of them was that they were about

the happiest bunch of kids I had ever seen. Some were almost normal in some areas, but severely lacking everywhere else. Some came from broken homes; two came from a local Presbyterian orphanage. All of them responded to love with love, and I was amazed at how much love they had to give. I was even more amazed to find how much love there was still in me, to give to others.

I hadn't realized it, but I needed to love just then—and needed to be needed. And knowing that, a caring God had given me these kids. Love was exactly what we all needed, and they needed as much as I could possibly give them. With normal kids, you had to be wise about the quantity and nature of love you gave them. With normal, willful, rebellious, lazy kids like I used to be, tough love in massive doses was the usual prescription. And the tougher the love, the more I seemed to thrive on it. Whatever success I achieved as a youngster, it was thanks to the wisdom of my teachers—and their willingness to administer spiritual cod liver oil, as necessary.

But these kids needed love so badly and responded to it so instantly, that hardly any discipline was ever required. I just loved them. It never occurred to me that this was therapy for my heart, as important to that muscle as cycling and swimming were to my legs. As I poured love into these kids, my heart was getting healed—of hurt and anger and bitterness and rejection—which for the most part I was not even conscious of.

We baked cookies for their parents, and once they'd learned how, they went home and baked them for me. I took them on field trips, when they wanted to see where I lived, I showed them my trailer; after that, two boys would arrive on Saturdays to mow my tiny lawn, or do anything that needed being done—basically they just wanted to be around.

As long as I was around them, my life was full and
happy. . . . But there were still the evenings—and alone
at night, sitting in that trailer, I would imagine what the
sisters were doing at the convent, and I would miss them
terribly. Then the pangs of guilt would return, and the
tears.

I would remind myself that what was done was done,
and that what He had given me now was the most
wonderful challenge anyone could ask for. And drying
my eyes, I would thank Him. It was usually better, after
that—until the next time I happened to see a nun in her
habit. . . .

Gradually, the fact that I had been a nun myself, leaked
out among the faculty. Before long, well-meaning women
considerably older than myself were giving me motherly
(and in some cases, grandmotherly) advice: "Well, we've
got to find someone for you; you're too attractive to go
wasting away with nobody." So they began to contrive
dinner engagements and other activities, in order for me
to meet various suitable gentlemen. Because they meant
well, I cooperated with their efforts, but in reality my heart
wasn't in it. I was only three months out of the convent;
it was simply too soon to think about the sort of relationship
that had been out of my mind for so many years.

Then one day, Mrs. Fowler, the school nurse mused,
"You know, Rita, there is one guy. . . you've got to meet
him; he has the broadest shoulders." As she thought about
him, her enthusiasm grew. "He's the principal of the
elementary school down the street, and the best-looking
guy—but you know what's even better than his looks?"

"What?" I smiled.

"He takes care of his mother! Anyone who takes care
of his mother has got to be a good guy!"

"Maybe."

"No maybe about it," she said, as if closing a file, "he's

the one. And best of all, his school shares our cafeteria; he brings his kids here every day for lunch."

Now I knew who she meant; I had noticed him walking the children here, usually with one hanging on either hand. I had noted that he was never annoyed with them, though they were constantly asking him questions and pulling at him. It was obvious that they loved him, and the feeling was reciprocated. This was a good man, I had decided.

"Well, look who's here!" declared Mrs. Fowler, as we were eating lunch in the faculty lounge. "Ron? Come over a minute; I want you to meet someone."

I blushed, feeling like I was on an auction block. But the other teachers were all laughing, and he didn't seem to mind. He had a nice smile, and kind, bright blue eyes. . . .

Next Saturday morning, as I was scrubbing the floor of my little trailer, the phone rang. "Rita? It's Ron Klaus; we met in the faculty lounge—would you like to go out?"

"Well—"

"To tell you the truth, I've wanted to ask you for some time, but until Mrs. Fowler introduced us, I didn't see how I was going to meet you."

I laughed—I didn't know what else to do; I was a little out of practice at this.

"I hear you're a Catholic," he went on.

"That's right."

"And you used to be a nun?"

"Yes." Where was this going? I was too nervous to realize that he was nervous, too.

"I'm Lutheran," he stated. "Is that going to be a problem?"

"No, we're just going out," I blurted. "It's not like we're getting married, or anything."

He laughed, and I thought, oh, good work, Rita; I hope

you have a nice time knitting Christmas presents tonight!

"Um, would you like to go to the symphony? Or do you like outdoor things?"

I mentally reviewed the choice of evening dresses in the tiny closet behind me. "Outdoor things," I answered.

"How about hiking?"

"Hiking's good." The doctor had said no running; he hadn't mentioned hiking. As long as there weren't any hills involved, it should be okay. "As a matter of fact, I'd love to go hiking!"

"That's it, then," he said, relieved. "I'll pick you up at one o'clock."

He took me to McConnell's Mills State Park outside of New Castle, about an hour's drive north. Covered with virgin forest, it had a deep, boulder-strewn ravine that had been carved out by a glacier and now had the Slippery Rock Creek running down through it. Where the ravine narrowed almost to a gorge, the river below became a rapids, and a covered bridge spanned it. Very picturesque.

What was more, it was the middle of October, and the leaves had just turned—yellow oaks, red maples, all translucent under the warm afternoon sun. It was as if we were in an open-air cathedral, strolling under a canopy of brilliant, fiery stained glass. *Very* picturesque—even (for those who loved to do outdoor things) romantic.

After telling me about his family, he admitted that he had noticed me often in school. "You always dress so nice and look so nice. But I have a question; why do you wear those clunky shoes?"

I hesitated before replying. "I—had an illness when I was younger. I'm well over it now, but it left my ankles weak, so I have to wear these for support." It wasn't the whole truth, but it didn't matter; this was just a date, and he was just a friend.

We had a good time that afternoon—good enough,

so that he called me again. And again. We did go to the symphony; in fact, we went often. His brother-in-law was a violinist for the Pittsburgh Symphony, so there were always tickets available, and I loved the symphony.

Ron and I became good friends, then very good friends. But the idea of marriage never crossed my mind. Early on, he had made it perfectly clear: with his mother to care for, marriage could never be an option for him.

"This will be a platonic relationship," he had announced. And that was fine with me: kids were the main reason I would ever consider marrying, and now in school I had nine of them. The world put enormous pressure on single women to buy into the romantic fantasy that marriage was happy-ever-after land. But I wasn't buying; I'd lived enough years with happy, challenged, fulfilled sisters to know that God's call to celibacy was every bit as valid and vital as His call to matrimony.

And so, we carried on at pretty much the same level for the next two years. We might have gone on indefinitely, were it not for the return of Bill McFarland.

24
Ron

Bill McFarland had been a teacher for the county, whom I had gotten to know about the same time as Ron. A year later he had left the country to take a job in Bangkok, Thailand, working for the International Schools system, and from time to time, he would write, describing how things were over there. Why would he write to me? Probably because he felt like writing and didn't have anyone else to write to.

One day at the end of May in 1970, shortly after he had come back to the States on home leave, we happened to meet at a teachers conference. "You know," he said, "we could really use you over there. You'd be a real asset to the International School."

That got me thinking: I was 30 now—and if I was ever going to travel and see foreign lands, this might be my last chance. The more I thought about it, the better it sounded, until finally I mentioned it to Ron. "—and I could see the whole world," I concluded, watching his face closely; if there ever *was* anything more for us in the future than platonic friendship, surely it would surface now.

He did have a strange look, but all he did was shrug and say, "Do whatever you want."

"Right; I'll give Bill a call."

Everything happened very quickly after that. Bill sent me the International School information the same day. As soon as it came, I called the International Schools' office in New York, and they urged me to come in immediately: at that very moment, they were interviewing teachers for the next semester. I called Allegheny Airlines: there was a flight leaving for La Guardia in two hours. I pulled together my transcripts and classroom observation reports and just barely caught it.

Vaya con Dios—was I going with God? I felt so. I prayed that if this was His will for me, everything would go so smoothly I would know it was Him, and would not have to make anything happen. So far, it was: I was a hick from Iowa, who'd never been to New York before, never seen so many people in such a hurry. Yet I never got lost or even confused: an endless succession of kind strangers made sure I got on the right bus and got off at the right stop, went in the right building on Fifth Avenue, took the right elevator, got off at the right floor. In my mind there was no question that God was with me.

During the course of my interview, I found that the position would entail teaching English-speaking embassy children in the morning and helping to train native teachers in the afternoon. It sounded perfect. And on their part, they were satisfied with my degree and impressed with my ten years of classroom experience and the observation report of my teaching supervisors.

At the end of the interview, the director of personnel opened a drawer in his desk, took out a contract, and handed it to me, beaming. "Welcome to the International Schools."

If my father were here, I thought, he would caution me to read this carefully before signing it. So I did.

"Two years is an awfully long time to be away," I

commented, perusing the third clause.

"That's true," the interviewer agreed, "but we're spending an awful lot to place you over there."

There was no denying that: the salary was more than double what I was presently making, and I would not have to pay taxes on the first six months earnings. Plus, they would give me a head-of-household allowance of $2,000, *and* provide me with living quarters, complete with a full-time maid. Plus, there was a two-thousand-pound shipping allowance, which meant I could take more than a few of my favorite things.

The biggest plus of all, however, was the unrestricted plane ticket: they would fly me home each summer, and going either way, I could get off and back on the flight wherever I chose, staying as long as I liked. In short, I could literally see the world—for free.

Finishing, I looked up. "This is an incredible offer," I acknowledged. "I just wish I had some time to think about it."

"You do," the interviewer smiled, glancing at her watch, "we're not closing for another hour."

I decided to go for a walk. At first I gawked and gaped unabashedly. I'd heard the skyscrapers were tall; I just hadn't realize *how* tall. Nor had I realized *how* elegant the shops on Fifth Avenue would be. But fifteen minutes of that was enough; I got the idea. Now it was time to get serious: Dear God, what do You want me to do?

I couldn't seem to get a clear answer—which didn't surprise me; on major life decisions, I was learning, He did not always give clear-cut guidance; some things He wanted us to decide by faith.

Well, I *had* cast a fleece, of sorts—and smoothly was hardly the word to describe how everything had fallen into place. In the end it came down to this: While I could not be sure that it was the center of His perfect will for me, I did sense He was allowing it, if I wanted to go. And I was pretty sure *I* did.

I looked at my watch: twenty minutes to go. All right, list the pros and cons. The pros were obvious; what were the cons? I would be awfully far away from my family, for an awfully long time. But, I reasoned, I already was far away from them—just not half-way around the world. And as for the time period, hadn't I been away from them for thirteen years? And I would be home for as much of the summer as I didn't spend traveling.

What about Ron? Well, what *about* him? Hadn't he told me to do whatever I wanted?

I went back up to the International Schools office and signed the contract.

There was dead silence on Ron's end of the phone, when I got home and told him what I'd done. Then, he said softly, "You really did it."

"Yes—didn't you say I should?"

"You really did it," he repeated in wonder and disbelief. More silence.

Then he was angry. "You're going to go over there and meet some fly-boy and get married, and I'll never see you again!"

"Well, that's all right, isn't it?" I said resolutely cheerful. "I mean, we'll still be friends."

Pause. "You don't know anything, do you?"

His anger was getting nasty, and it was making me angry, too. "Just hold on a minute: we have no strings attached; we've made no commitment to each other. Just 'platonic friends,' remember?"

"I'm coming over!" he shouted, hanging up.

I lived in an apartment now; the man I had been making the payments on the trailer to, had not been turning them over to the bank, and the bank had come to repossess the trailer (something else I never told my father).

Ron was at my door in far less time than it had ever taken before. "What have you done!" he demanded. "I was going to ask you to marry me!"

"*What?* You never said a word!"

"I thought you understood!"

"Understood what? How was I supposed to understand anything, if you never said anything?"

At that irrefutable logic, he calmed down. Neither of us said anything; both of us were absorbing the enormity of what had just happened. In that one exchange more had transpired between us than in the previous two years.

At length, he asked, "Can you get out of it?" His tone was modulated, but he was shaking with the effort to keep his emotions under control.

I shook my head. "I just signed the contract."

"You mean, you're really going."

"Yes," I replied, realizing it for the first time, "I'm really going."

"I don't believe this!" he said, shaking his head repeatedly, as if to clear it. "I just don't believe it!" Then he looked up at me, his eyes blazing. "All right, go ahead and go!" he cried and slammed out the door.

"Well, why didn't you say something!" I shouted at the closed door, after he'd gone. "Was I supposed to read your mind?"

I didn't sleep well that night; there was no way I could sort out the riot of emotions tumbling through me. And the strangest thing was, I sensed God smiling.

The next morning, the phone rang, and I hurriedly picked it up. It wasn't Ron. But it was his secretary, Aggie, who had become a friend. My school was over, but his still had another week.

"You know," confided Aggie under her breath, "you've really upset somebody."

"What did he say?"

"It's not what he's said; it's what he's doing: he's banging around here like a madman." She chuckled. "I guess you're really going."

"Yes."

"Well, I'm not going to tell you not to. To tell you the truth, I'm envious. If I were you and weren't married, I'd go in a shot! The future can wait."

"Thanks, Aggie," I said, meaning it.

But my sister Ruthanne's response was not as encouraging. Two days after I called to tell her, I received a hand-written letter from her, pleading with me not to go. It was covered with tear-splotches.

I called her back, reminding her that it was only June, and I wasn't due to leave until August 7; I would be coming home for a long visit, before then.

In the meantime, there was a lot to do. I turned in my resignation to the school, gathered up my records, terminated my lease on the apartment, and did some careful (frugal) shopping for appropriate apparel for Bangkok.

For a week after I had broken the news, Ron studiously avoided me. Then without warning, he suddenly descended on me. "Rita," he said with great difficulty, "can you change this? Can you cancel the contract?"

This man was driving me crazy! He still hadn't formally proposed; he hadn't even said, "I love you." If he was that afraid of commitment, what did that bode for the future?

"I'll call and see," I heard myself saying.

"You know," he said gravely, "the situation over there is deteriorating; in Bangkok, they're even throwing bombs in banks."

"I'd heard that," I admitted.

"Well, I'd think about it a whole lot more before I went, if I were you. But there's no point in telling you that," he said, getting angry again. "You'll do whatever you want, anyway; you always do!" he shouted. "You can't tell a McLaughlin anything! And I'll bet the rest of your family is just as bad as you are!"

That did it! "You leave my family out of this!" I shouted back. *"Nobody* insults my family!"

Slam!

"Great!" I cried at the closed door. "I think we've got a major breakdown in communication here."

I did call the International Schools. They were sympathetic, but they were in a difficult situation themselves: it was now too late for them to find a replacement for me. They would amend the contract to release me from my second year's obligation, but I would have to give them the first year.

I called Ron and told him. He came over. "I wish you could get out of it entirely."

"Ron, I tried. I just wish you had said something sooner."

"I have trouble expressing myself sometimes."

"That may be the understatement of the millennium. But at least you're doing better now," I added to encourage him.

He was recalling the past, more to himself than to me. "I went over and over it: yes, I can; no, I can't. The problem was—and is—my mother. What am I going to do with her?"

So, at last it was out in the open; this was the thing which had kept him from speaking. "I guess you are going

to have to decide who you love more, me or your mother."
He had not used the word love before, but, I figured,
that was what we were talking about here; might as well
call a spade a spade.

"That's not fair!" he cried. "Don't ask me to choose
between you and my mother. I love you both."

Oh, goody, goody! My impatience leaked out now (it
always did): "That is exactly what I am asking you to do!
Because if I am going to be your wife, I have got to come
first! Above your mother, above everything!"

"All right, all right, you'll come first."

He said it, but it didn't sound very convincing. And
suddenly I was just tired and depressed about the whole
thing. "Look, you've got to give me some space," I pleaded
in the vernacular of the day.

"You don't want to see me anymore?"

"That's not what I said; I just need some room to
breathe—"

"Well, maybe I don't want to see *you* anymore," he
retorted. "Maybe we should just not see each other for
awhile."

"All right," I sighed, "if that's the way you feel."

"It is."

"Then let's be perfectly clear: you date who you want
to, and I'll date who I want to. We have no engagement
here, right?" And no breakdown of communication, either.

"Right, we are not engaged."

This time as he left, he closed the door quietly—but
to my heart, its click was as loud as a slam.

I had imagined this enforced hiatus would not particularly bother me. I was wrong. To my intense surprise, I found I was miserable. Every time the phone rang, I leapt for it, like some goofy teenager. And each time it wasn't him, it was all I could do to keep the disappointment out of my voice.

Finally, a week later, it was him. "Well, I've thought it over. And I've decided you should come and meet my mother."

"I'd like that."

"Tonight?"

"Fine."

Ron's mother had prepared a magnificent German repast, from *sauerbraten* to *spatzle*. She and I had a nice time, though her son was too uptight to enjoy himself. But as I thought about it afterwards, I realized that the ball was now in my court. He had brought me home to meet his mother. That meant he was absolutely serious about our getting married. And he had accepted my sole requisite: that I come first.

So now I was in a quandary. By this time I was really looking forward to going to Thailand, and I sensed that it would be my last chance to see the world. But I really wanted to marry Ron, too. And I had the distinct feeling that wouldn't wait: if I didn't marry him now, I would lose him forever.

The next move was up to me.

Correction: the next move was up to God.

Father in Heaven, I prayed, I'm beginning to suspect that You allowed me to sign that contract, to bring matters to a head. Well, they're boiling nicely now, thank You. But what am I supposed to do now? I've given the International Schools my word. And I'm happy to go, if that's what You want for me. But if it isn't, if you want me to stay, then You'll have to arrange it in some way that I won't have to break my word.

A pretty good fleece, I thought—but I never could have dreamed the way things worked out.

Before I knew it, August, transition-month, was almost here. The International Schools had called to arrange a convenient day for them to come and pack the ton of stuff I could take, and to confirm my travel plans to rendezvous with their scheduled plane. It was due to leave JFK on August 7th and stop in Hawaii and Australia before terminating in Phnom Penh, the capital of neighboring Cambodia. From there, we would be transported overland to Bangkok.

But less than two weeks before that, the evening news had carried some alarming footage from Viet Nam. The rapidly-escalating war had now spilled over into Cambodia: Phnom Penh had been bombed!

The next morning I received a call from the International Schools' New York office: "You've heard the news?"

"Yes, we watched it on Walter Cronkite last night."

"Well, we are offering all our teachers bound for Thailand an option: if under the circumstances, you do not wish to honor your contract, we will understand. But you must put your decision in writing. Otherwise, we are arranging another flight, entering Thailand by a different route."

Was this an answer to prayer? It might be. . .

If I needed confirmation, it came from a chance meeting with a girlfriend whose sister happened to be on home leave from Thailand—where she worked in the Bangkok International Bank. When she heard I was trying to decide whether to go, she exclaimed: "Don't do it! They threw a bomb in my bank! I wasn't hurt, but it killed three of my co-workers! If you think I'm going back there, you're crazy!"

I wrote the International Schools and asked to be released from my contract, and they replied at once, saying that they would honor my request.

So now I had no job, no place to live, and no money— but I also had nothing preventing me from marrying Ron. We planned the wedding for the following summer.

In the meantime, I met another man—Timmy.

25
Timmy

In less then two weeks the school year would begin—
and I didn't have a job. I called the special education
office and explained what had happened. "I realize it's
awfully late, but have you got any openings?"

"I'm afraid we've already filled your position at Mars,"
said the administrator who would decide how I would
spend the next year of my life. "And everything else is
filled, too. Too bad," he added, "because you had an
exceptional record at Mars."

I was disappointed but not surprised. Duquesne, St.
Vincent, Robert Morris, Seton Hill, Bloomsburg, Wash-
ington & Jefferson, and Slippery Rock State Teachers were
but a few of the colleges in the greater Pittsburgh area,
not to mention the University of Pittsburgh itself. All of
them were turning out fine young teachers, which meant
that for every opening there would be a dozen highly-
qualified applicants.

"Is there anything at all?" I pleaded, suddenly realizing
that teaching was virtually the only work I was trained
for.

"Well—there is one opening, but I don't think you'd
be interested."

"What is it?"

"Well, under the new state law that *everyone* is entitled to an education, we are now required to at least attempt to educate even the most severely handicapped children. So, we are starting a pilot program at—" he named a residential "school" in a nearby town which was little more than a holding facility for youngsters, until they were old enough to be transferred to a state institution.

"I'll take it."

"I think you'd better see it first, Miss McLaughlin. We're not just talking about severe retardation here; we're talking about cases that have always been considered hopeless." He paused. "You know, you can always register as a teacher substitute. I'll make sure you get plenty of work, and next year I can just about guarantee you a top job."

"I'd like to see the school."

"Very well, but you're not going to take it."

He was wrong.

On the first day of school in early September, the director of the facility, Mrs. March, arranged for a nurse to take me on a tour of the wards. I was to pick nine children whom I felt could benefit from this new program. As we went from ward to ward, on a clipboard I made initial observations, building a new file on each of the children I selected.

As we entered the last ward, there was still one opening. Near the entry, away from the other children, was a boy in a crib. He was wearing a yellow crash helmet, and the bars on the crib were metal. Over the top of the crib was a metal grate; it was a cage, really. I soon saw the reason for the helmet: as we paused in front of his crib, he started banging his head against its bars.

"What's his name?" I asked the nurse.

"You don't want that one," she said, shaking her head. "He's violent. He does that banging all the time. He's also autistic; can't communicate at all. He'll never be able to do anything."

She walked on into the ward. "Now this little boy over here—"

But as I started to follow her, the boy in the crib reached through the bars and grabbed my clipboard. "Book!" he yelled. *"Book!* B-o-o-k! Read book!"

I was stunned. "I thought you said he was uneducable," I said to the nurse who was now returning.

"Oh, he yells like that all the time," she said, dismissing it.

"He's *spelling!* This child is communicating!"

"You call that communicating?" the nurse said contemptuously. "You take the lid off that crib, and I'll show you communication!"

"I want him in my class," I said quietly, surprised at the steel edge in my tone.

She glared at me. "We'll see what Mrs. March has to say about it. But I can tell you right now: she's going to agree with me. He will *not* be in your class." She turned back to the lad on the bed she had been approaching. "Now this little fellow is the one who should be in your class; he's no problem at all."

As I joined her, I could see why: he sat on the end of his bed, his eyes half closed, not responding to anything. I tried to get his attention, to no avail.

"Book!" shouted the boy in the crib behind us, and looking back at him, I was amazed: he was holding up what looked like a tattered Sears Catalogue. What was more, he was pointing to pictures in it and trying to spell them.

"He's reading!" I exclaimed.

"That's not reading!" the nurse retorted.

"How did he learn to do that?"

"How should I know," she shrugged. "I didn't think he could do anything."

"Did you ever stop to listen?" I shot back, no longer

caring whether my anger showed. "That child has taught himself the alphabet! There's something there!"

The nurse looked at me with a mixture of scorn and bemusement. "If you insist on this, he'll tear your classroom apart. And he'll keep you from teaching any of the rest."

"We'll see. I want him in my class, dressed, at 9:00 tomorrow morning. Now what's his name?"

"Timmy."

"Timmy," I called to him, "I'll see you tomorrow morning!"

The next morning he was there with the others. He was wearing his yellow helmet, and I realized I didn't know what color his eyes were, because he kept his head down all the time.

I had been allowed to design the classroom, and had asked them to paint it a calm, neutral green, put in sound-deadening carpeting, and erect acoustical dividers between each child's work station. Everything possible was done to minimize anything that might distract or disturb their focus.

But first I had to get them to focus at all. Most of them had their heads down on their desks; they were all so doped up on Thorazine they could hardly see me, even if they wanted to.

The head nurse was there; I asked her: "Are they always like this?"

"Like what?"

"This medicated."

"Of course."

"Well, how do you expect me to teach them? They can't even hold their heads up."

"It keeps them calm, Miss McLaughlin," she informed me primly. "It's easier to work with them this way."

"Not for me, it isn't; I have got to have them at least awake!"

"Well, I am not going to reduce their dosage without the doctor's approval!" she declared.

I was not making any friends here—but that wasn't why I had come. And I'd never had much stomach for getting along by going along.

So I went to see the pediatrician, Marybel McKelvey—and in her I finally found an ally.

"Well, we'll still have to consider the staff here, but let's try incrementally reducing the dosages, and see how they do. We won't be able to take them off completely; you'd have bedlam. But let's work to achieve an optimum balance."

So we did. As their dosages were lowered, the children came alive, laughing and enjoying themselves. And they were surprisingly eager to learn. Kids were kids I realized, no matter how severely retarded. Given attention and encouragement—and love—there was no telling what they might be capable of. They still couldn't analyze the way normal children could, and their ability to learn and retain was drastically impeded. But they could be brought to the place where they were able to take care of themselves and have such basic survival skills as elementary reading and the ability to follow simple directions. Our goal was for them to be able to live in a group home and work in a sheltered workshop.

But Timmy remained my special challenge. Every day of the first week, Mrs. March looked in on my classroom and pointedly asked if I wanted Timmy removed. I didn't. I was not giving up on him, until God told me to—and so far, I was getting only green lights.

The first day, all Timmy did was rock and bang his head. Then, as they started reducing his medication, whenever I gave him a book he stopped rocking. And so that became my primary motivator: whenever I wanted to make him happy, I would give him a book. He would whip through the pages pointing to objects he recognized, and spelling them: "t-r-e-e"—"b-a-l-l"—"d-o-g."

When I took the last book away from him, he pounded his head on the desk, shouting, "No book! No book!"

I went to the library and got a whole stack of books for beginning readers. Then, letting him hold a book, I would draw a picture of what the page was describing, and write the word of what I had just drawn, on top of the drawing.

Another method I used was to take his hand in mine and with it, point to me and then to him, saying, "Teacher loves Timmy." Then we would reverse it: "Timmy loves teacher." Back and forth we went, training his eye to follow his hand. Then I would spell out the words for him on his pad and coach him to say them.

One morning, as we were doing this, all at once he looked up at me, straight into my eyes. His eyes were bright blue. He burst into a grin, and I knew we had made a breakthrough.

We made progress quickly after that—we, because I now had Jean, a terrific teacher's aid, helping me. We would take turns, one working with Timmy, while the other worked with the rest of the children, all of whom were coming along beautifully. Timmy had come the farthest—but only because he had the farthest to come.

At Christmastime, his parents came to take him home for the holidays—and could hardly believe he was the same boy. His father, a professor at one of the colleges upstate, said, "We have enrolled him in school after school—and no one was able to do anything with him. Finally, we had to institutionalize him; there simply wasn't anything else to do." He paused. "I cannot thank you enough for what you've done. You've given us our son back."

At the end of the school year, Timmy had come along

far enough to go home. Out of gratitude, his father
arranged for my being included in *Who's Who in American
Education*. But the best part was to see Timmy going home
with his mother and father for good. I could not remember
being so happy about anything.

I thanked God for Timmy, and told Him that if He
ever had any others like him, I would consider it a privilege
to work with them. Over the years, He would answer that
prayer twice more. By His grace and with an endless supply
of His love, two more autistic children would be restored
to wholeness.

The end of school that May of '71, signaled a transition
in my life, as well as Timmy's: Rita McLaughlin was about
to become Rita Klaus.

26

The Plunge

Get me to the church on time—it was all I could do to keep from shouting the refrain from "My Fair Lady" at the windshield, as I was caught in traffic. What were all these people doing out on the streets? I imagined going up to their cars and getting them to roll down their windows: "Excuse me, but I'm conducting a survey: what brings you out on Saturday morning, and is this trip really necessary?"

Mine was. I was getting married this morning—in about five minutes! I had no one but myself to blame for cutting it so close: I was the one with the hair down to her waist who'd forgotten it took five hours to dry, when she arrived at the hairdresser's at 8:30.

Technically I was still not late, I encouraged myself. But that was a cup of hollow cheer; it would be at least another ten minutes before I reached the church. And given how tense everything was, I should have been at least twenty minutes early.

As I peered through the streaming windshield, trying to will the traffic into moving faster, my life flashed before my eyes—not all of it; there wasn't time for that. Just the past couple of months. . . .

We had told Ron's mother first. Full of enthusiasm I started to describe my parents' church in Cedar Falls, where the wedding would be, when she held up her hand. "Sonny is going to be married in my church," she informed us.

"But the bride's parents always do the wedding; it's traditional."

"No. My two daughters married Catholics—in their churches. I will not have my son married in a Catholic church, too; that would kill me!"

I looked over at Ron, but he was studying his shoes.

That was that: the wedding would be in her church. I wondered what had happened to our understanding that I would come first—but rationalized that we weren't married yet.

So—I had to go see my pastor, Father Shaeffer, at St. Killian's, and get permission to be married in a Lutheran church. Fortunately, the Church had just recently broadened its position on such marriages to non-Catholics, and he was able to grant me this permission. (Later that year, Father Halley would formally bless our marriage.)

When we went out to Iowa for Ron to meet my parents, our visit coincided with a McLaughlin family reunion. There were so many, it had to be held outdoors, and it was decided to have a picnic in a nearby park. To see aunts and uncles and cousins and second cousins I hadn't seen in years—I couldn't wait!

"Which group is yours?" asked Ron, as we pulled into the parking lot. There were several hundred people of all ages and description, laughing, chatting, pitching horseshoes.

I surveyed the entourage, looking for faces I knew. "All of them!"

Ron went ashen. "They're *all* McLaughlins?"

"Sure!" I clambered out of the car and ran towards them. "Aunt Helen? Uncle Hank? Over here! It's Rita!"

That day was all sunshine for me—and acute culture-shock for Ron. "I can't believe this!" he whispered to me once. "They *all* talk as fast and as much as you do!"

"Yes, isn't it great?"

"Staggering."

The McLaughlins were all extroverts, totally free and possessing the Irish gift of gab in double measure.

By the end of the day, my fiance was on the verge of collapse. All the laughter, the singing, the sheer exuberance of my family—and there were so many of them! I had to remind myself that Ron's background and childhood were totally opposite mine. His father died in a car accident when he was young, his two sisters were much older than him, and all the rest of his family was still back in Germany.

Two days before the wedding, Iowa came to Pennsylvania. Everyone arrived—and I mean, *everyone;* the bride's side of the church would be overflowing.

We had the rehearsal dinner in the house that the three of us would share. Originally we had planned to buy a house a few doors down from his mother's, but Ron soon came to see that it was be almost impossible for him to look after two houses. It only made sense for her to sell her house and move in with us. Actually, we would be moving in with *her* after the wedding, from our respective dwellings. For we had moved her in first, so that she could become comfortable in her new surroundings.

But my mother was gravely uneasy about how this menage was going to work—me in the same kitchen with a woman who hated Catholics. Indeed, the meeting of the two future mothers-in-law was about as icy as it could possibly be. My mother was tall and outgoing, the head of every church committee back home, and about as far from the grandmotherly type as it was possible to be; in fact, she was no older than Ron's oldest sister. The two women could not have been more opposite, and in this case opposites did not attract.

Nonetheless, despite the tension which hung like a pall over everything, the dinner was a thoroughly festive occasion. The McLaughlin men outdid one another with their eloquent, heartfelt, and moving toasts, and more than a few eyes were moist.

When it was over, everyone pitched in with the clean-up, just the way we always did at home. At a dinner party, you never left the dishes and mess for the hostess to clean up afterwards. Everyone took care of it right away, so you could relax over coffee and conversation, with nary a thought to the enormous task waiting out in the kitchen. And with many hands making the work light, there was laughter and joking—indeed, half the fun of a dinner was the banter that went with washing, drying, and putting away.

But that was *not* Ron's mother's way. She preferred to do it alone, as she had for most of her 74 years— in regal solitude, never allowing anyone in the kitchen with her. And now here she was, surrounded by noisy, cheerful strangers, in a kitchen so small that the pantry shelves were in the basement. And here were the McLaughlins rushing up and down the basement stairs, putting her pots away where they didn't belong. . . . I looked across the crowded room at her. She wasn't smiling; in fact, her lips were compressed in a thin white line.

Now she summoned me over. "Tell them to get out of my kitchen!" she demanded in a voice that was hardly a whisper.

I looked her in the eye. "This is my kitchen, Mum," I replied quietly but firmly, using the name I was trying to get used to calling her. Then I smiled. "This is the way we do it in Iowa," I grinned, "everybody helping."

"This is not Iowa," she testily declared. "It's

Pennsylvania. And in Pennsylvania we do it *my* way."

Well, this was not the time for a showdown; with a sigh I started graciously ushering folks out of the kitchen. "Mum wants to finish this herself. I think she just needs some quiet and a little space."

When they were all out of earshot, and there were just the two of us, she said, "This is my kitchen."

"No, Mum, it isn't. This is our house, and you are going to be living with us, and we will share the kitchen."

She glared at me, and I turned and went in the living room. Where my mother, ever discerning, took me aside: "You see what just happened? Haven't I been warning you all day about this arrangement of her living with you?"

"Yes, Mom, you have."

"Well, your father and I—"

"Mom," I cut her off, "I really don't need this now," and I gently extricated myself.

Ron, seeing how upset I was and surmising the cause, got angry. "It's none of their business how we choose to live our lives!" he said under his voice.

"They mean well," I whispered, trying to placate him. "It's just that they love me and are concerned for me."

But he would not be mollified. "When are they going to realize that you're not their little girl anymore?"

About the time you realize you're not Sonny anymore, I nearly shot back. But to speak those words then, would mean no wedding, tomorrow or ever. And that wedding was going to happen, come hell or high water.

Or Noah's Flood, I thought ruefully, as the church came into sight between sweeps of the windshield wipers. I pulled up and jumped out into the deluge, grabbing my veil and running into the church. A couple of people were looking at their watches as I burst in, and were visibly relieved to see me. It dawned on me then, that they must have thought I'd changed my mind.

In a few minutes I was veiled and composed, and the familiar strains of Lohengrin's Wedding March began. Down the aisle I went on my father's arm, to where the minister was waiting with the man who in a few minutes would be my husband. I smiled at Ron—and my smile froze: giant hives had erupted all over his face, swelling around his eyes. Until that moment, I had not realized the depth of the trauma he was going through.

But once we had exchanged our vows, the hives started to subside, and by the time we kissed and went back down the aisle, they were almost gone.

At that point I wouldn't have noticed anyway; everything was a blur of smiling faces, a blizzard of rice, a friend's Mercedes festooned with cans and junk, waiting to take us to the reception hall.

The hall was all that I could have hoped for—all white linen and gleaming crystal, and in the center of the head table, the most beautiful wedding cake I had ever seen, surrounded by cherubs spouting fountains of golden water. My brother Russ, a fine professional photographer now, was doing the photography, as one of his first assignments. Everyone was having such a wonderful time, we didn't want to leave.

Then with a shower of rice and a rattle of cans we were off for a ten-day honeymoon at Rehoboth Beach. It proved to be ten days we would not soon forget—but would like to. After a mistake in reservations, a near-deadly encounter with riptides, a missed ferry, and three trips to the doctor's, we were both glad to be back in Wexford, ready to settle down to marital bliss.

27

With a Little Help

The honeymoon was over—traditionally, that phrase had an ominous ring to it. But for me in that summer of '71, all it spelled was relief. At last Ron and I could settle down to just learning to live with one another, without the excess baggage of romantic expectations.

There was just one problem—the one my mother had intuitively anticipated. . . .

When we arrived home, Ron's mother had the house all spic and span. But the next morning as I started getting breakfast ready, I couldn't find any of our wedding gifts. The blender, the toaster, the new glasses, the crystal pitcher which would have been perfect for orange juice—we'd unpacked it all, so that it would be ready to use. But where was it?

"Mum? Where are all our things from the wedding?"

"Oh, I boxed them up for you and put them in the basement. No sense ruining all your pretty new things; we'll just use mine, and then on special occasions, you can bring yours up and use them."

My Irish came up like a flood. "Those things are for me to use now, not later. I want them in the kitchen. Now."

Her German came up as quickly. "Well! I thought I

was doing you a favor. But I see there's no pleasing you."

Should I back down? For the sake of peace, let her have her way? No. If I gave up the kitchen, I might as well give up the house—and any life Ron and I might have together, as husband and wife. I went down in the basement, found the pitcher and glasses, and brought them upstairs.

When she saw them, her lips compressed into that thin, white line. "Sonny?" she called out to Ron. "Sonny, will you come in here?" When he didn't appear, she called louder: "Sonny, *come here!*"

Ron entered the kitchen, and immediately she started telling him what I had done.

But he held up his hands, refusing to be drawn into it. "Girls, girls!" he pleaded. "I love you both, and you're both going to have to work this out."

I shook my head. "In Scripture, it says: the man shall leave his father and mother and cleave to his wife, and the two shall be as one." (Matt. 19:5)

Ron's mother glared at me. "Well, I thought it was going to be the three of us!" she declared, stalking out of the kitchen.

Ron turned to me. "Go down and get your things. Only— try to leave some of her things here; maybe just bring up just the things you really want to use," he said with a placating smile.

I did not smile back.

"She'll get used to it," he added, without much conviction.

Then he sighed. "Two women in the kitchen—maybe your mother was right about my mother living with us."

"Leave my mother out of this!" I snapped. "She's in Iowa; we're here!"

"All right, but—you two are going to have to work things out."

Without answering, I went down in the basement and started sorting through our gifts. I didn't like this one bit! Where was the cleaving? The more I sorted, the madder I got.

And fearful, too—because Ron and I both believed that "till death do us part" meant exactly that: divorce was not an option. We were in this marriage now for the duration, for better or for worse. Well, it was already worse than anything I had foreseen—and I didn't see any way it was going to get better.

When I had left the convent three years before, my confessor Father Halley had cautioned me never to regard the time I had spent there as wasted. Now, as I stood in the midst of the basement shelves fuming, I could see what he meant. Because all those years of living in community had taught me the quickest, best way out of any inter-personal conflict: prayer.

"Dear Jesus," I murmured aloud, "I know You know what's happening here. And I know You love Ron's mother. And You know that I don't. So—You're going to have to put some of Your love in my heart. And give me patience, too; help me to see her side in all of this, that her treasures are as dear to her, as mine are to me. Actually, they're a lot dearer, because she's had them all her life, and I've only just gotten mine. . . ."

Even as I prayed, I could feel my heart softening; in fact, it almost made me mad that He would answer my prayer so quickly! But He did. The anger that had crept into every corner of my being, dissipated now—like a swamp fog under the first rays of the morning sun.

Prayer was amazing, I thought, climbing the basement steps to find Mum and make up.

But I had no idea what God had been doing upstairs, while I'd been praying. . . .

"Rita?" Mum called out. "Is this space okay? Can your

dishes fit in here?"

In the dining-room, I discovered that she had opened the china closet and begun removing her dishes and putting them in boxes. She smiled at me, proud of the shelf space she had already cleared.

"Oh, Mum, I really appreciate that!"

"Well, we never use them anyway; they're from the old country. But these—" she held up two red crystal champagne glasses, "these are the glasses my husband and I toasted our marriage with. I would really like to keep them out—"

"Of course you can! They're *beautiful!*"

And so, with a little help from God, we began to work things out. It wasn't always happily-ever-after, but whenever we had a problem, I knew what to do.

The next two years passed peacefully and uneventfully—and that was the only problem: no Blessed Events. We both wanted children, and while the term "biological clock" had not yet come into vogue, we both knew that my child-bearing years were drawing to a close. In April of 1973, four months after my 33rd birthday, we started exploring adoption procedures.

And—within a week, in the middle of one of my classes, I got a phone call from my doctor. When I hung up, I went back in and yelled to Jean, my aid: "I'm going to be a mother!"

The kids went bananas! So did Ron, when I told him that evening—and so did Mum; in fact, her reaction was the most touching of all: "My own grandchild," she whispered over and over. "I can't believe it!" And she started to cry.

All three of us went right to work, of course, creating a nursery, and in those next few weeks it seemed like God was handing us one bouquet after another. And then one Monday morning at the beginning of June, the enemy handed us one.

I'd gone in to school early, preparing some papers, when the nurse called down: "Some of the children are not feeling well this morning, but they're not really sick, either. So we're going to give them some aspirin and send them down; they're not really sick enough to keep upstairs."

Two hours later, I noticed that two of them had red blotches all over them. I called the head nurse down, and she said, "Oh," she said, "I guess it was more than just a little headache," and she took them upstairs.

That afternoon Dr. McKelvey, the pediatrician, diagnosed it as rubella. I had not told the head nurse I was two months pregnant, but I did now. "Oh, you'll be all right," she said. But I wasn't. Ten days later, I was covered with red blotches, too.

When blood tests confirmed that I had rubella, my OB/GYN said, "We can do an amniocentesis to determine if the rubella is in the fetus's bloodstream; if it is, you can elect to have an abortion."

I looked at him without answering.

"Am I getting vibes here that abortion is not an option?"

"You can forget your amniocentesis; I am carrying this baby to term, if it's God's will."

"Do you know what you are saying?" asked the doctor angrily. "If it lives, it could be deformed and severely retarded! You *teach* children like that!"

I changed doctors.

We decided on natural childbirth, and Ron and I attended the Lamaze classes, to get ready. I did one other thing to get ready: I cut off my hair which had been growing for the seven years since I had left the convent, and donated the cut hair to the Cancer Society, to be made into wigs for people who lost their hair during chemotherapy.

In August, a sonogram revealed that the child I was carrying had no deformities which was a relief; it also revealed the child's gender—which we chose not to be informed of. Since the baby was due around Christmas, we decided to name it Christopher, if it was a boy, and Kristen, if it was a girl.

But Christmas came and went. And so did New Year's, and Epiphany. On the morning of the 12th, my water broke, yet still there were no contractions. Ron called the doctor, and he said to come into the hospital immediately, which we did.

"How far apart are the contractions?" he asked, when we arrived.

"There aren't any," I replied.

He gave me something to induce them, but when nothing happened after fourteen hours, he elected to deliver by Caesarian. (I learned later that because of the MS, all my abdominal muscles had atrophied; there was nothing there to contract.)

Kristen was born at 5:30 in the morning—healthy, no deformities, a beautiful baby!

And so was Ellen, eighteen months later—another caesarian delivery. She was the tiniest little baby, not even five pounds. And she remained undersized that first year—but she was walking before she was 11 months old.

The two girls played well together, and Nana loved them dearly. What tensions had occasionally arisen from loving the same man in different ways were by now largely a thing of the past. We were in a new home, up in the foothills of the Alleghenies, about an hour north of Pittsburgh, and life could scarcely have been better.

It was topped off by the arrival of our third child, Heidi, on August 1, 1978—also a caesarian, also healthy. And she would be our last, as I was going on 39.

When I was released from the hospital, there were still a couple of weeks before Ron had to start the school year, so we decided to do our favorite thing: we hauled our pop-up tent-camper up to a campsite on the south shore of Lake Erie. It was an idyllic setting. We had a rubber raft for the girls (and ourselves), and we built sandcastles and cooked out and threw the frisbee for Mitzi, our Golden Retriever trapped in the body of a Doberman.

One night, after we had been there about a week, Ron was putting Kristen and Ellen to bed in the camper, while I sat out under the stars, with Heidi asleep in the port-a-crib beside me. It was one of those special nights— moonless, breezeless (and fortunately, humid-less)—in which all nature seemed expectant. The surface of the lake was perfectly still—a black mirror reflecting the myriad stars cast across the sky.

It was, in fact, so much like another night at another lakeside campsite two summers before, that I half-expected a repeat of what had happened then, when all at once, a great shooting star had roared up into the heavens and streaked across the sky—the most breathtaking I had ever seen.

It had reminded me then—and its memory reminded me now—that I had been so busy with children and diapers and cooking, I had forgotten to pray.

"Dear Jesus," I whispered now, glancing over at the camper where Ron was telling the two older girls a bedtime story, "thank you for my husband, for this beautiful family—for everything."

An immense peace settled over me then, a perfect peace. It would be the last peace I would know for a long, long time.

28

Downhill

The following evening at the campsite, the baby was asleep, and Ron was sitting at the picnic table with the girls, cutting up a long loaf of Italian bread. The pasta was my department, and I checked the pot simmering on the portable campstove, to see how it was doing. It was ready; draining it carefully, I carried it over to the table.

I was just about there, when I tripped over a little maple root and stumbled forward. Primarily concerned that I not dump our dinner in the dirt, I managed to slam the pot down on the end of the bench, though I caught my side on the corner of the table in the process.

Ron jumped to his feet. "Are you all right? How are your stitches?"

"They're okay," I replied. "I hurt my side, but otherwise I'm all right."

I was more puzzled than scared. I looked down at the little root that had tripped me: I was sure I had stepped over it.

During the remainder of our stay, I must have stumbled on that darned root half a dozen times; Ron even took to calling me "Klutzy Klaus." And that single step up into the camper—it caught me a time or two, also, pitching me headlong into the camper. Which was weird, because

I had distinctly stepped high enough to clear it.

Still, it was a wonderful vacation, and when we got home, Nana was delighted to see all the sun we had gotten (suntans were still a good thing, back then). Our cat Tucker was glad to see us, too, though she refused to show it at first, punishing us for leaving her behind.

That September and October I grudgingly came to appreciate why God customarily gave babies to younger women; I was a little old to be getting up in the middle of the night to care for a new baby while also coping with a two-year-old and a four-year-old. I didn't like having to admit that, not when I was up for Wonder Mom of the Year (an award for which I seemed to be perpetually in the running). But the bone-weariness I was feeling was making me acutely aware of every one of my 38 years. I was getting more and more worn down, and not even a good night's sleep, when Ron got up to take care of Heidi, seemed to make any difference.

Then one day in November, I was standing by the wall phone in the kitchen, listening to my friend Marianne (we called each other pretty much every day) and sipping from a mug of coffee, when—the mug went crashing to the floor.

"What was that?" asked Marianne.

"I just dropped my coffee."

"How could you do that?"

"I don't know; it must have slipped out of my hand, somehow. Let me clean it up, and I'll call you back."

I hung up and looked down at my right hand—the feeling in it seemed to be gone. I clenched and unclenched the fingers, trying to bring it back like a foot which had gone to sleep. As I knelt down to clean up the coffee on the floor, I had the strangest feeling that this had happened before. And then I remembered: it had—in Massena.

An icy chill spread through me, as the details came back: I had been taking a morning coffee break with Sister Mary Clementia, when the same thing had happened: the cup had slipped out of my grasp without my even being aware of it. It had been the first undeniable evidence that something far more than fatigue was at work in me.

"But that was 19 years ago!" I cried aloud, throwing the coffee-sodden paper towels in the trash. I sat down by the phone, and now thoughts started pressing in on me faster than I could brush them away: "Klutzy Klaus," the fact that I couldn't drive at night anymore because the headlights of the oncoming cars would double. The fact that I couldn't sew in the evenings, because I couldn't see the stitches, and when I forced myself, my right hand started to shake. The numbing tiredness that no amount of sleep seemed could allay. . . .

I began to shake. The—thing—was coming back.

An hour later, however, the feeling in my hand had returned, and after another hour I had convinced myself that it was just an aberration. After lunch I got the girls down for a nap and took one myself, and by suppertime I felt back to normal.

Three days later, I had the girls outside in the backyard playing frisbee with Mitzi, with Heidi in our little wagon, wrapped up in bunting. The afternoon had started out warm and sunny, but had soon reverted to form (Pittsburgh gets only 59 days of sunshine a year). The temperature dropped precipitously, and a fine rain began which was threatening to turn into sleet.

"Time to go in," I called to Kristen and Ellen.

"Aw, Mom, do we have to?"

"Never mind 'aw, Mom'—it's too much for the baby, and for you, too. Now c'mon, I'll make us some hot cocoa."

I reached down to lift Heidi out of the wagon, and

as I did so, my right arm suddenly felt strange—and I dropped her.

Kristen was horrified, and started jumping up and down and screaming: "You dropped the baby!"

Heidi was crying, but fortunately the bunting was thick and protected her. My right arm was completely numb; I couldn't pick her up.

"Kristen, stop that! Now help Mommy pick her up."

She helped me to get her into my left arm, and I carried her into the house.

"I'm going to tell Daddy!" Kristen shouted. "You wouldn't let me hold her, but you dropped her!"

"No," I said in my authority-voice, *"Mommy* will tell Daddy."

Only Mommy didn't. That year the school system had done away with building principals, which meant that Ron had been forced to take a pay-cut—at a time when we desperately needed the income. So when he came down for supper and started telling me the problems he was having at school, I decided he had enough to worry about. I would tell him tomorrow. . . .

But by the next day I felt normal again. And nothing more happened, until the evening that my friend and neighbor Peggy and I went grocery shopping for Thanksgiving. When I told her of the trouble I was having driving at night, she said, "Let's leave the guys home with the kids, and shop together; it'll be fun!"

It was—at first. But as she pulled into the Shop 'N Save parking lot, and I started to get out of the car, suddenly I felt a sensation down the back of my neck and down my spine—like electricity, ripping through my body. Instantly paralyzed, I lost control of arms, legs, bladder—everything.

"Oh my God, oh my God!" I screamed, and Peggy came rushing around to my side of the car.

"What is it?"

"I can't move!"

"Sounds like a stroke—we've got to get you to a hospital!"

"No, I want to go home!" I wanted Ron; I needed him.

So she drove me home, and together they got me into the house. Ron called Dr. McDonnell, who said to come in right away. On the way, he said that for some time it had been obvious to him that something was wrong, and he reminded me that two weeks ago he had tried to get me to see Dr. McDonnell.

By the time we got there, most of the feeling had returned, but I was terribly weak. After testing my reflexes, Dr. McDonnell referred me to an orthopedist, who booked me into the hospital where they ran test after test. The next day, he came into my room with the consensus: there were still some more tests they wanted to do, but everything pointed to a ruptured spinal disc in the cervical area.

Ron looked at me, astonished: "How can you be grinning like that? He just told you that you've got a ruptured spinal disc, and you look like that's good news!"

I just smiled and shook my head. Deep inside, I was so relieved! Oh, thank you, God!

"Of course, we're going to need to do a myelogram," the orthopedist was saying. "We need to find out exactly where it is. But a disc *can* be surgically corrected; you're going to be fine."

Three days later, Sunday morning, I was waiting for Ron to come take me home, when the nurse came in. "Your doctor's here," she said, mystified. "He *never* comes in on Sundays; it's his one chance to play golf. But he's here now."

Dr. McDonnell came in then, and just stood at the end of my bed, looking at me. Finally he spoke: "You don't have a ruptured disc. Your spine is just fine." He paused and rubbed his chin. "We did another test, just routine; we took some spinal fluid and—" he fixed me with his gaze. "Rita, how long this has been going on?"

"Pardon me?"

Since I was obviously unready to admit to any knowledge of what he was talking about, he asked, "When is Ron coming in?"

I started to cry.

Dr. McDonnell frowned. "He doesn't know anything about this, does he."

"No," I managed, "he doesn't know a thing."

"Well, we're going to have to tell him. You need to have a CT scan, and I gather you're going to need household help and extensive physical therapy."

"Does this all have to be done right away?"

He nodded. "The sooner the better. The more debilitated you get, the less chance we have of recouping any of what you've lost. I'd better have a talk with Ron."

"Don't tell him about the MS; let me do that."

"All right," he agreed, "but I think you'd better tell me the whole story now."

When I finished, Dr. McDonnell said, "Well, I can understand now why you did what you did. I have a sister with MS; under the circumstances, I might have done the same thing. I can't say what you did was right—but I can't blame you for doing it. And you're right: you weren't 100% sure you had it."

He sighed and smiled at me. "But here you are, and what are we going to do about it?"

We decided that he would talk to Ron when he came to get me, and I would tell him about the MS, when we got home.

When Ron arrived, Dr. McDonnell explained the situation. "You're going to have to get some help in the household; your wife needs a lot of rest."

"Well, there's my mother, but she's 81." He shook his head. "I don't think we can afford household help."

"Ron," said Dr. McDonnell, "you may have to get a second job."

"Get another job? How can I do that *and* look after the kids?"

Dr. McDonnell shook his head. "These things are never easy, but it's what has to be done. I know you love her; somehow, you'll find a way."

That evening, after the kids were in bed, I said, "Ron, we've got to talk. There's something I have to tell you—something I should have told you a long time ago."

I told him. When I was done, he said, "Is that *all* of it?"

"That's everything."

He got up and walked to the front door. "I want a divorce," he said, slamming out of the house and driving away in his car.

Sitting alone in the living room in the gathering darkness, the enormity of what I had done to this man finally began to sink in. I had been so wrapped up in my own feelings and in being Wonder Mom, I had never stopped to consider that the lie I had been living might in any way jeopardize our relationship. So completely had I rejected the possibility that I might have MS, it never occurred to me that one day my dishonesty might cost me my marriage.

It was occurring to me now—in spades. The specter of divorce, of the break-up of our family—of ultimately being left alone, as my condition progressively deteriorated—was shattering. I could not move; I could scarcely breathe.

Two hours later, the headlights of a car coming up the driveway swept the darkened living room.

I felt a sense of relief—but also forboding, because I didn't know what was coming. I managed to turn on the light just as the door opened. He stood there in the doorway, looking at me: "You know," he said slowly, "sometimes, I'm not a very strong person. God knows, I'm no saint. But I'll try." He shook his head. "No, change that: *we'll* try."

When he said *we*, I felt such relief, I couldn't speak.

He came over and sat down next to me. "I want you to tell me why you didn't tell me."

"Well, in the beginning, there was no reason to; we were just friends—platonic friends. And besides, I had convinced myself that I was one of the three in twenty who would never have another episode; by the time we were about to get married, more than three full years had passed without a slightest symptom. In my mind, the whole thing was just a bad dream, best forgotten. Once I did think of mentioning it, but what if it wasn't true? I would be throwing away the marriage and any chance for a normal life—for nothing."

For a long time he was silent. Then he said, "Well, I can see where you're coming from, but—Rita, I'm not angry about the MS; I'm angry that you didn't trust my love enough to risk telling me. That's what hurts: husbands and wives are not supposed to have secrets from one another. I was totally honest with you; I thought you were with me, too."

He looked out the window. "Well, what we've got to do now is find out the best way to help you."

We didn't have much time, because things started going downhill fast in the ensuing months. I couldn't walk down the driveway to get the mail anymore, even with the cane Dr. McDonnell had given me, because I could never get back up again. Even if we hadn't been up on a hill, the dirt-and-gravel driveway was too uneven for me to walk on; I was tripping over everything these days.

Grocery shopping with the children was a misery. We had a front-pack which Heidi would ride in like a baby kangaroo, and at the supermarket I would put the other two kids in the shopping cart. It took forever to run the simplest errands—but it was preferable to not being able to run them at all.

And now there was another complication: excruciating pain. The muscles in my right leg had atrophied to the point where there was such imbalance that my bones were completely misaligned and pressing in on the sciatic nerve. I was in agony.

It was almost a relief, therefore, when I was hospitalized in the spring of '81. A new CT scan showed where the lesions were in the myelin sheathing in my brain, and X-rays revealed the extent of the bone deformities in the right leg. Things had reached the state where the only thing that could be done now, our orthopedist explained, was to perform a radical retinacular release. He would cut the tendons that held the kneecap in place and clean out the whole knee cavity. This would remove the pressure on my sciatic nerve, and the pain would cease. But it meant that from now on, I could no longer walk without support— either from a walker or Lofstrand crutches, the kind which held your upper arms from behind at the biceps.

The alternative was to simply live with the pain, which was unbearable—and getting worse. So there *was* no alternative.

As I recovered from the operation, I was taught how to plan my day and space my activities, to conserve what little energy I had. I went home, totally depressed.

Some nights later, we were all in the living room, watching "Little House on the Prairie." I was on the couch with my feet up, and my skirt, where my knees were, showed only one bump. Because my right kneecap had slid around to the inside and was facing my left leg.

I wasn't paying much attention to the program, clipping bargain coupons out of the Sunday paper (at least I could do *that* to help!). But Kristen, who was five now, was watching closely, as in the story a student's mother died. Now she climbed up on my lap and looked up in my eyes: "Mommy, are you going to die, like that mommy?"

I summoned all the control I could muster, to keep my voice calm and reassuring. "No, honey," I smiled, "I'm not going to die." But inside I was raging at God: how could You do this? How could you put this fear into this little girl's heart?

It had been a long time since I'd prayed; the well of bitterness was too deep. Nor was there much joy in going to church; all I did there was argue with Him.

If You had to do this to me, why did You wait until I had a husband? Or children? If You had done it earlier, I never would have gotten married, and they would have been spared this. And I repeated the words of Teresa of Avila to God: "If this is how You treat Your friends, it's no wonder You have so few of them."

But that was back when I was still speaking to Him. Now, I just hated Him.

29

The Bottom

My anger and bitterness gradually worsened, until it spilled out over everybody. Ron and his mother (who was 86 now) were doing their best to cope, and all I could do was see where they had failed. If Ron scrubbed the kitchen floor, I would point out that he'd missed the corners. I saw every spot on every glass, every crumb on the carpet. I felt like my house was dirty, and everything around me was falling apart, because I couldn't keep it the way I wanted it.

One day I was alone in the living room, lying on the couch as usual, when I noticed there was a spider web in the corner of the ceiling. And of course, once I had seen it, that was all I could see, whenever I took my eyes off the book I was reading (I still liked Agatha Christie). Heidi was in with Nana, and it would be hours before Ron came home with the girls.

I was supposed to be resting—but how could anyone rest, with that ugliness up there? So with a great deal of effort, I sat up and got my crutches under me, lifted myself up and went out to the kitchen. I found a rag and tied it to the tip of one of the crutches. Back in the living room, I reached up with it and wound the offending web onto it. As a result of that endeavor, I slept most of the afternoon, but it was worth it.

At night, Ron would bring me the laundry to fold; he knew I enjoyed doing it (and I had been so caustic about how he'd done it, the last time he'd tried). But by the middle of March, my upper body muscles had atrophied to the point where I couldn't do even that little chore. My arms felt like lead.

One time, I determined to do it anyway, by sheer force of will. My two arms were soon shaking, and I could not make them do what I wanted. In total frustration I threw the shirt on the floor, and just hugged myself and wept.

"What's the matter, Mommy?" asked Heidi, who was four now.

"Shut up! Just shut up and leave me alone!"

"C'mon," said Kristen (eight, now), putting an arm around her little sister and guiding her out of the room. "Let's leave Mommy alone. She's not feeling good today."

Then I would feel so horribly guilty that all I wanted to do was give them hugs. But wait a minute, I would think: *I'm* the one who needs hugging around here! I did hug little Heidi whenever I got the chance, wishing as I did, that I was her, being hugged.

As for Ron, I poured out such contempt on him, it was a miracle he did not walk out. (I did not realize until later, when I joined an MS support group, how true that was: many husbands, unable to cope with their wives' increasing bitterness, simply walked out.) There was a wall growing up between us, and I was the one building it, brick by brick. Part of it was out of guilt for the deception on which our marriage had been founded; a lot of it was pride, because I had always been fiercely independent, and was now totally reliant on him. And there was jealousy, too: here was Annie Oakley, who once could shoot and ride better than anyone, now a pathetic, dependent blob.

Whatever the reasons, the wall was there. "I talk to you," Ron would say in desperation, "but you never hear me. The whole time I'm speaking, you're thinking about what you're going to say back to me, to get even." Which was true.

But the worst jealousy was focused on Nana. Kristen would come home from third grade, Ellen from first grade, and Heidi from nursery school, and they would run to her little apartment, and knock on her door. "Nana! We're home! Would you like to see what we did in school today?"

And I would yell from the living room, "*I'd* like to see what you did today!"

I would wait and wait, until they came to show me, and then in a fit of jealousy I would make a great production out of putting their artwork or spelling efforts up on the refrigerator with magnets. But I still felt like I was second in line, the second mom. Nana not only had the kitchen now, she had the whole house, and now she had my kids, too.

She even had my plants! She would stick little plastic roses in my ferns and philodendrons. I hated plastic flowers and would yank them out—only to find them back in the next day. The War of the Roses went on for months.

So when Nana would come in and say things like, "Would you like some tea?" or "Can I get you a pillow?" I was barely civil, and I had no patience at all for her attempts at small talk.

Finally I'd had enough. One day when Ron came home, I had it out with him: "Please! Get her to leave me alone!"

But instead of simply doing what I'd asked, he defended her! "Rita, you can't see yourself, the way you've become, the way you really are. She's only trying to help you—"

"You're not here during the day!" I shouted. "You don't know what goes on here! You can function; you're off at school! I'm stuck here all day, at the mercy of your mother!"

Nothing made me angrier than when he tried to counsel me. One time (only once) he made the mistake of trying to show me the truth: that I was drowning in my own pride. I was so furious that the next morning as soon as he'd left for school, I called my parents and told them I was coming home. Hatred gave me extra energy, and somehow I got a suitcase out and started throwing clothes in it. When the kids came home from school, I told them, "Go get your favorite things out of the closet and put them in the car, because we're not staying here anymore. And don't tell Nana!"

Fortunately Ron came home just at that moment. He took me and held me close and said softly, "I can't believe that you would take my family, everyone I love, and just leave me with nothing."

I began to cry, and just cried and cried. He hated it when I cried, and came completely unglued. I didn't try to check my tears; I wanted him to feel as miserable as I did.

To make matters worse (if that was possible), the bills were mounting up. The therapy sessions and the whirlpool bath and the electroshock muscle stimulation sessions were all expensive. But we had no choice: the doctors felt it was vital to retain as much motion as possible. Our medical coverage didn't begin to cover it, and 90 days after I was released from the hospital, it didn't cover anything at all. We had to pay for it out of our meager savings—which ran out after a year.

It reached the point where we were receiving government assistance for our children's lunches at school, and were only able to pay off the doctors' and therapists' bills at a rate of $5 each a month.

By the spring of 1983, the debilitating effects of the

MS had so weakened me that I had to back into the hospital for intravenous cortisone therapy. At that time I was also fitted with leg braces—as light as possible, because they wanted me to be able to move them with the little upper leg strength I still had. From then on, I would need them *and* Lofstrand crutches to get around.

Getting upstairs to our bedroom was a major operation, one that took Ron and one of the girls to get me there. My right leg was utterly useless. Standing next to me, Kristen or Ellen would lift my left leg up to the next step. Then pushing down on my crutches and using what little strength remained in that leg, and with Ron lifting behind me, I would raise myself up to the next step, where we would repeat the process. There were fourteen steps; getting up them took five minutes.

Something else happened to me while I was in the hospital, something so horrible I never told anyone about it—and which now haunted me.

The evening before I was due to be discharged, a new orderly had come in to make up my bed. When he had finished, he asked me if there was anything he could get for me for the night.

"No, thanks," I said sweetly (I could still be sweet to people I wasn't jealous of). "But what is that thumping up there?" I nodded toward the ceiling. "It sounds like they're playing basketball up there."

"Oh," he laughed, "that's just the MS crazies."

"The what?"

"You know, the ones who've lost all their marbles, because of MS."

I nodded numbly, and he left. Until that moment, it had never occurred to me that MS could affect the mind. I had seen plenty of people with MS by then, but never had I seen one whose mind was affected. I listened to the frenetic thumping overhead. Their minds weren't just affected; they were *gone!*

Earlier, when I had first faced the reality that the MS was back with a vengeance, I had tried to strike a bargain with God (this was back when we were still on speaking terms). "Dear Jesus," I had prayed, "if You must take my legs, then—I give them to You. And my arms, too, if You require them (dear, noble, Saint Rafe). In fact, you can have everything—below the neck. All I ask is that you leave my intelligence intact."

My vaunted intelligence, the seat of all my pride—I stared at the ceiling and listened to the thumping. . . .

Never in my life had I ever felt so alone and scared and hopeless.

30

Hugged by God

It was good being home with Ron and the kids again, and Mitzi and Tucker, and even Nana. But the good feelings soon wore off; I saw to that: before long, my jealousy and bitterness had my tongue once more flicking poison in all directions. And then would come the guilt, because I could see the hurt in Ron's eyes when my darts hit home, and could see the kids starting to avoid me again. The guilt only made matters worse—because I hated myself most of all.

So I was in a perfectly foul mood, when my friend Marianne called. "Rita? Listen, there's going to be a healing service over at St. Ferdinand's next Wednesday evening—want to come?"

"You can't be serious!" I replied, my voice dripping with contempt. "Marianne, I thought you were more intelligent than that! I can't imagine anyone with half a brain—"

"It's not like you think," she pleaded. "I was skeptical, too, but—"

"I'm a scientist," I interrupted. "I don't believe in healing; that stuff happened 2,000 years ago."

Marianne did not give up easily. "It's not like you think," she said again. "It's really beautiful—"

"It's a bunch of fakes! I've watched them on TV, those televangelists shouting: 'You in the green dress! Come up here and be healed of your arthritis!' And the people who come up, they're all plants. Don't you know anything?"

She tried to respond, but I was on a tear. "And when they lay hands on people, and they fall backwards—you don't think they're really 'slain in the Spirit,' do you? They've been pushed—and they're too embarrassed to get up."

Marianne sighed. "Well, that was pretty much the way I felt, too, before I went. But honestly, it's not—"

"You think I want a bunch of religious kooks praying over me? Is that what you want?"

She was hurt. Finally, I'd wounded her; I'd certainly tried hard enough. "Well, just think about it," she said, hanging up.

For a moment, I felt badly—but she shouldn't have tried to foist that quackery off on me.

Ron came into the kitchen then. "I heard the end of that—what are you so angry about?"

"Oh, it's Marianne; she wants me to go some stupid healing service! Can you believe that?"

"I think you ought to go."

"*Et tu, Brute?*"

"Seriously, is it going to hurt you to go?"

I looked at him, incredulous. "I can't believe you're serious!"

"Look, Rita, we've been to every doctor we could find; none of them have been able to help you. There's nothing they can do. This can't hurt you—I want you to go for me. Will you?"

I was fuming! But then I thought: here's this Lutheran, wanting me to go to a healing Mass—well, he's put up with a lot; he deserves something. All right, I would do it. I wasn't going for God, that's for sure; but I would go for him. But *no one* was going to pray over me; none of that kooky stuff! I wasn't going to ask God or anyone else for any physical healing, either.

With a weary sigh I nodded, and called Marianne back.

By the time we arrived Wednesday evening, St. Ferdinand's was packed, with people standing against the walls. There must have been more than a thousand—oh, brother, I thought, just exactly what I was afraid of!

I was standing in the back in my braces and Lofstrand crutches, when a young usher came up to me: "There's room up front," he said, smiling.

"I don't want to go up front," I replied, smiling.

"But that's where the room is," he insisted, taking my arm.

"I am *not* going up front!" I insisted, taking my arm back. "I am not going to make a spectacle of myself!" I wished Marianne were there, but she had her twins with her, and after I'd made it clear I preferred to remain in back, she'd taken them forward to join the rest of her family.

Before I realized what was happening, the young usher had grabbed me again and was propelling me down the center aisle. "This is far enough!" I hissed, planting my crutches.

The pew we had stopped next to was full. The usher whispered to the man on the end: "Could you make room for this lady?"

At first the man looked insulted, then seeing my crutches, his expression changed. He nodded to the others in the pew, then to me, and they scrunched over. Deeply embarrassed, I sat down, and the usher laid my crutches in the aisle alongside the pew.

No sooner was I seated, than the organ started to play, and everyone one stood up. Determined not to make myself conspicuous by remaining seated, I grabbed the back of the pew in front of me and started to pull myself upright. But I could not feel the heels of my orthopedic shoes slipping on the terrazzo tiled floor—the next thing I knew, I was sliding off the seat and almost under the pew with a great clatter.

Instantly hands reached out to me from all directions—rescuing me, raising me, offering me my crutches which I obviously needed. Everyone was craning around to see the cause of all the commotion. I could not believe this! The very thing I had feared the most had come upon me: I was Number #1 spectacle for the evening!

They were singing a hymn now, and the person next to me extended a hymnal for me, holding it open to "Abba, Father." I was scarlet; would the humiliation never cease? This was Ron's fault; why did I ever listen to him?

At the back of the church, the priests who were going to concelebrate now started down the aisle. Everyone began to sing "God, my Father"—everyone, that is, except me; God was not my Father, right then.

As the priests passed my pew, I was surprised at how many there were. My count reached nine when I heard a loud whisper behind me: "Wait, wait!"

The priests stopped and turned, wondering what the delay was. Then the one who had whispered put his arms around me from behind. I looked down; the arms were clad in the sleeves of a white alb—some priest, a big one, was giving me a great bear hug. What *is* this? What's going on?

I twisted around, and here was this huge priest with his eyes closed, praying for me. And now everyone was reaching out towards me. Several were able to touch me; the rest just elevated their hands, raining their prayers over me, while the rest of the congregation kept singing.

Oh, God, this was worse than my worst nightmare! This sort of thing was supposed to happen *after* the Mass! And I had no intention of going forward! But they didn't ask my permission; they just did it! I was in a rage.

And then—all of a sudden, it was like an ocean of peace inundated me. It flowed through me, filling every part of me. . . . It was like being hugged by God.

I never felt so—*loved*—in all my life! It reminded me of when I'd almost drowned—the only comparison I could think of.

And I found myself praying the first real prayer I had said in months, years: "Dear God, I don't know what this is. I don't know what You're doing. But whatever it is, it's okay."

I was not really aware of the service after that, or of anything else; just of this astounding peace—which did not leave.

When we went out of the church, the peace came with me—all the way home. I was not physically healed, but I didn't care; the peace was there—to stay. All the anger, the bitterness, the despair—it had all dissipated, and I felt loved—and truly happy, for the first time since the onset of my illness. I might still be crippled on the outside, but inside I was whole.

And grateful! Oh, God, how long has it been since I have been grateful? If I had been You, I would have washed my hands of me long ago! How could You possibly still love me? I was so mad at You, I wouldn't speak to You, and—You just picked me up and hugged me! Oh, God, I love You!

Ron was waiting at the front door, as Marianne helped

me out of the car. "How was it?" he asked.

I just grinned.

"I take it, it was okay," he chuckled. Then he noted that I was still in braces and crutches. "Did anything happen?"

"Yes."

"Well—what?"

I started to laugh. "I'm not sure; but I've never been so happy in my life!"

I thanked Marianne profoundly, and when Ron and I got inside, he said, "Well, tell me all about it."

I did.

He shook his head. "I don't see how a priest hugging you could make such a difference."

"It wasn't a priest; it was God."

"You mean, the priest was taking the place of God."

"No—I can't really talk about it."

He smiled. "Well, the main thing is, you're happy. You have no idea how long it's been!" And then he frowned. "I wonder how long it's going to last?"

I answered from the depths of my heart: "Hopefully forever."

31

Uphill

If this were fiction, from this point on things would get better and better—but how often does real life stick to our script? Things got worse and worse. Only on the outside, though; on the inside, the peace *did* get better and better—till it truly passed all understanding.

My physical condition continued to deteriorate. With the strength in both upper legs now completely gone, I had to be fitted with heavy, full-length steel braces. And because there was no longer sufficient upper body strength to use crutches very long, the wheelchair became an increasingly frequent helper.

I didn't mind. Inside, I was infused with Christ; it was like we were dancing together, for joy.

The first new thing I did after the healing service was go to confession. How long had it been since my last confession? Two and a half years! Since I'd had no desire to give up my anger at God, there was no way He could forgive me, so what was the point of going?

Now, I confessed all that—and was ashamed to also admit that I still had selfish, unhumble thoughts. But after the words of absolution were pronounced, and I came out of the confessional and with my crutches scissor-gaited over to my place at the end of the pew, I felt so cleansed and relieved—and so grateful for this sacrament! I just thanked Him over and over, weeping.

The grieving for my sin went on for several days. And nights: I would lie in bed with Ron sleeping beside me, and I would weep for all the pain I had caused him, all the deliberate hurt I had done to him. I grieved for what I had done to my children, to Nana, to everyone. And to God—most of all, to Him.

Night after night, I went through this process with the Lord, praying the prayer of St. Ignatius: I ask only for Your grace, and that alone will be sufficient to me.

In return, I repeatedly gave Him everything. Body, mind, soul, being—it was all His. Family, friends, work—His.

One night, after crying myself to sleep in sorrow for what I had done, suddenly there in front of me stood Christ. He had His back to me, but I knew it was Him. Then He turned around, and His eyes were huge. They were the most beautiful eyes I had ever seen—and they were all I could see. I had loved Him before, but now, looking into those eyes, I was *in* love, just wanting to be with Him.

He spoke. *You have not given me everything.*

"Lord, I have," I insisted. "I have nothing left to give You. I completely trust in You."

Then give me your sins.

As He spoke, I felt this tremendous relief—wonderful, unburdening relief. And I was free.

After that, I no longer cried myself to sleep; I prayed and rejoiced.

My physical condition may have been failing, but things around me were definitely improving. One day Ron's Mother, 86 now, came and sat next to me on the couch. "Do you know how much you've changed?" she asked.

"Well, Mum, you've changed, too."

"We've both changed, because that's what God wants.

He wants us to love one another." She hesitated. "I know you love me now."

"I do, Mum, I truly do." I hugged her, and we both cried.

"I'm so happy," she said, dabbing her eyes. "I'm just so happy."

"Me, too."

So was Ron. Finally, there was peace in his home.

I got a job! Wheelchair and all—in our own parish church school, where Kristen was in third grade. One day, I just thought, why not ask? So I called our pastor, Father Charles Bergman who said, "You know, this is amazing; one of our teachers has just turned in her resignation. It looks like you're going to be teaching second grade, come September." When I hung up, I glanced at our kitchen calendar. It was May 22, the Feast of St. Rita.

The next year, when they found out I had a science background, I was transferred to the fifth and sixth grade, to teach science and religion—which in my classroom were surprisingly compatible.

I was also in our choir now, one of the soloists, in fact. They made a special choir robe that I could wear in the wheelchair, shortened so that I would not run over it, and with the sleeves modified, so they wouldn't get caught in the wheels. For the Christmas season, I wrote and directed an Advent Cantata, which our young students performed the Sunday before Christmas.

Nana asked to come to that, which was a surprise. And on Christmas Eve, even though it was 16 degrees below zero, she pleaded to come with us to Midnight Mass. We got there early, so she would have a good view. There was the traditional candlelight procession, and the carols were never more exalting. When it was over, she was in tears. "That was the most beautiful thing I have ever seen! Thank you so much for taking me!"

That whole year was a year of grace. The peace never left, and the habit of prayer—usually the hardest habit to get into, and the easiest to break—seemed to come naturally. In fact, I was pretty much living in a state of communion with God—and I sensed that this was what He might have meant, when He encouraged us to pray without ceasing.

By now the bills were astronomical—but thanks to my new job, the State of Pennsylvania was helping us. I didn't know if other states had similar programs; all I knew was that the State of Brotherly Love was living up to its motto. The Office of Vocation and Rehabilitation was committed to keeping handicapped persons (like me) usefully employed as long as possible. This meant that they helped with therapy costs, provided an electric wheelchair which cost about ten times what we could afford, modified the controls of my car, and was ready to modify a van (when we could afford one), putting in a hydraulic chair-lift and raising the van's roof by two feet—modifications which were going cost more than the van itself. At school, they put in an electric chair lift, and were in the process of measuring the stairwell in our home for a similar lift. They were even making plans to install a third one outside, to get me from the van to the front door.

Incredible! And all to keep me on the taxpaying side of the state ledgers. At least, that may have been the official motivation—but I liked to think that there was some spiritual machinery at work here, too. For of all the original Thirteen Colonies, the one which put the greatest emphasis on Christian charity and tolerance was the one founded by William Penn. It seemed to me that some of that heritage continued to the present day.

By the spring of 1985, we needed all the assistance we could get. For as Ron said in despair one evening, "We're not even holding even. We do all this therapy, and it's so painful for you, and we keep losing ground."

My heart went out to him. He helped the therapist administer the stretching exercises, designed to keep my Achilles tendons from tightening and shrinking. They were extremely painful, and I tried not to cry out, because I knew how badly it made Ron feel, but he could still see the suffering on my face.

Finally the therapist lost patience with him: "Mr. Klaus, if your wife is going to maintain any mobility whatsoever, we have got to do this. Now if you can't bear to see her face, then put a bag over her head!"

But as was so often the case these days, just when it looked like we couldn't go on, God would open another door. On Ash Wednesday of '85, I was admitted for a four-week, comprehensive evaluation to Harmerville Rehabilitation Hospital, the best facility of its kind in the state—and perhaps the country. Their final diagnosis: progressive spinal MS; quadraparalysis (incomplete paralysis of both arms and legs); chronic bladder and bowel syndrome (which meant I had no control of either function); spasticity (involuntary muscle contractions); severe loss of muscle tone—the list went on, but about there was where I tuned out.

"What's the prognosis?" I asked Dr. Vincente, the physiatrist who was also head of the neurological unit.

"Well, it's progressive, I'm afraid."

"Which means?"

"Which means that eventually the paralysis will be complete; you'll have no movement at all."

"How long do I have?"

"That depends. . . ."

He didn't have to finish; from the different therapists I'd worked with, Ron and I had gathered that it was probably three years—five, at most.

"Any chance of remission?"

"No." On that, he was definite: he believed in honesty, and that it was cruel to raise false hopes. "The damage that's been done is permanent, 'non-reversible,' as we say. All feeling in your legs is gone and cannot come back. The bones themselves are distorted and out of alignment. As for your bladder, well, it, too, is beyond repair, but we can give you some training that will help."

I didn't ask him for the prognosis after the paralysis had become complete; I didn't want to know.

Nana died the Sunday after Mother's Day. She was 88, and her last years were her happiest. A few months before, I had taken her around to visit her friends. She had a few really nice things, and she wanted them to go to those she loved, to have the fun of seeing their faces, when she gave them to them. And they loved it! We knew Nana was with the Lord now, but we still missed her.

That summer, Ron took us down to Hunting Island State Park—on a barrier island, off the coast of South Carolina. It had wheelchair ramps and other special facilities for the handicapped. But even if it hadn't, it would still have been our favorite by-the-water campground. It was just beautiful! The air was soft, and the pines fragrant, and even the surf seemed somehow gentler there.

Ron would push my chair as close to the water as we could get, before the wheels got stuck in the sand. Then he would help me with my crutches over the short distance to the water, and position the air mattress for me. Once we were deep enough, I could hold onto the mattress and still make a little "swimming" progress—but Ron was right there, in case, there was any problem. How grateful I was for him.

How grateful I was to God, just to be there! It was a healing time for all of us, after Nana's funeral. That was the only bad thing: when we went home, she and Tucker would not be there to greet us. (Our next-door neighbor and good friend, Anne Martin, who used to visit Mum every day when we'd go on previous trips, had been kind enough to take Tucker in, while we were on this one.)

I was almost daily confronted with the further deterioration of my upper body. I used to love to write letters, but by the fall of 1985, I could no longer hold a pen. For that matter, I could no longer raise my right arm above my shoulder.

So now, instead of writing my family and friends, I called them (until we got the phone bill). Even with the State of Pennsylvania's magnificent assistance, finances were still a problem. We were doing everything we could possibly think of to conserve, like buying as much of our food as possible, at railroad salvage. These were damaged seconds, cans without labels. There were bins full of big cans of beans and soups and stew that were only ten cents a can—but you had no idea what was inside, until you opened them. It made dinnertime a real adventure.

One evening, as I was about to open a can, Kristen asked, "What are we having for supper, Mom?"

"Food," I said. "Good food."

As it turned out, it was sauerkraut, and so was the next can. Then, peas.

"Ugh," said the girls, eyeing its contents.

I got angry. "Don't you ever make a sound like that about food! Not when there are people on this earth starving to death! Now you will sit down, and you will eat it, and I don't want to hear a single complaint!"

They did. And Kristen even got to like sauerkraut—a good thing, because we ate a lot of railroad salvage sauerkraut that winter.

In February, 1986, an article in *Reader's Digest* caught my eye: apparently six children in a remote mountain village in Yugoslavia were seeing the Blessed Virgin Mary—every day! It was happening in a place whose name, Medjugorje, defied pronunciation. But as I read the article, something in my heart told me it was true.

In the past year I had become very devoted to Fatima, reading all I could about how Mary had appeared to three young people in that town in Portugal, in 1917. This new apparition which was (and is) still going on, seemed to be a continuation of the one at Fatima, carrying it forward to the present. Somehow, it was deeply comforting to know that God was so concerned for the conversion of mankind in these twilight years of a darkening century, that He sent His earthly mother on such a mission.

About that time someone gave me $20 and told me to spend it on myself. What I wanted was two books on Fatima. What I needed was clothes; we were so destitute that I felt guilty even thinking about the books—until I remembered what the person had said: "Get something you really want!" The books won.

When they arrived, however, there was a credit for $9.95, which had to be a mistake. But no, they sent a catalogue and said check off what I wanted. There was a book by Father Rene Laurentin called *Is the Virgin Mary Appearing in Medjugorje;* with shipping, it came to $9.95— I had them ship it. When it came, I devoured it—and knew in my heart that it was true. Through the visionaries who saw her daily, she was appealing for five things: conversion, prayer, fasting, reconciliation, and penance. That was the message of Medjugorje, and I longed to go there.

Meanwhile, I could certainly do what she asked. Thanks to Fatima, I was already praying the rosary every day for world peace. But I was not fasting, and after praying about it, it seemed that I should. So for Lent, I decided to fast as she suggested—on Wednesday and Fridays, on bread and water.

Reason, of course, objected immediately: you can't fast; you're sick! This is ridiculous! You're a poor, sick person.

A poor, sick, heavy person, I replied; one whose doctors had tried everything, even to putting her on 800 calories a day for the four weeks at Harmerville. Net loss: 7 pounds.

I did the Medjugorje (Med-jew-*gor*-yay) fast, seemed to gain energy in the process, and by Easter, to my doctor's amazement and delight, was down 14 pounds.

Summer came, and as soon as school was out, I enrolled in an intensive two-week Scripture course at La Roche College, entitled the Writers of the Gospel. To maintain the diocesan accreditation necessary to teach in parochial school, every five years one had to accumulate 90 hours of instruction in Scripture and Theology. This course which met five mornings a week from 8:00 to 12:30, satisfied half that requirement.

To get there, I had to leave the house at 7:15. Ron would help me to our stationwagon which had hand controls, then fold up the wheelchair and put it in the back. When I got to the college, my friend Laverne who was also taking the course, would be outside waiting in the parking lot. She would get the chair out, set it up, help me get in it, and wheel me in.

That June of '86, Pittsburgh was experiencing a record heat wave. It reached up into the Allegheny foothills, where normally we were cooler than those down below—and with it came a dreadful humidity which made us wish the Klaus Haus had at least one room with an air-conditioner in it.

Wednesday, the 18th, I was having a particularly bad day. I had the kind of MS which was heat-reactive—what little muscle tone remained in the few muscles still working, vanished. Every movement was like moving through wet cement. Moreover, my eyes were crossing and I was getting double vision, so that leaving the college, I had to pray hard just to make it home safely.

When I got there, I told Ron I was simply dead. There was nothing to do but go to bed, and he and Kristen helped me upstairs. It was too hot for covers, so I lay on top, and Ron set up our two fans to move the sodden air in one window and out the other. Then he soaked some washclothes in cold water and put them where they would be handy. He went downstairs to look after the girls, hoping that I could get some sleep.

I couldn't. It was a long, miserable afternoon. At 6:00, Ron brought up a chef's salad for supper and changed the washclothes. At 9:00, the girls came in to kiss me goodnight before going to bed. At 9:30 I started my quiet time with the Lord, as I had every evening since the healing service three years before. I tried to read, but my eyes still wouldn't focus, so instead I said the rosary, and kind of dozed and daydreamed, waiting for it to be 11:30, when Ron would come up.

And then I heard the voice. It said: *Why don't you ask?*

32

The Feast Day of St. Julianna

Looking around the bedroom I could see there was no one there. The clock radio was off, and the TV downstairs, where Ron was watching the eleven o'clock news, was an undiscernible, barely audible hum. But someone had spoken.

You didn't hear that, my reason told me.

But I *did* hear it, my heart insisted. It was a soft, gentle, almost pleading voice: *Why don't you ask?*

What was I supposed to ask for?

No sooner had the question formed in my heart, than I was given the answer. The words were there instantly, whole and complete, and I found myself speaking them out loud with no prior knowledge of what they were:

> "Mary, my mother, Queen of Peace, whom I believe is appearing at Medjugorje, please ask your Son to heal me in any way I need to be healed. I know your Son has said that if you have faith, and you say to the mountains: move, that they will move. I believe. Please help my unbelief."

303

The moment the last word, "unbelief," was out of my mouth, I felt electricity course through my body, engulfing me, like bubbly champagne. It was pleasant, and it was particularly strong on my right side.

Instantly, my reason informed that this was not happening. Not to me. This cannot happen.

But I'd just about had it with my self-exalting intellect; my heart knew it *was* happening, and that what I was experiencing was some kind of healing. And with that I immediately fell asleep—so deeply that I never heard or felt Ron come to bed.

I was not aware of anything, until I woke up in the morning, the 19th of June—The Feast of St. Julianna. I looked at the clock whose digits said: 7:02—*7:02?* The alarm should have gone off an hour ago! I had to leave in thirteen minutes—eighteen minutes, max!

I woke up Ron, who was enjoying his summer sleep-in, but even with his help, there was no way I was going to get to class on time this morning! In fact, I was going to be so late, there would be no one there to help me get in the building!

As he lifted my legs with their heavy braces into the wagon and stowed the chair in the back, he said: "Now, look: I know you're in a hurry. But you're going to be late anyway, so five or ten more minutes isn't going to make that much difference. So just take it easy, okay?"

"Okay," I called out the window—and roared out of the driveway like I was leaving pit row at the Indy 500. When I got to the college, the parking lot was full of cars, but as I'd feared, there wasn't a soul in sight. In desperation I started beeping the horn—until a cafeteria worker finally came out to see what the matter was. She got my chair out, helped me get in it, and wheeled me into class.

I was half an hour late—and mortified. Father Patrick O'Brien, Th.D., was lecturing; 60 students were taking notes; and one wheelchair person was distracting everyone. I wished for the cloak of invisibility—or at least the ability to take notes, so I could lose myself in productive activity. But I couldn't hold a pen; all I could do was concentrate. Except that this morning I had been in such a rush, I hadn't had time for the big mug of coffee which was the backbone of my usual breakfast. So now on top of causing a disruption, I was getting a caffeine-withdrawal headache. All I could think about was hanging on till the mid-morning break, when there would be coffee available.

From 7:02 until this moment, I had absolutely no recollection of what had happened the night before.

Finally, it was ten o'clock break-time, and I could see Laverne across the hall, coming over to wheel me into the cafeteria.

All at once, I felt this unbelievable rush of heat roar from my feet, spread up through my legs, and up through my whole body, and I thought: Oh, my God! What is this?

It passed through me like a wave, and as it did, I began to itch, everywhere it had gone. It felt like a million pinpricks, like your leg does when it has been asleep and starts to wake up.

I reached down to scratch my right leg which itched badly, and as I did so, I noticed that my toes, which also itched, were going up and down inside my orthopedic shoes.

They had not moved in years.

Now, on top of everything else, I was experiencing muscle spasms, and what was this? My right leg, where I was trying to ease the itch—I could feel my fingers scratching!

That leg had been like a wooden post since 1983.

I began to scratch all over the leg—and everywhere I scratched, I could feel. The leg felt far away and cold and prickly—but it did feel.

As Laverne came up, she began profusely apologizing for not waiting for me; she had waited fifteen minutes, then assumed that something must have happened.

I didn't tell her what was happening right now—because I wasn't sure what *was* happening. For the rest of the class, my concentration was not on Father O'Brien; it was on just how extensive this new sensation of feeling was. I could feel my feet. I could feel myself moving my toes. I could feel the insides of my shoes. I could feel the braces on my legs.

I peered over my knees and down at my shoes. I wiggled my toes—and could see the tops of my shoes moving. Hi, guys; long time, no see.

At last the class was over, and Laverne wheeled me out to the car. "Are you okay?" she asked. "You look kind of—funny."

"I feel kind of funny," I admitted, grinning at her. "But—I am definitely okay."

I drove slowly most of the way home. But then I started to go a little faster, because I had to use the bathroom.

That was another first: I'd had no signal like that from my bladder in more than two years—which despite incontinent precautions made for miserable nights and demeaning and humiliating "accidents" in the daytime.

When I got home, our van was gone, and there, under the shade tree by the driveway, was the beach chair with my Lofstrand crutches on the railroad tie beside it. I remembered that Ron and I had decided he would take the girls strawberry-picking that morning. He had left the chair and crutches for me, in case I beat them home.

The signal from my bladder was more urgent now, so I grabbed the Lofstrand crutches and pulled myself upright. The braces locked in place, as they were supposed to, holding me in the vertical, and I did the scissor-gait towards the three steps up to the house. The doctors had forbidden me to attempt them alone, not just because my arms were too weak to support myself, but because my sense of balance was gone. The combination made it likely I would topple over, and if I broke a bone—well, my circulation was so bad, it would take forever to heal.

But things were definitely urgent now, so there was no time for caution. I went up the steps with the crutches, and when I arrived at the front door, I was astonished: that should have exhausted me—but I was not even breathing hard! This was some kind of strange remission! (I still had no recollection of the night before.)

In the downstairs bathroom, I raised my skirt to unlock the keepers on the sides of my braces, so that they could bend at the knee, and I could sit down. As I did, I thought my right leg looked strange. When I was finished, I looked more closely. It was strange! Strange, because it wasn't deformed! And my right kneecap was on top of my knee! The two legs matched!

I screamed.

This was no remission! This was a miracle! The biggest one I had ever heard of!

Still screaming, I grabbed my crutches and swung myself out to the living room, where I took off the braces—and stood up without them. "Oh my God! My leg is straight! *My leg is straight!*"

I unrolled the long stockings, so I was bare-legged and barefoot, screaming and thanking God the whole time at the top of my lungs—and yet still not realizing the extent of the healing.

I tucked my skirt up in my waistband so I could see my legs, and grabbing my crutches I swung myself to the foot of the stairs. As I looked up at the steps which had been the site of so many arduous ascents, suddenly my whole life flashed before me—but the scenes were only the beautiful things that had happened, nothing horrible.

It began with the time in the pool when I saw the Blessed Mother, followed by the day I made my vows, that autumn afternoon when I first went out with Ron, the moment of birth for each of the girls, the healing service when the priest hugged me, the dream in which Christ asked me to give Him my sins—at each scene, I was given to re-experience the same emotions, the same joy and euphoria, as I had at the time they had occurred.

Then came a scene which I now remembered: the voice of the night before, the prayer I had subsequently prayed, and the inner galvanizing feeling I had experienced—which had all been blocked from my memory until this moment.

And that was when I knew that I had been completely healed.

"Well, if I *am* healed," I said aloud, "I can run up those stairs!" I laid the crutches aside and took a deep breath. What if—Never mind what if! Up the stairs I raced, as fast as I could run. I think I made it in under five seconds—about sixty times faster than the last time I had gone up them!

I started screaming again, and flew down the steps, flinging open the front door and running outside. It was another one of Pittsburgh's 59 sunny days; the sky was azure and perfectly clear, except for two puffy clouds directly overhead. Looking at them, I shouted, "Thank you, God! Thank you, Blessed Mother!"

Our dog Mitzi who had never seen me run before, was delighted with this new game and bounded around me, as I ran over to the woods and down to the creek, jumped across it and jumped back, running up to the house again.

Finally I came to a halt, panting, and looking up at the sky, shouting over and over, "I love you, God! I love you, I love you, I love you!" until I was completely out of breath.

Then I thought: I've got to tell somebody! I ran into the house, and grabbing some tissues (for by now I was sobbing for joy), I tried to use the phone, to call our pastor. Ever try to dial, when you were frantic? Same thing happened: I kept getting it wrong. A recording kept telling me I couldn't do it that way. Then, I kept getting a busy signal—until I realized I was dialing my own number.

Taking a deep breath, I slowly pointed to each digit—and got through. When Father Bergman (who does not remember this conversation at all) came on, I started yelling, "I can run, I can run! I don't have MS anymore! I can run!"

"Who is this?"

"I can run, I can run!"

"I heard you," he replied, "you can run. Now who is this?" And then it must have struck him. "Rita?"

"Yes, and I don't have MS! I can run!"

"All right," he said in a soothing voice, "now, Rita, is there anyone there with you?"

"No, Father."

"All right, I want you to get some aspirin and take two of them. Then I want you to sit down and call your doctor, all right?"

I hung up. He doesn't believe me! He thinks I'm nuts! (I was, of course, behaving in a wildly irrational manner, but never mind.)

I called my friend Marianne who was also a teacher at St. Gregory's and used to drive me to work every day. By the time she came on the phone, I was crying so hard I couldn't speak. But she knew who it was.

Two minutes later (the drive usually took four), her car was pulling up the drive. She had her twins with her and told them to stay in the car; there was no telling what she was going to find in our house.

What she found was indeed quite a sight: me in the

living room with my skirt tucked in my waistband, twigs in my hair from running through the woods, and mud splattered all over my legs from jumping back and forth across the mucky creek bed. What was more, I was praising God and jumping up and down—in all, she had good reason to be alarmed.

Finally it dawned on her what was wrong with this picture: no braces and no crutches. Her eyes widened, and then she ran to me and hugged me. And now we were both jumping!

"I'm healed, I'm healed!" I shouted, as we jumped.

"I can see that!" she shouted back. "How did it happen?"

We both calmed down and sat down, and I told her.

"Where are Ron and the girls?"

"Strawberry-picking, I think."

"Well, we've got to show them."

I looked down at my muddy feet. "I don't have any shoes—I know, I'll use Kristen's sandals."

I cleaned up my legs and put my skirt down, and we set off in Marianne's car.

"Does Father know?" she asked.

"I called him, but I don't think he believed me."

"Well, let's go see him; it's on the way."

At the church, Father's secretary, Marianne Thompson saw us first. She took an involuntary step back, and all the color drained out of her face. "Oh my God! Wait, I'll get Father!"

In a moment he was there. He was stunned and kept murmuring, "Oh, praise God."

"Sit down," he admonished me, "before you hurt yourself."

"Father, I haven't felt this good since I was seventeen! I've never had so much energy in my life! I feel wonderful!" And it was true: while I had not experienced the major symptoms of MS until I was 20 in Massena, for at least three years before that, I had been experiencing its pre-symptom: the dragging weariness that I couldn't shake.

"Well, do sit down."

"I can't, Father. I'm on my way to find Ron and the girls. I just came for your blessing."

So I knelt down before him, and he gave me a blessing and said that he would talk to me later. "Take it easy now!" he called after me, as we went out to the car.

When we got to the strawberry farm, it had closed, so we headed home—where the van was in the driveway. Ron and the girls were in the house, undoubtedly worried; there were Mom's braces and crutches—but no Mom.

"You'd better stay in the car," said Marianne. "I'll go prepare them. This is going to be quite a shock."

She got out and went up to the house. "Rita's fine," she called to Ron. "Everything's okay; she's in the car."

Ron came out with the girls behind him, and I got out. "My God!" he exclaimed.

I walked up to him and hugged him. "I'm healed!" I shouted, and hiking up my skirt I started dancing an Irish jig.

Kristen and Ellen were crying, and I hugged them and danced some more. The whole world was sparkling!

But little Heidi was perplexed. "What's the matter, Heidi ho?" I hugged her. "Your mom's healed—see me dance?"

"Mom, Mom! Stop! Moms aren't supposed to act like that!"

"I can't help it, honey. Jesus healed me, and I'm so happy. I don't have MS anymore."

"Oh, good!" she exclaimed, relieved. "Now I won't have to do any more work!"

"Well," said Ron, "let's go in the house. I want to hear all about this."

With a promise to call, Marianne took the twins home,

and leaving the girls outside to play, Ron and I went inside. I told him what had happened.

It was difficult for him to assimilate, especially the part about the voice. "It was like it was inside of me, but also surrounding me," I tried to explain. But from his expression, I could see he was having trouble with it.

I tried again: "It was like I was in a bubble—the voice was in me, but I was also in the voice."

The prayer I had prayed was equally difficult for him, though he confirmed that I was fast asleep, when he'd come up; I never moved. When I told him about what had happened that morning, as I had sat in the wheelchair in Father O'Brien's class, he just shook his head. "Look," he said, "you're just going to have to be patient with me. That's more supernatural input than most people have to absorb in an entire lifetime. No, make that five lifetimes!"

33

After the Healing

When Jesus called Lazarus out of the tomb and had them unwrap his burial windings, the expressions on the faces of his friends must have resembled the ones I was now seeing on mine. Shock and stunned amazement first—and then either delight and joy, or fear and anger. The latter surprised me, until I thought about it.

If what happened to Rita Klaus was a miracle, then it had a lot of heavy ramifications, starting with the inescapable fact that God was real. And He cared. And He was still in the miracle-working business.

The ramifications had ramifications: if God was real, then so was heaven. And hell. And eternity. And all those absolutes of which the Bible spoke, and which were so unfashionable today. And if Scriptural absolutes were reality—then what did that do to the reality we chose to perceive?

If God cared, then it meant He really did have a plan for each of our lives. It would, if we chose to follow it, bring us great joy and peace, or misery if we chose to ignore it. But it was an either/or choice: there was no more middle ground, no more complacency or rational-ization or procrastination. There was only the one or the other.

And if God could reach down and instantly heal someone from an illness that medical science stated categorically
was incurable and irreversible, if He could do the
impossible, when and wherever He chose, then He truly
was omnipotent. And omniscient. And omnipresent.

God.

Faced with that ultimate reality, there was only one
choice to make: conversion. Which to some was a
frightening prospect. For it meant forever changing their
lives, their motivations, their responses. It meant forgiving,
relinquishing, foregoing. It meant accountability.

It also meant experiencing love, beyond all human
comprehension—but too many, confronted with the reality
of God and fearful of how He might react to their sin,
forgot that the God of judgment was also a God of mercy.

So to some, my healing was not a cause for rejoicing.
It was a profoundly disturbing skewing of their reality,
one best ignored.

And to a few, it posed a threat.

When I woke up the next morning, Friday, and started
my prayers, I had just gotten to "Father, Son, and Holy
Spirit, I profoundly adore You," when the thought came:
Boy, that was some dream I had last night, about being
healed! That was so real!

I stopped praying and thought about that. I'd had such
dreams in the past—that I wasn't handicapped, that I was
running. Sometimes the dreams were so real, I could feel
the wind on my face as I ran. And then I would wake
up—and not even be able to roll over in bed. I would
lay on my back, and I would have to offer it all up to
God again. All right, Father, whatever You want.

So I'd apparently had another one of those dreams.

But it was so real, I thought sadly; couldn't it—couldn't it just possibly be true?

I was afraid to lift off the sheet and see if my leg was really straight. But I had to. If it was just a dream, then I would offer it up again. I lifted the sheet—

My God, it *was* straight! It had all happened! I was healed!

And now I was afraid. In all the excitement and wonder of yesterday, the true significance of what it meant had not dawned on me. Now it did, breaking over me like an enormous ocean wave. God, why? Why me?

Fear rained down on me like ice cubes; my whole body was throbbing with it. And then, in the midst of this chaos came a calm interior voice: *Why are you afraid?*

Instantly I felt the most beautiful peace come over me.

The voice went on: *I am the same today, as I was yesterday and will be forever. I have asked you to be a sign to my people, of the heritage that they are in danger of losing, the heritage which is rightfully theirs, won by my own precious blood.*

There was more: *I want you to give me all your yesterdays, all your todays, and all your tomorrows. To trust me completely. And to be generous in whatever I ask of you.*

In my heart, I said yes to that. I accept.

A few moments before, when the fear had been pounding through me, I had said to myself and to Him: why me? Why not one of the handicapped children I had worked with? I'd had a wonderful childhood and a wonderful life, and I was content with my lot now. For just one of those little ones to get up out of a wheelchair and live a full life—why not one of them?

Now He rebuked me: *You are not to question. I give in the way I choose to. I give you what I choose to give, and who are you to tell me what I can and cannot do?*

I'm sorry, Lord. I will try not to do that again.

It was time to get up. I asked God's forgiveness for

having doubted and been afraid to pull back the sheet. And also for the decision which Ron and I had reached last night about this morning.

Today was the final day of the course at La Roche College, in which Father O'Brien would summarize all that he had been imparting to us for the past two weeks, and give us our last test. If I didn't go, I would be throwing away all that work—and the course credit that went with it. But if I did go, if I walked in there and took a seat, it could destroy the class.

"Well," Ron had said, "there is one way. . . ."

"I can't get back in the wheelchair! That would be denying what God has done!"

"It would certainly mean swallowing your pride."

I searched for another solution, any other way, but there was none.

"Well, I'm not going to wear my braces!"

"Fine," said Ron, "I don't think anyone will even notice. Or if they do, they won't think anything of it."

He was right; no one did. Later I came to see that there was a lesson in it: there would be times when it would be inappropriate for me to share the testimony of my healing. I had to let God show me where and when. And if He said, *Go, and tell no man,* then I would be obedient.

There was great peace in my life now, but there was still some anxiety: Who was I, to be a sign to anyone?

What came to me was the example of the Blessed Mother: she, too, had been afraid at first, when the angel had come to her and announced God's plan. But then she had said, "Be it done unto me, according to Thy will," and had simply been obedient. That's what I would do, too.

I prayed about going to church on Sunday. I was to go. Upright. Walking.

Well, in that case I would need some shoes. We had so little money, I decided I would get one pair that would serve for many occasions—white ones. I went to the shoe store, and the woman who usually waited on me and helped me pick out orthopedic shoes, came over to me now.

I didn't know her name, but we had become good friends, nonetheless. She was a good Christian, and over the years, over many pairs of shoes, we had talked about how we felt about religion and Christian education and bringing up kids. I was sitting down now, and as she pulled the little stool up and sat down in front of me, she didn't notice at first that there were no braces on my legs.

Then she did notice. "Did you have an operation, or something?" She looked around for my crutches, and not seeing them, almost shouted: "Are you in some kind of remission? Please tell me; I've got to know!"

"I've had a healing," I smiled.

"You mean, like in the Bible? Like when Jesus healed the sick?"

"That's right."

"Oh, my God!" and then her eyes filled. "This is going to be the best pair of shoes I've ever sold! I'd give them to you, if I could."

She laughed. "What kind do you want? Pretty ones, right?"

"Right. White."

She brought me a pair of beautiful white pumps. I put them on, and they fit perfectly. I got up and tried them out, walking around the store. My friend started to cry.

After I paid the bill, she handed me my parcel, saying, "I cannot begin to tell you what this has meant to me— you've made my day. No, you've made my life. You've given me hope. Not that I didn't believe before but—you know how it is."

She walked me to the door. "It's so good to see somebody who's a real, living sign," she added, as we said good-bye, "proof that God is with His people."

Now I understood what He had meant.

Sunday morning, as we entered church and walked down the aisle, I could hear the gasps and whispers behind us. I tried to keep myself in the presence of the Lord, and when the Mass started, every aspect, every element seemed to glisten, like it had just been washed. I heard the liturgy and the singing, as if for the first time.

The Gospel was about the man who was born crippled, whom Jesus healed, and who went dancing through the streets. Father Bergman's voice broke as he read it, and next to me, Ron had tears streaming down his face. He gave my hand a squeeze and whispered, "That message is for you."

I would have to tell him afterwards, I thought, that the reading had been selected a long time ago and was also being read in thousands of other churches that Sunday. But—in a way, it was for me.

Monday we went to Harmerville, to see Dr. Vincente. We had called him, of course, to tell him what had happened, and he must have told his colleagues; half the staff in the outpatient department was waiting for us, when we got there.

You could tell the Christians among them right away: they were the ones praising and thanking God. The others were nonplussed. When Dr. Vincente came out, he was dumbfounded. He mentioned that some of the doctors over the weekend had speculated about the possibility of an identical twin sister, as had occurred in a recent TV drama. Heidi was with us, and now she piped up, "My Mom doesn't have a twin sister. She has two sisters, and they both have black hair, and live in Iowa!"

Dr. Vincente took me into his office, where he did a complete neurological exam. Everything was normal. When he finished, he just shook his head. "I don't know how to explain this. In fact, I'm not even going to begin to try." He paused. "How many times did you pray? How many times did you ask?"

"Once."

"Did you use up all your prayers?" he asked a little wistfully. "Do you have any left for me?"

I smiled. "I will pray for you every day, doctor. I already do."

"Well," he said, resuming his professional tone, "you've been given a second chance at life, like being born all over again. Now here's your doctor's recommendation: first, you and Ron and the girls go home and get on your knees and thank God. And then, whatever money you have left in the bank, take it out and go on a long vacation."

And so, we followed doctor's orders.

It was late on a warm, sunny afternoon by the time we arrived at Hunting Island—but not too late to find a campsite, set up camp, and go for a swim. How good the water felt! How good it was, to be able to swim with Ron and the girls!

We stayed in the water the remainder of the afternoon. We played tag, and Ron taught the girls different strokes, and after awhile, I drew off a little and just stood there, looking at the family God had given me, the calm ocean, the white sand, the still pine trees and palmettos.

Parts of the puzzle were finished. God turned them over now, and showed me why the pieces had gone together the way they had. He showed me the incredible picture that they made, and how His plan, which at times had seemed so wrong, had been so right.

I looked up—above us, the clouds, fired by the setting sun, were a brilliant rose-copper hue that stretched from horizon to horizon. And because the surface of the ocean was now perfectly calm, it mirrored the sky—so that looking out, there was no division between sky and sea. We were suspended in a world that was shading to a soft crimson. . . .

All at once, little fish began to flip out of the glass-smooth water all around us, thousands of them, sparkling like silver coins in the last rays of the setting sun.

Suddenly Ellen called, "Look, Mom! Behind you!" We turned, and less than a hundred yards further out, dolphins suddenly broke the surface—four, five, six of them! And they weren't just swimming; they were leaping and dancing on their tails. And they kept doing it, while the little fish kept flipping.

Awestruck, Kristen said, "It's like all nature is rejoicing!"

It went on for several minutes, as tears streamed down my face and Ron's. Then finally the fish settled down, and the dolphins gave their last little splash and disappeared. And there was silence.

Postlude

Two years later, I received a phone call from Father Halley, inviting me to come to Omaha in June, to give my testimony. From the conversation I could tell that he had no idea that Rita Klaus and Sister Mary Raphael were one and the same. When he finally did realize it, he was thrilled as I was.

When I arrived and found that I had been invited to stay at the motherhouse, I was delighted. As my friends Ann and Earl Jones drove me up the drive, it was hard to accept all the changes that had taken place since I had been there. I wanted it to still be 1968—but you can't go home again. When I left, the motherhouse had been a farm, on a hill out in the country, where it had reigned in solitary splendor.

But in the twenty years which had passed, the city had reached the hill and gone up it, surrounding the motherhouse with high-rise apartments. Ann explained that many of the sisters had left their vocations in the wake of Vatican II, and the order had come on hard times. It had been forced to sell off more and more of the land, in order to support the remaining sisters, many of whom were old now and infirm. I had a flash recall of the elevator reserved for the O&I—and for me, that time I was in the wheelchair.

At the front door we were met by Sister Mary Suzanne who was as delighted to see me, as I was, her. She asked if I would be willing to give a talk that afternoon to the sisters, and I said, of course. But before I did anything else, I excused myself and slipped into the chapel—and smiled; some things, at least, the really important ones, didn't change. I gazed at the Pieta above the main altar, where the Blessed Mother held the broken body of her Son, and then at the statue of St. Julianna, patron saint of the Servite Sisters, then at dear St. Philip. I remembered then that the last time I had seen these friends was on that morning when I had left. And from the ache that I could feel in my heart, I knew why God had brought me back here.

When I emerged from the chapel, Sister Mary Suzanne asked, Would I like a tour? Very much, I replied. The main part of the convent had been turned into a giant infirmary, as most of the sisters who were still there were well into their 70's. I met some old friends—Mother Paula, Mother Dolors, Sister Benedicta. . . . They hadn't changed; there was the same love, the same holiness. We were all just a little older.

It was time for lunch. We went down to the refectory. It was different now; the U-shaped table with its stools had been replaced by conventional tables for four. And there was no reading now, nor any rule of silence; conversation was encouraged. A few of the old sisters still wore their habits, but all the others were in civilian clothes.

At lunch Sister Mary Suzanne asked that, when I shared my testimony that afternoon, I be totally honest, when I came to the part about leaving the convent. "You're not the only one who has come back. Others have shared. Those were painful times—as painful for us who stayed, as for you who left. But we have learned; it is different

now. And this afternoon will be part of that healing—
yours, and ours."

There was an hour before I was due to speak, and I
knew what I had to do. I excused myself and walked out
and up through the pines to the cemetery.

There was a breeze; the pines were whispering. . . .
Look who's back. We missed her. Do you think she missed
us?

I traced the same path through the old stone crosses
that I used to take, stopping at each grave to pray for
the sisters, as I had done so often before. It hurt—terribly;
but it was a good hurt.

Then I came to crosses which had not been there
before. With a shock I read the names on them. . . Mother
Liguori. . . Mother Annunciata. . . Mother James. . . Mother
Loyola. . . .

My shoulders shook with silent weeping. All my mothers,
who had meant so much to me, whom I had loved so
much. All here.

I knelt down. "Thank you, all of you," I whispered.
"Thank you, more than I can ever say. I still pray for
you. Please pray for me. I know you can hear me—and
I need your prayers now, even more than Sister Mary
Raphael did."

The breeze moved through the pines. They seemed to
be answering. And as I looked around, I could almost
make out the figures in their dark habits, against the pines.
They were there, praying with me. All my sisters.